The Ideal Real

The Ideal Real

Beckett's Fiction and Imagination

Paul Davies

Rutherford • Madison • Teaneck
Fairleigh Dickinson University Press
London and Toronto: Associated University Presses

Associated University Presses
440 Forsgate Drive
Cranbury, NJ 08512

Associated University Presses
25 Sicilian Avenue
London WC1A 2QH, England

Associated University Presses
P.O. Box 338, Port Credit
Mississauga, Ontario
Canada L5G 4L8

The paper used in this publication meets the requirements of the American National Standard for Permanence of Paper for Printed Library Materials Z39.48-1984.

Library of Congress Cataloging-in-Publication Data

Davies, Paul.
The ideal real : Beckett's fiction and imagination / Paul Davies.
p. cm.
Includes bibliographical references and index.
ISBN 0-8386-3517-2 (alk. paper)
1. Beckett, Samuel, 1906–1989—Fictional works. 2. Imagination.
I. Title.
PR6003.E282Z62475 1994
843′.94—dc20 92-55028
CIP

PRINTED IN THE UNITED STATES OF AMERICA

To Rashid

. . . even those who give much of their time to reading, yes, and writing about, the greatest poetry, frequently reveal their sense of its "unreality" as compared with the rest of the life around them. Where will it end? When the real is taken as unreal, and the unreal as real, the road is open to the madhouse.

—*Owen Barfield,* Poetic Diction

Contents

Acknowledgments

This book has been in the making for seven years, and there are many people I would like to thank for their help, direct and indirect, during this time. My debts to John Pilling, Reader in English at Reading University, who was my doctoral research supervisor, are perhaps the most difficult to convey simply because they are so numerous and various. His support and generosity have been unstinting. As taskmaster, academic mentor, editor, colleague, and friend, he only grows in my regard. James Knowlson, Mary Bryden, Audrey McMullan, and Michael Bott, also at Reading University, have been the friendliest of people to work with over the years, and have done much to help, in diverse ways. I am grateful, too, to Kathleen Raine for her interest in my work and her encouragement; and to Owen Barfield, with whom I once had an interesting conversation about Samuel Beckett and much besides. Another remarkable person without my meeting whom this book could not have been is Richard MacEwan, formerly of Chisholme House. Amongst many people to whom my debts reach further back in time are John Newton, Christopher Ricks, Peter Andrews, and, it goes without saying, my parents and my brother. A very special thank you also to Anthony Davis, who may well have sown the seed of my interest in Beckett by throwing a copy of *Six Residua* through my window one stormy October night.

Permission to quote material from the following institutions, publishers, and copyright holders is gratefully acknowledged: the Beckett International Foundation (extract from *The Ideal Core of the Onion* on pp. 229–37); *Temenos* (reprint of part of an essay which appeared in vol. 11); John Calder Ltd., and Grove Press Inc., (passages from works by Samuel Beckett quoted on pp. 47, 102, 113, 139); Oxford University Press (extracts from Owen Barfield, *What Coleridge Thought,* quoted on pp. 90–91); and Rudolf Steiner Press (extracts from Owen Barfield, *Romanticism Comes of Age,* quoted on pp. 144–195).

Notes and Abbreviations

Footnotes are indicated by asterisks. Endnotes, which are references only and contain no comment, are denoted by superscript numbers.

Works by Samuel Beckett are referred to in the endnotes by title only.

All page references in the text, footnotes, and endnotes are to the editions described in full in the bibliography.

The following abbreviations have been used:

CSP	*Collected Shorter Prose, 1945–1980*
M	*Molloy*
MD	*Malone Dies*
U	*The Unnamable*
RUL MS	Manuscript in the Beckett Collection, Reading University Library

Preface

Fay Weldon said recently that writing is usually a much more unconscious process than critics allow it to be. Regarding Beckett, I agree with her. But Beckett is in a particularly special position. He wrote fiction obviously not with the aim of entertaining a large public, nor of making a fortune, nor of aggrandizing himself, nor of solving the riddles of philosophy. He never gave a final explanation of what he was doing, and in this respect, he is an example of Jung's view that artists should not be called upon—are not always indeed able—to give the explanation so desired by their public. If the voices who narrate his stories and novels are to be believed, they at least, if not their author, appear to have very little conscious idea of what they are doing or why. Beckett, and Jung's artist, say: I cannot explain my work. It means what it says.

Art of this kind, which the artist cannot explain, is the outflowing of the creative imagination. Understood properly, the work of imagination in literature takes language into a mode and onto a level that is not discursive, explanatory, and rationalizing, or at any rate certainly not only these. If explanations could be given, says the art of imagination, there would be no need for the artwork. The communication would succeed without it.

Beckett said little, leaving interpretation open to the critics, who since his death are possibly freer still to offer readings which he might have ruled out had he been the kind of writer who offered his own "definitive" views. That fact, the weakest of excuses for yet another book on Beckett, gives place to a stronger justification, which is that a new book can offer to interpret the gestures and images which Beckett cast into fictional form, and intend a commentary rather than final explanation.

Beckett has been done a disservice by many critics, but he partly brought it on himself. By keeping silence, he ran the risk of having a reputation made for him by others, so that the world heard the critics' reviews before they heard Beckett's voice, and many who never heard his voice still attributed the critics' views to Beckett. The meaning of his works has been foreclosed by others perhaps even as a result of his very determination not to foreclose it himself. He has sometimes suffered badly at the hands of the media and cultural history, being popularized almost beyond recognition.

On the other hand, Beckett's universality is reflected in the amount of interest shown in his work by many of this century's major schools of thought—psychoanalytic, existentialist, linguistic, structuralist, philosophical. The trouble starts only if a member of one or other of these movements adopts Beckett as its spokesman: suddenly, then, Beckett appears diminished.

The artist of the imagination—and Beckett was one—is beyond adopting party attitudes, whether cultural, political, or intellectual. An imagination truly alive to its times will never ignore them, but it is always active from the perspective of an order which is not exclusively conditioned by them. The beauty of Beckett's works of imagination is that they invite both a contemplation of their strangeness and a curiosity as to their meaning. I can certainly say that it was the former impression Beckett's work first made on me; writing this book has been to some extent a response to the latter. One of Beckett's novels, *Watt,* is openly concerned with these opposing impulses, one to still oneself in face of the strangeness of an experience, the other to explain it. This relation between being involved in a thing and reflecting upon it is one of the springs of creativity in human consciousness: it offers writer and reader, speaker and hearer alike the chance to transform the entropic, self-canceling dynamics of opposition and conflict into the energy-releasing potential, or flow, latent in polarity and paradox.

The Ideal Real

Introduction
What Is Man? The Search for Reality

Some writers and even philosophers tell us we have no business to enquire where we came from, what we are, and where we are going. They say that these are unaskable questions. Yet Beckett did not shy away from asking them. Drafting a piece called "The Voice" in 1977, Beckett directly echoes Job in asking "What is man?"[1] And earlier, in his trilogy of novels, if the narrator's plight of "not knowing where you came from, or where you are, or where you're going"[2] did not bear blunt witness to a search for the meaning of existence, little else could. *From an Abandoned Work* asked the same: "With so much life gone from knowledge, how know when all began, all the variants of the one . . .?"[3] That Beckett, whose intelligence was more than equal to it, did not become a scientist, academic, or philosopher suggests that the imaginative medium held for him a potential the other disciplines lacked.

The limits to discursive reasoning have been noticed by writers, artists, thinkers, visionaries, musicians, and healers since very early times, not only since the advent of the Age of Reason of the eighteenth century. In the medieval Middle East, in the European Renaissance, in the works of Dante, Shakespeare, Milton, and the Romantics, and of certain writers and artists of the late nineteenth and twentieth centuries, there has been a constant stream of voices with the same message: that the springs of creativity have something more to do with—and more to give to—our relations with existence than discursive reason and analytical philosophy could possibly indicate, and yet these latter continue to advance our culture in a certain direction, dominating and impoverishing it at the same time. Beckett was born into a century where an exaggerated faith that the power of positivist science and rationalist thought would give all the answers still could not prevent an extraordinary sense of emptiness and isolation, especially so amongst those whose very aptitude and potential for becoming conscious of the meaning of existence made them feel the lack of, or desire for, such development all the more strongly.

The sense of emptiness comes from trying to cope with a real assent to the claim pressed on us by our education system and by specialists, by a positivism which says that, in a nutshell, all that can be called *real* is the material universe (seen as other than the observer) and that consciousness, mind, and sense of self are epiphenomena of the physical body, matter. The assumption common to analytical psychologists, behaviorists, sociologists, historians, and biologists, by all who would claim to be materialist, empiricist, or positivist, is that matter is anterior to consciousness. According to this view, all that comes into existence does so by chance, or "by mistake," and has therefore no innate potential or purpose. It is the psychic and emotional upshot of these postulates which is all too familiar in the arts of our time. Beckett's scenarios and stories unarguably illustrate and express what it is for a human being to bear these thoughts and conditions—isolation, emptiness, purposelessness, sense of meaninglessness, a great hole empty which should be filled. These are the kinds of images of Beckett that have gained widespread public currency from his plays. In this context, Beckett shows an unremittingly bleak and suffering world, as it would be dishonest not to do, given the postulates suggested about the human's state.

There is a different view of humans' place in the universe, spoken of by the traditions and arts of the imagination. And to describe it too in a nutshell is painfully inadequate (not least because the kernel must burst the shell if it is to grow into a tree). From this point of view, matter is the epiphenomenon of consciousness, not the other way round. Here nothing happens by chance; there is no such thing as chance, conventionally understood. Physical existence is the expression of forms and potentialities which precede, are prior to, the physical universe. This view is not a crude determinism, because humans must still choose what to do in certain situations, and their choice is instrumental in the going forward of the universe. But what is not in doubt here is that the material/physical is one of many levels *in* reality, not the only reality there is. Although this perspective does not eliminate the suffering in the world, it makes a different attitude to it possible. One term which has been used to refer to this view is the *philosophia perennis,* mentioned by Spinoza, Aldous Huxley, Frithjof Schuon, C. G. Jung, and many others.

At this point I can imagine some theorists and critics saying that this nonpositivist worldview is simply an instance of organicism, religion, transcendentalism, or mysticism, that is, pap to feed anyone who cannot stomach the idea of a meaningless universe. To them I would say, leaving aside the fact that the only thing humans literally cannot stomach is *poison,* that such a judgment of the alternative perspective is precisely the stock response of the entrenched classifier, the logical empiricist who, if he can assign something to a category or an *ism,* thinks he knows all that matters about it. It is the response of one who by so doing gets as far from what is indicated in the *philosophia perennis* as it is possible to get. For in the *philosophia perennis* the starting point is the unlimited, the unconditioned, which gradually takes to itself its means of manifestation and gives birth to the apparent multiplicity and mass of particular phenomena.

This alternative view, known also to science as the *holistic* and to the religions as the *initiatic,* far from being described, can only be obscured by labels like *organicist* or *transcendentalist:* for they classify whereas the core of the world picture in question is an experience, not a category. I know one can go on and classify that as *experientialism,* but then we are still farther from it than we were before. Long ago, category, rule, and reason contributed to the mutation of gnosis and direct intuition into the dogmatic mainstream religions; and conversely, a disproportionate hatred of the intellectual powers turned mysticism into what might be called misty schisms, movements characterised by vagueness and attachment to personalities. Hence comes Beckett's profound distrust of religion and mysticism, which of course the cynically minded amongst commentators have been quick to mention at the expense of his equally tireless curiosity about those very topics.

It is on Beckett's ground, the arts of the imagination, that the deep explorer of consciousness can avoid the limiting judgments, dogmas, and prejudices present both in established religion and conventional science. This is, I believe, why Beckett chose this ground and dedicated himself to it, often at great personal expense.

What a great many critical accounts of Beckett ignore is that it is on this ground, a sacred space within the magic circle of imagination, where Beckett's narrators experience the many "sudden gleams" of inspired perception which steal in on their mechanistic, "reason-ridden" normal consciousness and transform it completely. Beckett's evocations of this state balance the nihilistic state that is always talked about as Beckett's only mode. They give a new (or restore the original) meaning to the cliché *The light dawns:* this ideal metaphor for the advent of transformation or renewal of perception is also present in the terms *illumination, enlightenment, seeing the light.* In this metaphoric complex is recognized at its clearest the birth of human possibility. *I first saw the light*[4] is a phrase that refers to birth—the initial possibility of existence in human form—and at the same time to enlightenment, the state beyond which one cannot pass in one's lifetime.

No critic would dispute Beckett's lifelong fascination with birth. It amounts to an attraction polarized by a repulsion, neither of which poles Beckett is ever prepared to side with. And this articulate sensitivity to the polarity involved in physical existence after birth Beckett shares not only with other artists but also with alchemists, homoeopaths, mystics, platonists, initiates, and saints.[5] Jung, along with lesser-known but equally qualified writers such as Arthur Guirdham,[6] has discussed the same paradox at length in a psychological context. Although this book is certainly not a Jungian reading* of Beckett, it is worth remembering how close an affinity subsisted between the emergence of Jung's work and Beckett's, an affinity not only of content but of time and place. Beckett at one time attended a Jungian practice and heard Jung lecture; they both had work published in the same issue of *transition* in the thirties. Jung is the "mind doctor" described in the anecdote in Beckett's play *All That Fall.*[7]

Although detail must be reserved for the following chapters, I shall suggest here that Beckett's interest and Jung's coincide on the issue of locating the self—whether it should be identified with the acculturated "personality" or with something deeper which neither parents nor education and milieu can do anything to define or modify other than to expedite or frustrate its development. These two possible "selves" have rarely been more explicitly contrasted than in Beckett's short pieces "Afar a Bird" and "I Gave Up before Birth."[8] Here one self (the real or higher self) expresses a resentment nothing short of stinging toward the other "social," "cultured" self which lived a life at the expense of the real self, which was stilled early on into almost total suspension. This question, as Beckett saw, is not the province of the psychologist alone. Perhaps Jung also appealed to Beckett precisely because he refused to exclude the arts, music, religion, alchemy, cosmology, and myth from his investigations of human identity, and indeed increasingly saw that the greatest need of our time was to give these things a central place in psychological work.[9] It is significant that the journal *transition*[10] explicitly devoted itself to the areas of art and culture marginalized by positivism, as did the 1980s review *Temenos,* which published one of Beckett's last poems and a short interview with him in 1990.[11]

---

*Mary A. Doll offers one in *Beckett and Myth: An Archetypal Approach* (1988).

To a reader new to Beckett's fiction, the following chapters may appear more of a maze than they will to Beckett devotees. Nevertheless, the book treats his work chronologically and by title, with very few exceptions. Also, I can identify two complementary principles which the entirety of this book, in one way and another, is concerned with exploring. A single principle governs them, namely that they find expression on many different levels and in many different discourses and images, and cannot really be covered in digest form. As I said in the Preface, contemplation and explanation are two expressions of this polarity. The list could continue, expressing the polar syzygy of fancy and imagination, classification and synthesis, measurement and taste, separativity and unicity, quantity and quality, breaking down/decomposition and conception/gestation, mechanism and organism, flesh and spirit, relative and absolute, consciousness and unconscious; the how-muchness and the whatness; the isness and the outness; the mystery of the positive and the negative, which is summed up in the fact that all desire is for a positive which nevertheless cannot subsist in the absence of a negative. Expressed in far more various ways by Beckett and the other authors and ideas mentioned in this book, this polarity is a principial seesaw which all Beckett's works, in their special ways, energize.

It may be a surprise to hear that Beckett's treatment of polarities makes them easier, not more difficult, for us to assimilate. He may be thought a difficult writer, but his illustrations are always of what it is for a person to experience the presence of those balances and oppositions: he not only poses the question of what knowledge of self may be, but also illustrates what it means for a person to pursue it. A fair opening gambit might be to suggest that from the angle described here, Beckett is not a "difficult" writer at all.

* * *

The path traced in the next eleven chapters follows Beckett in his search for reality. His work is especially pertinent in an age in which terms such as *reality* and *truth* are fast approaching the status of cliché, or are being limited to economic forces by dialectical materialism or—subjected to the dubious prescriptions of "value-free" research—discarded altogether, at least until after hours. It may be a point of interest that amongst these terms of qualitative attribution, one distinction has not fallen into such doubt as others have: that between the genuine and the fake. These terms are still trusted in a way the others—amongst them good and evil—are not. Hence the overwhelming consensus amongst philosophical skeptics in favor of Beckett's integrity. Alvarez, for example, often disgruntled about Beckett's artistic statements and acquiescing with a too easy bitterness in their dark side, nevertheless affirms Beckett's genuineness.[12]

Beckett's search begins with the condition of uncertainty, which is also the square one of philosophy from Plato to Wittgenstein. If the frequency with which such terms as *reality* and *knowledge* are used seems to have outstripped their relation to anything we can agree they refer to, and if a writer of such obvious integrity as Beckett continued all his life writing and saying *how it is,* his work is, if the idea is tenable at all, grounded in uncertainty. "Jahrelang ins Ungewisse hinab": Hölderlin's words are sounded at the beginning of Beckett's fiction-writing career, at the end of *Watt.*[13] The uncertainty has certainly been borne out as yearlong, but its direction was not simply worstward. In the earliest works (discussed in chapters 1 and 2) the uncertainty is that of the empirical skeptic, but in the very late writings, it has undergone such a transformation as to make uncertainty very much more a necessary abeyance of that certitude which restricts knowledge to fixed data and limits the imagination merely to arranging them. As Keats knew, uncertainty can thus inspire as well as frustrate. To account for the impression left by reading the entire range of Beckett's fiction one might very well agree with what Arthur Guirdham has said about mystics: "the contemplative, through all his vicissitudes, is nearly always accompanied by a feeling that however much he fails he is nevertheless on the right path."[14]

E. B. Greenwood, writing in *Essays In Criticism,* avers that a "redrawing of the *boundaries* of appearance and reality is often the basis for a metaphysical system as well as for a novel or poem."[15] Beckett's redrawing of these boundaries succeeds—precisely because it is not theoretical but imaginative—in avoiding what critical theory and philosophical terminology are always prone to: the laziness of jargon and cliché, in Coleridge's words "that dislike of vacancy and love of sloth which are inherent in the human mind."[16] A cliché allays vacancy; it offers us something to hold on to, but in doing such a minimum, it also promotes sloth. But Beckett's artistic characterisation of metaphysical issues is anything but slothful, partly because it is so good at dismantling clichés. Although many of his characters are conspicuously apathetic, his art is one of unparalleled alertness.

Such an interest in redrawing the boundaries of reality motivates a critic like Geoffrey Hartman:

> One wager remains to haunt us: can "denken" (*noesis*) and "dichten" (*poesis*) be joined again, though they have given rise to separate, often antagonistic disciplines?[17]

And a philosopher like Wittgenstein:

> Philosophy ought really to be written only as a *poetic composition*.[18]

If *noesis* (thinking) and *poesis* (imagination) were joined again, their common share of reality would no longer be in such doubt. As it is, *noesis,* in the form of scientific rationalism and clinical psychology, has declared *poesis* unreal. *Poesis* has not died out because of this, but it has come to occupy the status of a pleasant illusion rather than of an element of reality or agent of knowledge. Hartman continues: "To restore a connection [between *noesis* and *poesis*] is the one move towards foundations I would not find regressive." To put a major concern of the following chapters in a nutshell—to concede to sloth for the sake of convenience—would be to say that in this century, no writer has been more progressive in this respect than Beckett.

The near approach to cliché of the concept *real* probably owes something to an undue emphasis on the rationalistic kind of knowledge, a knowledge which, far from gravitating to reinforce our interpretation of *reality,* makes it seem, if anything, more and more *un*real. Heidegger remarked:

> The technological scientific rationalisation ruling the present age justifies itself every day more surprisingly by its immense results. But this says nothing about what first grants the possibility of the rational and the irrational. Perhaps there is a thinking which is more sober-minded than the incessant frenzy of rationalisation and the intoxicating quality of cybernetics. One might aver that it is precisely this intoxication that is extremely irrational.[19]

The antagonism of *noesis* and *poesis* thus presents itself as something like a historical emergency, to which a response has been made not only in philosophy but also in literature, unlike science in that it is mainly the domain of *poesis*. Such an emergency forces a writer sensitive to it into emergency measures. Those measures, while their aim is obviously to respond to the problem, nevertheless state it in embodying the very unease to which they are a reaction.

Uncertainty is an area of common ground between philosophy and literature, for it has profound imaginative appeal, whether grim or comic, to a mind like Shakespeare's or Beckett's, and is a point of departure for metaphysical analysis for Plato or Wittgenstein. Uncertainty also has this peculiar characteristic, that in addition to its primary meaning, lack of certainty, it suggests, as soon as it is situated in the structure of a human thought or action, that some kind of journey or investigation is in train or to be undertaken. It is transmuted into perplexity. It is impossible to ignore how predominant the investigation and journey are in Beckett's fiction, from the perfunctory travels of Belacqua in *More Pricks Than Kicks,* through *Watt*'s investigations into appearances and realities, to the disembodied travelers in *Worstward Ho* tramping a "groundless" abyss (Can any writing absolutely be *grounded* in uncertainty? this work asks). Uncertainty, if it is connected to life of any kind—even if that life is seen, as by Beckett or Thomas Mann,[20] as a death-process so slow as commonly to seem its opposite—never stalls. It moves on. It does not give in or up; it does not rule out inquiry, amplification, articulation, and description. It does not rule out literature, in short, though to be faithful to a sense of uncertainty is for Beckett an excruciating challenge: "nothing to express, nothing with which to express, together with the obligation to express."[21]

We may agree that uncertainty is an incendiary or at least unstable state, a more or less severe form of psychical suffering, and it can be transposed into forms of pleasure such as wit or tragedy. But some transposition must take place and the uncertainty be thus got on terms with, if not got rid of. In Beckett, one of the first steps, often a hilarious one, is a bid for certainty, skirmishing and random in manner, often feebly desperate, often bungled. Nevertheless, like a sentence begun, a bid for certainty is a spur to action: it is something after which, and in relation to which, something must come. And this is especially true of uncertainty in writing. To stall completely is not to write, and to write at all is to cover paper and, by extension, to cover ground, to make a journey of sorts. "The only way one can speak of nothing" says the collected if highly uncertain voice of *Watt,* "is to speak of it as though it were something."[22]

Part 1
Getting a Grip, Blundering on
(1935–1945)

1

Trusty Things? (*More Pricks Than Kicks*, *Murphy*, *Watt*, *Nouvelles*)

Things and Oneself

The material object has always saved the West, at least temporarily, from uncertainty. Our language is furnished with numerous examples of unconscious recourse to this form of rescue, one old tomb of a once-live thought being to *find a foothold,* in which is suggested a falling or climbing body, probably a person, in need of a projection, snag, or hole to stay the destructive work of gravity. To find a foothold is to get certainty from uncertainty, and whenever the phrase is used, it denotes relations presumed necessary between a self or subject and something else. It is no coincidence that the something is inanimate. Johnson's stone, kicked in order to asseverate *reality* in a day when, if not a cliché, the meaning of the word was certainly in question, is fittingly, almost amiably, inanimate. The impulse to plainness is evident in philosophical discussion, where more often than not something of immediate contiguity—like a table—is posited as the ultimate in objects.* The animate object strikes the instinct less easily: "the faces of the living, all grimace and flush, can they be described as objects?"[1] asked Beckett in 1945. Both tendencies suggest the immediate reassuringness of material and of dead objects. Our daily lives are full of them. Hazlitt said of the English that "they cling to external objects for support, . . . as one means of ascertaining their personal identity."[2]

"Only a small amount of what is said can be verified," says the

*For example, Bertrand Russell's *Problems of Philosophy* (1912), which opens with a discussion of a table.

voice of Beckett's *Company.*[3] But, for the empirically minded, a material object is more verifiable than an intentional object, what is thought or said. The wish or need to verify, which is implicit in the regretful, wry admission from Beckett, is a bid for certainty made from a state of uncertainty. Beckett's early works voice this:

> Almost at once gas . . . began to pour through the radiator. This could not alarm him, who was not tied by interest to a corpse-obedient matter and whose best friends had always been among things. (*Murphy,* p. 108)

> " . . . a charming man, he sends me objects . . ." (*Murphy,* p. 58)

> Things and himself, they had gone with him now for so long, in the foul weather and in the less foul. Things in the ordinary sense, and the emptinesses between them. . . . (*Watt,* p. 81)

> I saw the familiar objects, companions of so many bearable hours. The stool, for example, dearest of all. The long afternoons together, waiting for it to be time for bed. At times I felt its wooden life invade me, till I myself became a piece of old wood. There was even a hole for my cyst. (*The End,* p. 52*)

Beckett affirms the source of comfort that objects per se afford his characters. But the tone is not so straightforward as to allow us to stop at that simple conclusion, nor merely at the sense of affirmation. There is a play of ironic tension in "companions of so many bearable hours." The silently indicated *un*bearable hours are too close for us to get a sense of repose; we feel they have been nudged only just out of the way. But it is undeniable that in a world of so many unbearable hours, these particular hours accompanied by familiar objects must be special, considerable, to be singled out at all. Given a second thought, is "I felt its wooden life invade me" in fact such a positive suggestion as at first encounter? In the passage as a whole, the gestures of deep involvement, even love, are all there, "the long afternoons together, waiting for it to be time for bed." But the touch of languor and stasis, betrayed in that verbless sentence, would only be an unequivocal delineation of engrossment if that commitment were not elegantly, perversely held off by the hint of double entendre preceding it, the offhand, cool "The stool, for example"; or the addition, as though to complete a picture and at the same time expose it as something of a

*All page references to the four novellas *(First Love, The Expelled, The Calmative,* and *The End)* apply to the *Collected Shorter Prose.*

sham, "There was even a hole for my cyst." "Dearest of all"? Well, at any rate, familiar objects are meaningful; they persuade the narrator's voice to lift in some sort of praise; and even parody is homage of a kind. Murphy's *friends,* likewise, were among things. The unpredictable gas fire does not trouble him, though it kills him later. It is perhaps for him also "dearest of all" because it is a thing, possessing a high-handed independence of man, its supposed possessor:

> He stood back to imagine it lit. Rusty, dusty, derelict, the coils of asbestos falling to pieces, it seemed to defy ignition. (p. 98)

But there is a hint—obscurely formulated in a way characteristic of *Murphy*—that the object isn't as consoling as it seems: elsewhere Murphy refuses to be "tied by interest to a corpse-obedient matter," and he is a budding spiritualist. And wholly problematic is the apparent link between his not being thus tied and his having objects "amongst his best friends." For what are friends if not tied by bonds of friendship?

Watt, ever in transition, has nevertheless had these same habitual attitudes to things: "Things and himself, they had gone with him now for so long." Although the paragraph suggests that long-standing companionship is soon to end, it testifies to something as age-long as Didi's and Gogo's relationship. Watt had "never been a man's man"[4] and indeed until *Mercier and Camier,* no one in Beckett had been a person's person. They are all *things'* people, particularly Murphy and Watt, and to a lesser extent Belacqua. For them the presence of objects sustained relations of close contact. But the narrator of *Watt* holds off from commitment to the idea, a reserve made available by irony again: "things and himself . . . they had gone with him now for so long, in the foul weather and the less foul." As in *The End,* we find ourselves asking questions: questions about the fair weather, and why there is none of that. Beckett's nimble overturning of a cliché—*through fair weather or foul*—by perversely altering its old meaning refreshes it and offers at the same time something new in terms of message. In fact it almost offers the contrary, on the surface. Again meaning has been split by irony, and the pleasure of such writing is the way in which the narrator's voice dares us to choose between meanings, while knowing full well that the verbal web it has woven makes the choice impossible.

In the pretrilogy prose, things or objects are an attribute of habit, in the sense in which it is outlined in Beckett's *Proust:* objects are mediums of constancy in the environment, and a change in them, their appearance or arrangement, brings about suffering in the self or subject. Beckett cites the offense to habit which a new room represents to the Proustian consciousness.[5] Similarly charted in Beckett's own fiction is the habit Celia finds broken on the death of the old man upstairs. For the Beckett writing *Proust,* "habit maintained" equals "comparative well-being maintained." In his first stories, *More Pricks Than Kicks,* we can see the inception of such a habit and perhaps account for what Beckett later so often did, and does, in the quoted passages: turn objects into friends, by a trick of language turning inanimate into animate, and thereby edging into consciousness the idea of meaningful relationship.

> She had a coarse manner, but she was exceedingly gentle. She had taught all her more likely patients to wind bandages. To do this well with the crazy little hand-windlass that she provided was no easy matter. The roll would become fusiform. But when one got to know the humours of the apparatus, then it could be coaxed into yielding the hard slender spools, perfect cylinders, that delighted her. All these willing slaves that passed through her hands, she blandished each one in turn. "I never had such tight straight bandages" she would say. Then just as the friendships . . . seemed about to develop . . . the patient would all of a sudden be well enough to go home. Some malignant destiny pursued this splendid woman. Years later, when the rest of the staff was forgotten, she would drift into the mind. (p. 181)

This is one of the first important passages in Beckett where an object is explicitly associated with an affective impulse. The windlass and bandage, not only familiar and friendly in themselves, also become grounds for friendship between nurse and patients, delight to the nurse herself and affectionate memory in everyone, long after the occasion has been forgotten. The activity and relationships centering on the object become symbolized by it, and not least for the narrator; "drift into the mind" is not simply the feline exactitude of a self-conscious narrative voice. *The* mind is the generalized mind, the living memories of all those "more likely patients," and the minds of all readers who have understood the passage itself. Those humanizing qualities integral to the paragraph—humor, delight, friendship—are complemented by its tone, as against that of the rest of the story ("Yellow") and its companion pieces, a tone either testily, self-consciously virtuoso or obsessively and indiscriminately subversive. That predominating tone, foreshadowing the more controlled and purely Beckettian fury ("what I would have liked was hammer strokes, bang bang bang, clanging in the desert"[6]) evident in the novellas and trilogy, is absent from the *More Pricks* passage. It is remarkable how pure the nurse is allowed to remain, considering the way in which the authorial voice maims most of the women in the book. "She was exceedingly gentle. She taught all her more likely patients to wind bandages." There is the later Beckett speaking in and under these lines: silently suggested—that is, with the very opposite of bravado—is a causal link between the first sentence and the second (as if "gentle" *because* "she taught") and how, with that tactful equivocation, determined not to sentimentalize or oversimplify, the *unlikely* patients are excluded. Many people are *kicked* out of the book, but the nurse and her likely patients remain in it, and we are tempted to think they remain by virtue of what occasioned their coming into contact: the bandage winding, the "crazy little hand-windlass." The impatience of "crazy" is kindly rather than exasperated or vindictive. "Years later . . . she would drift into the mind." This is rare composure for the Beckett of *More Pricks,* and the link between man and object established in the passage is a link which, whenever it reappears in later books, occasions composure, a cooling of the blood and fury.

It is usual by the time of *First Love,* in which

> her image remains bound, for me, to that of the bench, not the bench by day, nor yet the bench by night, but the bench at evening, in such sort that to speak of the bench, as it appeared to me at evening, is to speak of her, for me. (p. 7)

It is usual for Mr. Knott, also:

> When Mr. Knott moved in the midst of his garden, he did so as one unacquainted with its beauties, looking at the trees, looking at the flowers, looking at the bushes, looking at the vegetables, as though they, or he, had been created in the course of the night. (*Watt,* p. 203)

And for Watt:

> And yet every now and then he did forget something, some tiny little thing, so that he was obliged to return and fetch it, for he could not have got on, through his day, through his night, without it.
>
> . . . wherever else his duties might take him, in the pleasure-garden up and down, or in a tree, or sitting on the ground against a tree or bush, or on a rustic seat. (*Watt,* pp. 115, 116)

But none of this composure is blind; the ironic poise, particularly in *Watt,* is so finely maintained that all the statements fall just short of assent. There is mischief, almost, in the specificity of "he did forget something, some tiny little thing" and of "through *his* day, through *his* night' as though they were no one else's. The stylized environment of *Watt*—pleasure gardens, rustic seats, trees and bushes placed as if by a God, in a paradise, to lean or urinate against—is as questionable as it is beautiful, like its stylized prose. Compare the pretty garden to the remark "Of these two explanations Watt preferred the latter, as being the more beautiful" (p. 35).

Pacts with Habit

The style of *Murphy, Watt,* and the novellas asks us to contemplate the relations that a man or woman can have with an object, preferably a familiar one. The more familiar the objects are, the more tempting it is for the voice to ascribe living properties to them. It is not a coincidence in this connection that the objects are often plants and animals, pointedly described by Beckett as having all the advantages of the animate over the inanimate as well as all the advantages of the inanimate over the human. If an early Beckett man wants life, as likely as not he selects for his relationship a rat: Watt's "last rats," *The End*'s "water rats, exceptionally lean and ferocious." Beckett's unwillingness to commit humans to these relationships is at once a reluctance to see humans as objects (insofar as that fails to account for their intelligence) and also a fear that human intelligence is too bare and too complex to cohere into a relationship. This fear is markedly expressed in the chapter of *Murphy* in which Murphy takes leave of Mr. Endon, if that harrowing meeting or nonmeeting of eyes can happily be termed a leavetaking. Murphy would have it so, but he knows at the same time its impossibility. "Mr. Murphy is a speck in Mr. Endon's unseen" (p. 40). The fear is as strong in Celia's thought: "She felt, as so often with Murphy, spattered with words that went dead as soon as they sounded: each word obliterated, before it had time to make sense, by the word that came next. So that in the end she did not know what had been said. It was like difficult music heard for the first time" (p. 27). Perhaps Beckett hints that there would be hope for Celia and Murphy if they gave their words the second and third hearings that difficult music needs. But the prospect for that person-to-person relationship is not good. The dropped hint does not pick up the load of obliterated words dropped beforehand.

Objects offer the Beckettian consciousness a reference point, an *idea*—if not a reality—of certainty. Mr. Knott's establishment is eminently an idea, much more questionably a reality, of a certain way of things. But its ontological status is obscure; every linguistic gesture in the book aims for that effect, so that it becomes a matter of course to name the house no less readily an establishment than a house. And this insecure ontology is what governs the ironic play pervading all those fond descriptions of objects. That the fondness is foolish is as strongly implied by the narrative voice as the fondness, the concern, itself is. *Proust* calls it "horribly comic, . . . the madness which holds a conversation with the furniture."[7]

By the time of *Murphy* and *Watt* the ambiguity has become a source of pleasure, and in *Watt* a source of narrative itself; but its first stages are again to be seen in *More Pricks:* as a nervousness about describing the environment of objects in any terms but the most scathing. The scathingness is really an escape from its objects instead of a coming to terms with them:

> They followed the estuary all the way round, admiring the theories of swans and the coots. (p. 28)

> Wicklow, full of breasts with pimples, he refused to consider. Ruby agreed. The city and the plains to the north meant nothing to either of them in the mood they were in. A human turd lay within the rath. (p. 100)

> . . . no loss of pastoral clamour . . . (p. 115)

> Now the sun, that creature of habit, shone in through the window. (p. 170)

The gestures are characteristic and have the newness of shock tactics. But the engagement is not subtle or penetrating on the whole. The sparks of nonconformity are not integrated into the writing, as they begin to be in *Murphy*. ("Seen from behind, Murphy did look fairly obliging, the kind of stranger one's little doggy would not mind being held by.")[8] But what they, and the better ironies they lead to, do reveal is that there is an obstacle, and a limit, to the "long afternoons together" that a Beckett character can spend with an object, much though Miss Rosie Dew might delight in being sent "objects" by Lord Gall of Wormwood.

Habit, as it is explained in the *Proust* essay, is a composure for which the subject pays a price. Just as the harsh tones conflict with the tender in *More Pricks,* so there is no neat opposition between, on the one hand, the familiar objects in Proust's room providing comfort and, on the other, the unfamiliar objects in a new environment producing suffering. It all depends on the value ascribed to each pan in the trembling balance. The comfort is habit; the suffering is a basic condition for art. "Habit then is the generic term for the countless treaties concluded between the countless subjects that constitute the individual and their countless correlative objects" (p. 19). Every now and then, according to changes in the environment, the treaties are renewed, and in the moment when one has become inapplicable and the other is not yet established, the "boredom of living" is replaced by the "suffering of being." In this, Beckett is a true Romantic; it is only those interspatial moments that he is able to designate *real,* the "enchantments and cruelties of reality" (p. 22). But at the same time, Habit is the "lightning conductor of [man's] existence" (p. 19). To live in *reality* is to endure something like continuous electrocution, whereas the conductor of his existence prevents its edifices from collapsing every time they are struck. That is why the familiar objects, indices of habit, exert such a dubiously attractive influence on Beckett's characters in the early books. As Beckett has it, habit "hides the essence of the object in the haze of conception—or preconception" (p. 23). Thus Watt is not really happy leaning against a tree or sitting on his rustic seat, and likewise a pot cannot repose as a pot without a certain agony being occasioned in Watt. Even to name an object is to hide its essence in a haze, to rest one's head on a "pillow of *old words.*"[9] To name a thing is to be complicit in the veto that habit lays on our perceptions. If this is so, it has far-reaching consequences for a view and use of language as a referential medium, as we shall see.

Broken Habits

> Things in the ordinary sense, and the emptinesses between them. (*Watt,* p. 81)

> Here there was nothing but commotion and the pure forms of commotion. Here he was not free, but a mote in the dark of absolute freedom. (*Murphy,* p. 66)

> Were he to overcome his infatuation with the ginger, then the assortment would spring to life before him, in the radiant measure of its total permutability. (*Murphy,* p. 57)

> . . . or did it have no meaning whatever for Watt at the moment of its taking place, were there neither Galls nor piano then, but only an unintelligible succession of changes, from which Watt finally extracted Galls and piano, in self-defence? (*Watt,* p. 76)

> The nameless multitude of current quick—life, we dare almost say, in the abstract. (*More Pricks,* p. 125)

If "things in the ordinary sense" are the correlatives of habit, then the "emptiness between them" are the moments, the passages of time, in which reality, the "suffering of being," takes over from habit until a new insulation develops, hazing over essence with conception again. Watt, like most human beings, wishes consciously to escape suffering, but by doing so, he misses the essence of a thing or event. And yet, when he suffered the Galls' visit in its essence, as part of the continuum of "current quick" with no words to accompany it, he became uneasy. It is significant that Watt's inability to attach meaning to the piano-tuning incident is equivalent to his inability to put the experience into words, to make for it a "pillow of old words," an insulating habit. (What *new* words might do for him is not discussed.) In this experience there is no insulation; he himself is the conductor of what must seem, unnamed, an "unintelligible succession of changes." Watt has no power to recognize, let alone alter, this state of affairs, but the author Sam, whose story is a careful report of Watt's account together with deductions made from those details, is capable of mirroring, like Beckett the critic in *Proust,* the analogy of a mental process, if not the process itself. Allowing for the much lighter context of the biscuit-eating scene in *Murphy,* the "radiant measure of total permutability" is a gesture made in the same direction as that of Watt's experience of the Galls. It represents for Murphy a release from preconception, and the release of objects (the biscuits) into a kind of freedom they do not have when subjected to habitual categories of preference.

Habit represents and abets ease and all its dangers. An "unintelligible succession of changes" or "the emptinesses between" things suggests, on the other hand, a habit-free perception and, simultaneously, a kind of suffering. This is the voice of *The Expelled,* meditating, like the voice of Proust, on a change of living quarters:

> Now and then I would go to the windows, part the curtains, and look out. But then I hastened back to the depths of the room, where the bed was. I felt *ill at ease* with all this air about me, *lost before the confusion of innumerable prospects.* (p. 24, my italics)

First Love repeats the meditation, albeit more briefly:

> I surveyed the room with horror. Such density of furniture defeats imagination. (p. 14)

Compare *Proust*'s exposition of the Balbec-plage episode:

> He enters his room, feverish and exhausted after the journey. But sleep, in this inferno of unfamiliar objects, is out of the question—his *attention* has peopled it with gigantic furniture, a storm of sound and an agony of colour. Habit has not had time to silence the explosions of the clock. (p. 24, my italics)

It is no surprise, then, that objects "detached from the sanity of a cause, isolated and inexplicable in the light of ignorance"[10] are going to make a subject as ill at ease as the reader is made by that subversive twist, "light of ignorance," which merges ignorance and wisdom into one. And so, for Celia, when the old man has died upstairs, "an Aegean nightfall suddenly in Brewery Road could not have upset her more than this failure of the steps." All the new objects the Expelled, too, encounters stand in the light of ignorance, just as the events and objects Watt comes across, and is troubled by, are all detached from the sanity of a cause. The whole novel enforces this impression. Yet it is not mere insanity. It is part of a vision which Beckett can alternately identify as the "enchantments of reality" *and* as "the suffering of being." In both cases we assume that the referent of "being" and "reality" is the same. Notice how, with the exactitude characteristic of Beckett, the word *attention* is pointed. Attention is the opposite of habit; just attention peoples a room with monsters. Ease is inattention, a kind of sleep.

These considerations are all implied in a reading of the passages quoted on page 28, in which things are a source of consolation in a world of uncertainty. The irony of such passages, that ambiguous stance and distance indicated in the play of words, clichés, and stock phrases—"the long afternoons together," "dearest of all," "just one little thing"—does not cancel the meaning of the passages but rather enriches it. "A worthwhile irony is always to some degree true in both senses" writes Christopher Ricks, echoing Empson, in an essay on clichés;[11] nowhere is the idea more applicable than here, where much hangs on either side of the fence, on an assent to and a dissent from the relationships between self and objects so suggested ("I felt its wooden life invade me"). Where assent predominates over dissent—but without doing away with it—the "light of ignorance" fades a little (into that darkness so beloved by Beckett's "heroes" when they want to think), and the search for certainty, knowledge, is a little further advanced:

> He watched his legs as under him they moved, in and out. "I stand first on one leg," he said, "then on another, so, and in that way I move forward." (*Watt,* p. 252)

> Erskine's voice, wrapping up safe in words the kitchen-space. (p. 80)

But occasionally, dissent grows and then the danger of the repose of habit is intimated. One is tempted to think of Keats's "easeful death"[12] and to associate habit with death in the Beckettian context as well. Habit is a great deadener even before *Waiting for Godot*'s coinage. Bob Dylan is thinking of habit in the Proustian or Beckettian sense when he says "You fail only when you let death creep in and take over a part of your life that should be alive."[13] Read for "your life" Didi's or Gogo's or Watt's, and for "death", habit.

> Things and himself, they had gone with him now for so long, in the foul weather, and in the less foul. Things in the ordinary sense, and then the emptinesses between them, and the light high up before it reached them [pure attention? or the light of ignorance?] and then *the other thing, the high heavy hollow jointed unstable thing,* that trampled down the grasses and scattered the sand, in its pursuits.* (*Watt,* p. 81, my italics)

There is more than a hint of the demon in that image, blind and unspecific as the "thing" that the words portend. Or perhaps the words themselves are that demon; legendary monsters are always made of words. For the demon, play (scattering sand) and destruction are neither incommensurable nor opposite. The suggestion is left hanging as to whether this thing is in fact Watt's body from an ant's-eye view: but it is obscure and dangerous and not unassociated with the "things" of habit. Also, a note sounded in that more than usually serious and abstract piece, *The Calmative,* shows how real the danger is that Beckett so often treats with light, swift wit elsewhere:

---

*Cf. *Molloy:* "I turned angrily and saw, blurred by the leaves, this high mass bearing down on me" (p. 100).

> All that remained to me was the vision of two burning eyes starting out of their sockets under a check cap. *Into what nightmare thingness am I fallen?* (p. 42, my italics)

Later in Beckett's prose, the "horror," the "staring sockets" and the "nightmare" of "thingness" are brought into a much more explicit relationship to one another. But at this stage, the danger gets some of its strength from its very lack of definition. If *thingness* is in any sense implied in the characters' various bids—more and less successful—to establish relationships with objects and thereby approach certainty, then habit, the function of thingness, is from one point of view as much of a nightmare as the "storm of sound and agony of colour" that a break with habit represents for the writer of the *Proust* essay.

A question is raised by this, which it takes nearly all of Beckett's prose writing career to answer: Why is a perception of reality as much a suffering—the suffering of being—as is the threat of *un*reality in the false ease of habit?

Watt's Ancient Labour

> [Watt] did not desire conversation, he did not desire company, he did not desire consolation, he felt no wish for an erection, no, all he desired was to have his uncertainty removed. (p. 225)

This at the end of a book in which Watt has always been seeking certainty, and has always been hampered by not counting the things that would edge him towards certainty, which would indeed edge any consciousness that feels an affinity with Watt's toward certainty. The possibility that is felt whenever a Murphy or a Watt or a novella-voice comes across a congenial object is the possibility of relationship. The reasons why often a person is less suitable than an object will be considered later. But, as we have seen, the temptation is great for Beckett to humanize an object just long enough to allow the potential of relationship to be felt. This humanization is one of the few ways of defining knowledge that Beckett's incessant search can find at this stage, and even this possibility has come into question. A relationship is knowledge conceived of spatially: space becomes *tractable* when objects mark out its shape and boundaries, just as language structures become intelligible by virtue of the silent boundaries of grammar and punctuation, the "emptinesses between" words. *Knowledge conceived of spatially* is the silent law governing what may be said and what may not be said at a point like this:

> Of Watt's coat and waistcoat, his shirt, his vest and his drawers, much might be written, of great interest and significance. The drawers, in particular, were remarkable, from more than one point of view. But they were hidden, coat and waistcoat, shirt and underclothes, all hidden, from the eye. (p. 218)

Here of course the law, as it were, is toyed with, and other knowledges posited but not explored. But elsewhere the same law is simply assumed:

> In a sort of vision I saw the doors open and my feet come out. (*The Expelled,* p. 24)

> All I remember is my feet emerging from my shadow, one after the other. (*The End,* p. 56)

> Not a sound was made within earshot, that he did not capture, and, when necessary, interrogate, and he opened wide his eyes to all that passed, near and at a distance, to all that came and went and paused and stirred, and to all that brightened and darkened and grew and dwindled, and he grasped, in many cases, the nature of the object affected, and even the immediate cause of its being so. To the thousand smells, also, which time leaves behind, Watt paid the closest attention. And he provided himself with a portable spittoon.
>
> This constant tension of some of his most noble faculties tired Watt greatly. And the results, on the whole, were meagre. (*Watt,* p. 83)

So much for the meticulous empiricism outlined so punctiliously ("the nature of the object *affected*"—both felt and affected by certain agents) with regard to Watt and his strategies for achieving certainty. (The use of the word *paused* in the passage from *Watt* is interesting: it depends entirely on what is outside it for its effect. Pause depends on the actions to which pausing stands in relation more than the word *action* depends on the stillness on either side of it.) In spite of the puncture it suffers at the end, the passage is full of aspects of relation, antitheses, comparisons, reciprocities of terms. Out of this Watt gains his "meagre knowledge."

Just as in the lines from *The Expelled* and *The End,* the sight of the narrator's feet moving is the only evidence for knowledge of his going anywhere, and just as things ask Watt to observe their relations in order for them to exist (become objects of knowledge), so Mr. Knott

> needed to be witnessed. Not that he might know, no, but that he might not cease. (p. 207)

Perhaps Mr. Knott is a tranquil man because he is content with being rather than hankering after knowing. Perhaps, too, it seems a plain enough example of the Berkeleian *esse est percipi* that was spatially and visually elaborated in Beckett's *Film*. But it is not so. The above words about Knott

> halting, faint with dubiety, *from Watt's lips* they fell. . . . His habitual tone was one of assurance. [?!] (p. 207, my italics)

It is not surprising that Watt, in such a state, should so confuse a *listener* with the homophones *know* and *no*. And then Beckett, with lapidary skill, disposes of Watt's investigations thus:

> So, at first, in mind and body, Watt laboured at the ancient labour.
> And so Watt, having opened this tin with his blowlamp, found it empty. (p. 134)

A cruel blow for Watt, perhaps. He does not know the very thing you need to know if exploration and alertness are to be of use: what it is you want to find. So in the world of *Watt*, there is an obstacle to establishing knowledge on the principle of *esse est percipi*. For

> the few glimpses caught of Mr Knott, by Watt, were not clearly caught, but as it were in a glass, not a looking-glass, a plain glass, an eastern window at morning, a western window at evening. (p. 146)

To perceive Mr. Knott is to establish a relationship so tenuous as hardly to be a relationship at all, so that Watt's halting definition that Knott needed to be witnessed in order that he might not cease must be modified to

> that Mr Knott might never cease, but ever almost cease. (p. 203)

Broken Relationships

In the light of the above, the voice of *The Calmative* takes on a fresh significance:

> All the mortals I saw* were alone and as if sunk in themselves. It must be a common sight, but mixed with something else I imagine. (p. 43)

Is there something in the idea that someone "alone and sunk in himself," a "seedy solipsist" as *Murphy* has it—for whom objects to relate to are no more than "that residue of execrable frippery known as the non-self and even the world, for short"[14]—is bound to find that all things potentially inviting relationship (or a sense of certainty based on a spatial model of knowledge) never cease but ever almost cease, and create uncertainty all over again? If the subject is not able to act as one term in a relationship of two or more terms, his image of objects is indeed going to be as uncertain as a reflection in a twilight window. For a post-Cartesian consciousness, the guarantee of being depends on the self (mind) being shut off from body and world (matter).[13] Beckett is later (at the end of the seventies) to perceive much more far-reaching relationship between twilight and the absence of certitude.

Some relationships between self and objects are suspect because they may be pacts of habit, insulating us from the cruelties of reality but taking away its enchantments too. Others are suspect because the subject, like Watt or Murphy, is not capable of relating to anything, being usually too much sunk in himself. Murphy's ambition to "come out in his mind" illustrates the solipsist's problem in a nutshell. That ambition and its failure enact the necessity of subject-object relations if certainty is to be achieved: the ambition of mind alone incapacitates Murphy completely. One's inward thoughts do not easily become objects, and do not sufficiently resemble things for the subject to regard and relate to them. It is noticeable how the leitmotif "now I have nothing/no one" in the novel is applied to everyone except Murphy.

> You are all I have in the world, said Celia. (pp. 11, 14)
>
> Now I have no-one, thought Celia, except possibly Murphy. (p. 18)
>
> Now she had nobody, except possibly Mr Kelly. (p. 24)
>
> Now I have no-one, said Mr Kelly, not even Celia. (p. 68)
>
> Neary also had no-one, not even Cooper. (p. 68)

---

*If the narrator of *The Calmative* is assumed to be Beckett, then Watt is probably among them.

Murphy wants to "have" only his own mind, and it is too late when he begins to feel the pain of never being able to "have" Mr. Endon, much as he might have liked to. Shortly before his death, his solipsistic mind has taken enough knocks for him to attempt to summon both a picture of Celia and the possible relationship she had offered him and a picture of his mother, but finds "he could not get a picture in his mind of any creature he had met, animal or human [Meeting is the paradigm of relationship]. Scraps of bodies, of landscapes, hands, eyes, lines and colour evoking nothing, rose and climbed out of sight before him, as though reeled upward off a spool level with his throat" (p. 141). The belated need to relate is shown to be incapable of fulfilling itself.

Objects conduce to knowledge only up to a point. If Beckett's characters are in any way an embodiment of the mental tendencies of modern man, then it is clear that man's inability to establish relationships, together with the threats of habit, is responsible for complicating the subject-object relation to a point far beyond the idea of a consolatory table or Johnson's stone. Owen Barfield sees human intelligence—realization of an "islanded" self separate from its environment, able to contemplate its own body, conscious *of* rather than conscious *in* it—as both the hope and despair of twentieth-century consciousness.[16] But the route to such an impasse, which seems the lot of Murphy and Watt, has involved all efforts, as well as faced all the difficulties, possible to get on terms with objects. That such a complicated process comes to be noticeable—and readable—at all is due to the powers of Beckett's language to objectify, to hold and suggest ambiguities, and due also to the function of marking out mental spaces which Beckett implicitly ascribes to language. It is to this I will now turn.

2
Laughing at the Referent
(*Watt*, *Mercier and Camier*)

Form and Purport

Watt found that the attempt to establish certainty by naming things, or hearing them "wrapp[ed] up safe in words," was not the right or complete answer to his perplexity. Once Watt has grasped the complexity of Mr. Knott's leftover food and the dog, "how the food came to be left, and the dog to be available, . . . then it interested him no more, he enjoyed a comparative peace of mind, in this connection." (p. 75) . . . "For to explain had always been to exorcise, for Watt." (p. 114). Watt is a lazy man, despite being credited by Beckett as "a very fair linguist," and he is at his best when interested. The price one can pay for certainty is to be interested no longer, which is one of the reasons we suspect certainty as we suspect the glib and the cliché. With Beckett's guarded, equivocal attitude to habit in mind, we might do well to remember that nothing is more dangerous than playing safe.

The infinity of space, which is itself as unintelligible as Murphy's "absolute freedom," becomes intelligible when objects, or terms, begin to occupy it and mark out form. A point in infinite space is a step to knowledge; a line between two points is another; the introduction of a third or more points creates a separate space, a new one, which we feel oddly to be master of in a way we can never be of infinite space. (Murphy is mistaken to think his skull is a whole universe: it is a delineated, formed space within infinite space, just as a closed curve is.) The reading of the night sky as it is done by many civilizations is an analogue of this process by which knowledge is marked out from chaos: images and meanings emerge from the relationships drawn up between the points, the stars and planets.

There is a comparable linguistic infinite space, into which certain points and boundaries can be entered, and a sense not unlike certainty achieved. And one advantage of what happens here is that the resulting knowledge is not an exorcism, or extinction of possibility, or a certitude that, like habit, encourages you to be blind with it. It is a different knowledge:

> To think, when one is no longer young, when one is not yet old, that one is no longer young, that one is not yet old, that is perhaps something. (*Watt,* p. 201)

Instead of material objects acting as intelligible terms, linguistic objects are here the terms of relation. Watt, thinking the above words, may cease being worried by things devoid of meaning ("an unintelligible succession of changes") and avoid the boredom of lack of interest. He and the reader—since this is a book for readers as well as for Watt—can take pleasure in as well as interest from the idea that language proposes an entirely new level of subject-object relations in which the terms are linguistic rather than familiarly material, and meaning, even knowledge, a matter of the relations between those terms. Wittgenstein noted "the greater 'purity' of objects which don't affect the senses, numbers for example."[1] If, for the purposes of experiment, we suggest that the relations between a subject and the kitchen table are an example of the old ontology, and that the linguistic bounding of free mental space can be called the new, then the piano-tuning incident and its effect on Watt may be said to be a transitional point between the old ontology and the new.

> . . . a thing that was nothing had happened, with the utmost formal distinctness. (p. 73)

> . . . incidents that is to say of great formal brilliance and indeterminable purport. (p. 71)

Purport is the element belonging to the old ontology; *formal brilliance* and *distinctness* are the elements of the new in this transition. It is the formal distinctness rather than the purport of the words about youth and age that enables Watt to conclude, "That was something." Purport is referential rather than formal. The phrase "thing that was nothing" stands poised between the two ontologies, for it is at once of "indeterminable purport" *and* "something." It is toppled into the new ontology by the suffixed "had happened," however. What has happened is a sentence.

Before tracing this process, a fascinating one, any further, it may be useful to remind ourselves that one of the incidents of the greatest known brilliance and formal distinctness, and the most indeterminable purport, is music. Even the supposed exception to this rule, referential music ("program" music, opera, ballad), is only one class of music, and it is by no stretch of imagination or reason exclusively referential. A set of tones cannot refer to anything tangible, even if they accompany words that do so refer. As Beckett put it, "The other arts . . . can only produce the idea with its concomitant phenomena, whereas music is the idea itself, unaware of the worlds of phenomena. . . . This essential quality of music is distorted by the listener who, being an impure subject, insists on . . . incarnating the idea in what he conceives to be an appropriate paradigm. Thus by definition, opera is a hideous corruption of this most immaterial of all the arts. . . . The beautiful convention of the 'da Capo' is a testimony to the infusible and ineffable nature of an art that is *perfectly intelligible* and *perfectly inexplicable*" (*Proust,* p. 92, my italics).

As so often in comparing Beckett's early works, the phenomenon in question, and its literary and epistemological attractiveness, can be noticed in development from a more or less chancy and unsatisfactory beginning in *Dream of Fair to Middling Women* and *More Pricks Than Kicks* through to a more "seasoned" effectiveness in *Watt* or, as the trilogy period looms nearer, the four novellas. The expression "great formal brillance and indeterminable purport" in *Watt* represents the net effect or culmination of a transfer of ontological principles to the surface of the book (its language) from what it purportedly refers to, its "narrated." Earlier, in *Murphy,* the class of everyday objects—biscuits or furniture, for example—began to merge imperceptibly with a class of objects which cannot so familiarly be taken to be part of a "represented environment."

> For quite some little time Mr Endon has been drifting about the corridors pressing here a lightswitch and there an indicator, in a way that seemed haphazard but was in fact determined by an amental pattern as precise as any of those that governed his chess. . . . Beginning with the light turned off to begin with he had: lit, indicated, extinguished; lit, extinguished, indicated; indicated, lit, extinguished. Continuing then with the light turned on to begin with he had: extinguished, lit, indicated; extinguished, indicated, lit; indicated, extinguished and was seriously thinking of lighting when Murphy stayed his hand. (p. 138)

> Miss Counihan would not have minded going up to Wylie if Celia had not minded Neary coming down to her. Nor would Wylie have objected

> in the least to going down to Celia if Miss Counihan had not objected most strongly to going up to Neary. Nor would Neary have been less than delighted to go down to either, or have either come up to him, if both had not been more than averse to his attentions, whether on the first floor or the second. (p. 144)

This kind of writing is as conscious of itself as of its purport, and the question is whether, as readers, we feel it matters much what the purport is. (That purports mattered little to Beckett here is perhaps argued for by his failing to account for all seven of Murphy's scarves on the first page of the novel.) In Mr. Endon's change-ringing, the material objects—switches—begin to take on the status of grammatical objects instead, and their purport, along with their status as objects, fades somewhat.

It is important to realize that the two passages quoted, perhaps boring if there were too many of them, are examples of only one of the modes in which this "new ontology" operates. *Watt* is notorious for its specialization—indulgence—in this kind of linguistic reality making. Conducting a strictly "no knowledge assumed" narrative, *Watt*'s narrator has to try deductively for fuller knowledge from a very sparse selection of known details. The language of the book makes that bid for "fill-in" knowledge, and while failing as a traditional "literary" effect—some of the passages are virtually unreadable—it succeeds as a linguistic edifice and has the effect of, say, a population density indicator in an atlas. Swarms of words, like swarms of dots over London and New York, connote swarms of possibilities, and no one is expected to count them out one by one so much as to trust the analytic work has been done so that he can gaze on the "radiant measure of . . . total permutability." This process, in fact, gives another meaning to the phrase "wrapped up safe in words": there is a sense in which something ceases to exist altogether when concealed by wrap. At least on the basis of "to be is to be perceived," this is true of any wrapped object, including one wrapped in words. All we shall see is the words covering it.

Concerning *Watt,* one might rewrite Mr. Hackett's speculation on Watt's interrupted trip to the station—"Too fearful to assume himself the onus of a decision, he refers it to the frigid machinery of a time-space relation"[2]—as: too doubtful to assume himself the onus of a decision about reality, Beckett refers it to the mischievous machinery of grammatical relations. It is certainly grammatical relations that try to decide things for Watt himself. And they are not only to be seen as mischievous, trifling relations: the paradox is that telling the truth is a necessary condition for the existence of language. Whatever is said is cast as truth telling until it is retracted consciously with, say, "That's all a pack of lies I feel,"[3] which itself is a new truth told.

Risus Purus: The Laugh that Laughs at the Referent

All the exhaustive documentations of permutability in *Murphy* and *Watt* are more or less crude versions of a practice that becomes more and more sophisticated as Beckett grows, so to speak, into the method and finds it congenial. Those permutations are all permutations of an external order which, even if it does not matter much, nevertheless exists. Murphy's staying Mr. Endon's hand brings us back to "reality" with a bump, and is symbolic of Beckett's reassuming grasp on an external reality which his wit has tempted him to forsake. But when he completely forsakes it, as in this extraordinary passage from *Watt,* the results are stranger still:

> The fact remains and can hardly be denied, that he proceeds by what we call meals, whether taken voluntarily or involuntarily, with pleasure or pain, successfully or unsuccessfully, through the mouth, the nose, the pores, the feed-tube or in an upward direction with the aid of a piston from behind is not of the slightest importance, and that between these acts of nutrition, without which life as it is generally understood would be hard set to continue, there intervene periods of rest or repose, during which no food is taken, unless it be every now and then from time to time as an occasional snack, quick drink or light collation, rendered if not indispensable at least welcome by an unforeseen acceleration of the metabolic exchanges due to circumstances of an imprevisible kind, as for example the backing of a loser, the birth of a child, the payment of a debt, the recovery of a loan, the voice of conscience, or any other shock to the great sympathetic, causing a sudden rush of chyme, or chyle, or both, to the semidigested, slowly, surely earthward struggling mass of sherry wine, soup, beer, fish, stout, meat, beer, vegetables, sweet, fruit, cheese, stout, anchovy, beer, coffee, and Benedictine, for example, swallowed lightheartedly but a few short hours before to the strains as likely as not of a piano and cello. (p. 51)

There is no referent whatsoever in this galaxy of alternatives: its entire law and logic is archly implied by "as likely as not" in the last dozen words. The Civic Guard in *Murphy* was on a similar tack: "When would he learn not to plunge into the labyrinths of an opinion when he had not the slightest idea how he was to emerge?" (p. 29). But the narrator of *Watt* need not learn, although one day he must: his responsibilities now are not those of the Civic Guard. It is noticeable how, as soon as Beckett takes leave, as it were, of the world and jumps on the roundabout of language, the charting of possibilities is no longer the graphlike affair of the combinations of Mr. Knott's shoes and socks, which is a dead affair of dead objects, to say the least. Beckett's conjured eater is all the more alive for his being entirely illusory as far as the novelistic empiricist is concerned. He is confined to only one thing, the sentence (to which he is punctiliously faithful; there is no subversion of grammatical structure); otherwise he is entirely, gloriously free. He is coaxed forth from language and from imagination rather than limited to the conditions of a represented world.

This irrelevance of the external world to the business of writing the book is shown in other ways in *Watt,* for example, by means of a trick played on Watt and the reader concerning the dog and the leftovers. The more certain Watt becomes that his faculties of mentation have explained the situation reasonably, the more absurd appears the entire scenario, until we realize that Watt has probably "foisted a meaning" onto nothing all over again: it would be cheaper to throw Knott's leftovers away than to procure dogs in the way that Watt envisages as the most economical. But the foist has served its turn; moreover, it is a showing of Watt's "noblest faculties" at work. No doubt it tired him greatly, and one is almost grateful for it, considering the "limits to what Watt was prepared to do, in pursuit of information" (p. 110).

In chapter 1 (pp. 31–32) we glimpsed Watt's preference for a "more beautiful explanation". In the new order of object relations, the most beautiful is also the most *real.* Symmetry becomes a meaningful relation of grammatical objects.

> But he had hardly felt the absurdity of those things, on the one hand, and the necessity of those others, on the other (for it is rare that the feeling of absurdity is not followed by the feeling of necessity) when he felt the absurdity of those things of which he had just felt the necessity (for it is rare that the feeling of necessity is not followed by the feeling of absurdity). (p. 131)

"That is perhaps something." There is no agony of uncertainty here, just wry assurance and a certain grace, the verbal negotiation of a corner too often cut by "vice versa." One-way syllogistic equations are attractive in a like way, conducing to a certainty that is as much a satisfaction gained from the disposition of linguistic points as it is of the hunger for reference: "For though we could not converse without meeting, we could, and often did, meet without conversing."[4]

More Pricks Than Kicks offers us insight into Beckett's first essays into these modes of writing. Whereas in *Watt* the practice is so advanced as almost to constitute a new narrative code, the earlier stories concentrate, with rather a narrow range, on subverting the old codes, arguably to prepare the way for the new.

> Hairy, feeling father, brother, husband, confessor, friend of the family, (what family?) *and the inevitable something more,* did the heavy with the reeling groundsman. (p. 196, my italics)

> Now the sun, that creature of habit, shone in through the window.* (p. 179)

> . . . large tracts of champaign . . . (p. 111)

> Belacqua, holding gallantly back with the bag in his hand, enjoyed a glimpse of her legs' sincerity. . . . Certainly he had seen worse. (p. 99)

> There was nothing at all noteworthy about his appearance . . . (p. 29)

> If this Hunnish idea once got a foothold in his little psyche in its present unready condition, topsy-turvy after yesterday's debauch of anxiety and the good night's sleep coming on top of that, it would be annihilated. (p. 172)

These are mere shafts aimed at conventional codes, but they serve to show how conscious Beckett was at this stage of how many "given realities" were assumed and fossilized in certain glib usages and verbal gestures. *Sincerity* is never phonier than when it quotes itself by name (also compare "he made a vague clutch at her sincerities," [p. 27]); Beckett is determined to render the text fully conscious of its own doings and their consequences. Of particular interest in *More Pricks* is Beckett's mockery of that habit of bad fiction writing, to throw in the sponge at a certain—predictable—point and say the event, or emotion, or situation, is beyond words. "The inevitable something more" is a caddish needling of this ten-

*Cf. *Murphy*'s opening sentence, an improvement on this theme: "The sun shone, having no alternative, on the nothing new," and *Mercier and Camier*'s, perhaps less of an improvement: "It's the foul old sun yet again, punctual as a hangman" (p. 105).

dency, which is also burlesqued to perfection in the "Nausicaa" chapter of *Ulysses:* "There was that in her young voice that told she was not a one to be lightly trifled with."[5]

There is in Beckett's mockery a powerful defiance, perhaps a sense of being challenged by the past, which must have been difficult for him to maintain; for Beckett's work—as becomes ever clearer with the passing decades—sails closer to the wind than most, closer than most to the conviction that nothing can be said at all. He wrote less and less in each new book as a result of that conviction, but less and less of what can be said is more welcome than more and more profuse declarations about what cannot be said. It is that "literary" mixture of profusion and escape, a verbose shyness about the ineffable, that Beckett hates. The jibes in *More Pricks* are not intended to suggest that it is easy to bring a situation into words, but that it is a writer's responsibility to do so. No writing worth its salt can safely claim that language cannot cope with what it has had the impertinence to introduce. It is worth remembering how often tragedy is held to deal with things profoundly beyond words: but in fact it deals in words with emergencies that threaten to outrun the capacity of words. What makes tragedy is not a *failure* of speech so much as the effort to stretch words around an unusually intractable situation or object, or to mark out new, radically different relations between words themselves. It is the tensions on the axis of that very enterprise that make for the effect. One of the assumptions underpinning this argument is that to claim something as independent of or beyond words is a presumption for whose veracity the only warrant is the claim itself: "You can only speak of nothing as though it were something."*

Jibes at convention do not stop at *More Pricks*. The almost ludicrous "constructedness" of *Murphy*'s plot has often been commented on as at once an appreciation and exposé of classicism. And some of the more sophisticated tricks appear in the later *Mercier and Camier* (1946):

> Where do we plan to pass the night? said Camier. Under the stars?
> There are ruins, said Mercier, Or we can walk till we drop.
> A little further on they did indeed come to the ruins of a house.
> A good half-century old by the look of them.
>
> (p. 101)

*An alternative exists: to speak of something as though it were something else. An interesting discussion can be found in R. A. Johnson, *Owning One's Own Shadow* (New York: Harper Collins, 1991), pp. 104–15.

Here we are unsure whether Mercier has actually seen ruins ahead that Camier hasn't seen, or whether a "lucky chance!" is being sprung on us by Beckett. About the following case there is no such doubt:

> I'm cold, said Camier.
> It was indeed cold.
> It is indeed cold, said Mercier.
> (p. 21)

In *Murphy* there are jokes which depend for their effect entirely upon the kind of disjunction between word and referent that I have been describing. It is precisely the plethora of associations attached to *surgical* and their inapplicability to Murphy which makes Murphy's "surgical quality" "not quite the right word" (p. 39) and yet in terms of effect just the right word. We are teased likewise with the reasonableness of

> For an Irish girl Miss Counihan was quite exceptionally anthropoid. . . . It is superfluous to describe her, she was just like any other beautiful Irish girl, except, as noted, more markedly anthropoid. How this constitutes an advantage is what every man must decide for himself. (p. 69)

The effect is due, to use contemporary jargon, to focusing more of our attention on the signifier and less on the signified.* The same goes for all the preceding instances, particularly those from *Watt.*

But in *Watt*, *Mercier and Camier,* and the novellas the disjunction takes a further step, so that we can almost see the language of the books generating its own meaning, in the fashion suggested by the Saussurean model of language. This is actually what was happening in the *Watt* passage describing the eater. The referred-to had all but disappeared, as it has here also:

> These north-western skies are really extraordinary, said Mr Goff, are they not.
> So voluptuous, said Tetty. You think it is all over and then pop! up they flare, with augmented radiance. (*Watt,* p. 13)

*This model, useful in commentary on verbal discourse, breaks down with respect to music and mathematics, in which the signifier has no signified that is perceptible to the normal senses. So when Beckett's language takes on the beauty of music and mathematics, at the same time as departing from referentialism, the structuralist explanation becomes useless.

In part 3 of *Watt,* the language takes off independently once again, but drags with it a construct of a world so extravagant in its properties that we realize it is an enchantment, a spell of words, more than anything else. The garden, for instance:

> In it great pale aspens grew: and yews ever dark, with tropical luxuriance, and other trees, in lesser numbers. They rose from the wild pathless grass, so that we walked much in shade, heavy, trembling, fierce, tempestuous.
>
> In winter there were the thin shadows writhing, under our feet, in the wild withered grass.
>
> Of flowers there was no trace, save of the flowers that plant themselves, or never die or die only after many seasons, strangled by the rank grass. The chief of these was the pissabed.
>
> Of vegetables there was no sign. (p. 152)

The incantatory formality, the impertinent indulgence of adjectives—"heavy, trembling, fierce, tempestuous"—give something like this away: the renewed paragraphs enforce the impression that the narrator is not *pointing to* anything, but making it into an organized verbal tissue. The last sentence is particularly brilliant, bearing witness to a notion of vegetables at the same time as ruling that notion out. "Of vegetables there was no sign" is true of the scene that is supposedly, whimsically, portended: but it is not true of the foremost thing. Of vegetables in the text there is indeed a sign, for the voice has introduced them. Likewise, in the tact-mongering phrase "Far be it from me to say *x* is a bore, but . . . ," the very message that is being forwarded is disowned in advance. There is no way we can really get *bore* out of our heads, whatever might follow *but.* That other gambit, "with respect," likewise forgives the speaker in advance for what is often a minimum of respect. Beckett's texts are always alive to such considerations.

Incantatory displays of self-generated meaning occur in *Mercier and Camier* as well, one of the most obvious concerning Helen's parrot. "Shivers of anguish rippled the plumage, blazing in ironic splendour" is definitely more suggestive of the multiform, ambiguous surface of Beckett's writing than it is applicable to the feeble caged bird. The economical ironies of *Mercier and Camier* as a whole presuppose, in their distancing effect, a tenuous connection or nonconnection between language and material reality. "I sense vague shadowy shapes, said Camier, they come and go with muffled cries."[6] The English version of the book is from 1970, and the language has been sharpened and rendered more adroit by Beckett's work on the short texts of the sixties in which his style changed. Before *Imagination Dead Imagine* and the associated texts (1965–79), a sentence like "Every now and then the beak would gape and for what seemed whole seconds fishlike remain agape" (*Mercier and Camier,* p. 27) could not have been written, dispensing as it does with all need for commas and relishing the prefixed *a* (compare *astir, Company*). The English *Mercier and Camier* is not really the same book as the French of 1945.

Some of the very best of Beckett's humor is so entertaining because it ironically straddles the fence between referentialism and a model on which language itself (or at least a pact between the wayward forces of language and the contradictory or recalcitrant world of objects) produces and directs the text.* Often this irony is no more than just a hint, but sometimes, in *Watt* and the novellas especially, the process is absolutely clear:

> The chimneys of Mr Knott's house were *not visible, in spite of the excellent visibility.* On fine days they could be discerned, from the station. For Watt's eyes, when he put himself out, were no worse than another's, even at this time, *and the night was exceptionally fine, even for his part of the country, reputed for the fineness of its nights.* (*Watt,* p. 224, my italics)

> If [the figure] was that of a woman, or that of a nun, it was that of a woman or that of a nun, of unusual size, *even for this part of the country, remarkable for the unusual size of its women, and its nuns.* (*Watt,* p. 226, my italics)

Three times in a few pages we find reiterated this marvelously preposterous obedience of the "referred-to-world" to the whims of the sentence, to the system of language, instead of what is conventionally to be expected, the obedience of the language to the referred-to world.** Reality, insofar as that is the material environment, is held in such an ironic perspective that it can bow without shame to the demands of the linguistic system established by the first terms in each case, "the night was fine" and "it was that of a woman or . . . nun of unusual size." The law is *as likely as not*

---

*This is where Peter Murphy's antideconstructionist view of Beckett, mostly such a welcome reading, practically loses *Watt* altogether. His comment "The way of life, for the artist, necessitates a hungering for the words that will combine the fiction and the real and thereby authenticate the ontology of the fiction" (*Language and Being,* p. 55) would hardly persuade us—if we did not know the novel—that *Watt* is above all a very funny and enjoyable work.

**In similar vein, Coleridge remonstrates with one of his table-talkers: "You abuse snuff! It may be the final cause of the human nose" (*Table Talk,* p. 36).

rather than *more likely than not* or *what is beyond question the case,* both of which beg the very questions I think Beckett's language is trying to ask. The latter both assume a fixed, unalterable world.

The same thing is apparent in:

> Lady McCann, coming up behind, thought she had never, on the public road, seen motions so extraordinary, and few women had a more extensive experience of the public road than Lady McCann. (*Watt,* p. 29)

The last clause is defined less by knowledge, on the part of the author, of Lady McCann's years of travel than by the clauses that come before it—clauses necessitating an account to be given of their existence as clauses. Likewise, from *Mercier and Camier:*

> She was in bed, a trifle unwell, but rose none the less and let them in. . . . I'm a trifle unwell, said Helen. (p. 70)

Or from *The Expelled:*

> There were geraniums in the windows. I have brooded over geraniums for years. Geraniums are artful customers, but in the end I was able to do what I liked with them. (p. 23)

Here the only concession to referentialism is the first sentence of the three. The other two *play* as facts; indeed, the ultimate epistemological token, the verb *to be,* is common to all three sentences. Thus no difference really obtains between them except one established by extralinguistic preconceptions or customs. We think we know more about what "in the window" means than we do about what "artful customers" and "able to do what I like" mean. Thus we feel the first sentence is more referential, more about reality, than the other two. But from a grammatical point of view, there is nothing to bear that out.

Perhaps it is for these kinds of reasons that we elect more easily or instinctively to speak of the narrative *voice* rather than of the narrative mind (and to use, as I have done instinctively in this sentence, *speak* rather than *think* in many cases). The voice, like the wind or the Spirit, turns where it lists: it has no guaranteeable respect for the world, nor for a certain idea of *what* it talks *about:*

> . . . vast turfbogs, a thousand feet above sea level, two thousand if you prefer. (*Mercier and Camier,* p. 97)

> He was wearing a little harness, I remember, with little bells, he must have taken himself for a pony, or a Clydesdale, why not? (*The Expelled,* p. 26)

Why not indeed? similarly, the *voice* of the *The Calmative* effects a change in the posited external world that is usually held to be beyond change (perhaps precisely because it is *held* to be so), as those part-sentences in *Watt* changed their second halves:

> I succeeded however in fastening briefly on the little girl, long enough to see her a little more clearly than before, so that she wore a kind of bonnet and clasped in her hand a book. (*The Calmative,* p. 48)

The usual conjunctive phrase would be a present continuous, "see her more clearly than before, *wearing* a kind of bonnet," implying that whether the narrator saw it or not she would have been wearing it. But here it is *because* he sees her *that* she is wearing it; he sees her "so that" she wears it and carries a book.

Linguistic gestures inherently tend to perpetuate themselves and add to themselves, as in the simple phrase "extends, as far as the eye can see," in which the second clause can be seen as a product of the word *extend* rather than as a verifiable authorial intention to specify the distance. Allusive writing, too, owns that meaning is just as much language's, and history's,* as it is the author's:

> Recollecting these emotions with the celebrated advantage of tranquillity . . . (*The Expelled,* p. 32)

> Hardly had he done so, in the words of the inscription, when he was struck dead by a cannon-ball. (*Mercier and Camier,* p. 10)

> . . . when I composed myself (composed!) to sleep . . . (*First Love,* p. 14)

The rotation of a cliché is similar evidence of the fact that meaning cannot be regarded as the author's own:

> He had felt even worse, he was in one of his better days. (*Mercier and Camier,* p. 110)

---

*"Oscar Wilde's *mot*—that men are made by books rather than books by men—was certainly not pure nonsense; there is a very real sense, humiliating as it may seem, in which what we generally venture to call *our* feelings are really Shakespeare's meaning" (Barfield, *Poetic Diction,* p. 143).

> What they like above all is to sight the wretch from afar, get ready their penny, drop it in their stride and hear the God bless you dying away in the distance. (*The End,* p. 67)

Mercier is *in* better days, rather than having *seen* them: Beckett's renovated cliché is a just joke, showing how even the battered old Mercier, who self-evidently has seen better days, cannot be disposed of as obsolete: some of his days are still undeniably better than others, and he has a right to them, which would be denied outright if we were to think of him as *merely* obsolete. The almsgivers, likewise, not only want to "drop [a coin] in their stride"—as they pass by—but also *to take it in their stride,* that is, not to be self-conscious or seem patronizing about the gift. The subtle alteration of set expressions, so that the old meaning is echoed even while being jostled or denied by the new one—you haven't seen better says if you are *in* one of your better days—is a magnified, consciously cast analogy of the fact that no statement can be solely the author's own. It is hard to wrap things up really safe in words: they are too resourceful of meanings to be bound by the often limited intention of the speaker. In a sense, none of his words is his. They all belong, as it were, to the spatial and temporal union of language users.

From Object to Axis

Beckett's wit often wraps reality in a dangerous cloak rather than a safe one, suggesting that the referent of a word, far from being an object, might be a whole history of ideas, or the record of an irreconcilable conflict, or the expression of a truth that can exist only if expressed in a polar form. This is the reason for the power and justice of what might seem a superficial interest in wordplay: it posits the existence of another world. This world is independent of the senses, and therefore not dependent on the habit-forming sense of material objects that had come to seem such a dubious consolation for the empirical Beckett characters discussed in the first chapter. But it is also a basis for knowledge. The infernal amusement afforded by a work like *Murphy, Watt,* or the novellas is in large part due to the perspective of irony in which language is related to its "real" objects and at the same time to "intentional" and purely linguistic objects. The charge against such a method of writing may be brought that it invites a self-indulgent or shallow enjoyment, and that its consequent vices are lack of weight and lack of seriousness. Kierkegaard might have replied that "irony is the incognito of the moralist,"[7] and that it cannot therefore be judged negatively; it is certainly true that "weightiness" and "seriousness" are just as much characteristics of the fake morality as of the genuine morality. Moral and epistemological terms have become so jaded, so easily used for purposes of deception or unconsciously used to safe-conduct humbug that they alone are no longer an adequate medium for communicating any genuine or clear moral consciousness.

Empirical thought has encouraged us to see the referents of words in terms of objecthood. The finest of Beckett's ironies, however, help us to see them as axes rather than objects: as intersections of numerous conditions of being. It is as axes not as objects, that they are distinct and distinguishable. Beckett's twists make us alive to the dangers of a *habitually objectizing** mode of thought: this is why the experience of reading the early Beckett is infernal, as well as amusing.

Truth, knowledge, and *reality* are philosophical terms at just such a risk of being jaded. It seems to me that Beckett as philosopher as well as moralist in these texts has to tread philosophical areas, if he treads them at all, in an "ironic incognito." Like Socrates, the Kierkegaardian moralist claims not to know what morality is, and Beckett claims likewise to know nothing about knowing. But both stand a better chance of overcoming outworn modes, concepts, and ideologies and staying free of false consolations and hopes. Breaking free of them is not the same thing as running away from them: you can get on proper terms with clichés and ideologies only by asking what exactly they are. And once such an attempt has been made, one stands back from them at that "distance" which is one of the root meanings of *irony.*

Language can either perpetuate habit or offer release from it. Irony, if it is alive, is hard to immobilize or petrify. But irony is also the characteristic trait of a consciousness which is still separated from what it perceives, a consciousness which, in Owen Barfield's phrase, "feels itself to be alone, on an island, cut off from all sense and objective meaning."[8] The irony of Beckett's writing liberates for us more and more senses and meanings; but the irony in his personae islands them indeed and cuts them off from sense and meaning: that is their whole complaint.

---

*I have borrowed this term from Barfield, who in turn borrows it from Coleridge (*Biographia Literaria,* p. 148).

Part 2
Lying and Longing (1945–1965)

3

Lies in the Trilogy (*Molloy, Malone Dies, The Unnamable*)

It is useless to dwell on this period of my life. If I go on long enough calling that my life I'll end up by believing it. It's the principle of advertising. This period of my life. It reminds me, when I think of it, of air in a water-pipe.

—Beckett, *Molloy*

Language contains everything you want . . . It is a kind of drama of human destiny. Its forthrightness and treachery are a drama of the honesty of man himself. Language reveals life.

—Geoffrey Hill

Some of the greatest writers appear not to make it a priority to distinguish fact from fiction. We are used to imprecision about fact and fiction in the field of novels and poetry, but it surprises us when we notice the same imprecision pervading the life story of the writer. Biography can have the power to grip us in a way that fiction seems in danger of losing, partly because we choose to call the latter *fiction,* thereby placing upon it a set of assumptions. Readers have a disconcerting tendency to indulge a writer's apparent inability to tell fact from fiction, and in indulging it we underestimate its impact, patronize it, and run the risk of missing its real meaning. Much of essential value is denied by the use of such terms as *poetic license, fictional devices* and *make-believe,* which imply that something has been accounted for, taken care of, and in a sense defused. The popular usage of *poetic license* in particular carries the assumption that the poetic is necessarily mendacious, needing recourse to falsehoods.

The biography of a literary genius can sometimes insulate us from the disturbing power of the literary works themselves and from their essential equivocation over fact and fiction, because in the case of the biography, everything is supposed to have *really happened.* This glib thought invites another: that the works of, say,

Beckett are farther from *reality* than are the hard facts of his life. This disparity and our tendency to posit it are not easily shrugged off, as they often appear to be by commentary that assumes it is alive to the dangers and makes neat divides between, say, the life of the author and the life of the narrator in first-person narratives. Much literature has arguably been perjured by Coleridge's request to suspend disbelief willingly:[1] to do this while reading a story or watching a play is in fact a consent to beg nearly all the artwork's ontological questions. Everyone is avid for reality, although not everyone conceives the matter in these terms. But literature is generally thought to give us an exciting, or pleasurable, *alternative* to reality. Hence the term *fiction,* and its place between the covers of novels, and its supposed opposite, *fact,* which takes place outside. In libraries and by purveyors of books, fact is nervously retermed *nonfiction:* it carries the uneasy suggestion that for some reason, we hardly dare to call any print or writing fact at all. Beckett's writing exposes some possible causes of, or contributing factors to, this nervousness.

Literary works survive this "lethargy of custom" when their conventions do not appear as such (and invite indulgence) but work as discreetly as possible to transmit what they intend, or, conversely, when they raise into full consciousness all the issues hitherto hidden and assumed in them. From what appears to be their inability to tell fact from fiction, writers help readers to see the veracity of all fiction—its ability to compel—and the fictiveness of much that is assumed to be fact. Things are arranged carefully, in normal life, so that they have, according to that revealing cliché which so shakily shores up its failing resoluteness, "some *semblance* of order." If art were not guarded as an area of licensed disbelief, and thus rendered innocuous, we would find that the gusts of fresh air it created blew out of position all the conventions that had been so carefully established. As areas of licensed disbelief, most literary genres, like safari parks or Indian reservations, are outside the asserted domain of what is real.

Protected trips in the land of fiction are not what Beckett's narratives offer. Quite a lot of realist literature has been written with the protected trip in mind, and is thus, a priori, emasculated. It is not possible to read Beckett's fictions from the comfort of such a protected situation. They cannot gratify. But it would be hard to deny that they have abundant power to "please," in the sense in which Johnson used the word. They call for a suspension not of disbelief but of belief: of its nature, the suspension cannot be called a completely willing one.

The Trilogy: A Pack of Lies?

Running through the language of Beckett's novels, especially concentrated in the trilogy *Molloy, Malone Dies,* and *The Unnamable,* is a legalistic streak which is sometimes strong enough to influence the scenario itself. There are, to start with, many locations and instances of interrogation, often arbitrarily raised and pursued with a peculiar thoroughness and assiduity.* Moran and his son are stuck in this mode throughout their recorded partnership. Gaber has the right of interrogation also. Moran, in his employ, is himself a detective and engaged in the pursuit, with legal consequences, of the truth about Molloy. In *The Unnamable,* one of the substantial terms in the relationship of the protagonist's voice and the world at large is a group identified as "they," who attempt to squeeze out information from the voice and have a juridical severity. Like the searchlights on the characters in *Play,* they succeed in extracting "material." The speakers questioned are unable, usually, to resist: it is as if they are oppressed by obligation. In the whole range of novels up to the period of *The Unnamable,* recurring phrases are embedded in the prose, such as "it would be premature" or "in this connexion," which, whenever they are used, often preposterously, bring to mind the ordering of events needed for police notes or the proceedings at a trial.

> I speak without ceasing, I long to cease, I can't cease, I indicate the principal divisions, more synoptic. (*U,* p. 107)

Another aspect, which will become increasingly important, of behaving as though under orders to produce an account is that to act or speak under orders or duress actually frees one of much of the responsibility for what is said, and certainly delays the attribution of a motive. The onus shifts to the interrogator. Beckett often uses legal language as academics borrow terms like *a case to be made,* showing how secondary literature too can stage itself lin-

---

*The fifth of the *Texts for Nothing* represents the trial literally: "I'm the clerk, I'm the scribe, at the hearings of what cause I know not, . . . This evening the session is calm, there are long silences, when all fix their eyes on me" (*CSP*, p. 85).

guistically as a mock trial. Indeed, in public life it is revealing to find that the machinery of legal process—which depends so heavily on language, especially print, to weed out the truth from untruth or obscurity—is as rich in ontological equivocation as the fictional devices we allow poets to use because we assume they are incapable of telling the truth. But only the assumption that the law is concerned with and able to tell the truth could hope to make us overlook the paradox involved in, say, declaring that a photograph is a *true likeness.* Psychiatrists normally consider a failure to distinguish *"x* is like *y* from *x* is *y"* as a sign of derangement. Similarly revealing is the need for and cost of "legal fictions" in a trial set up in order to distinguish truth from fiction.

Concerning Beckett, the conclusion to be drawn from these equivocations is that, in the trilogy at any rate, the machinery associated with truth and the ways it is used to establish truth are close to indistinguishable from the agencies of untruth.* The notion is not new, any more than the legal process and its oddities are; the Greeks have left writings in which the ideas of the poet as a charlatan and as a prophet are equally valid.[2] What is interesting about Beckett is that he makes sure we are pressed as we should be by the closeness, in language and thought, of fact and fiction, truth and untruth. Neither the idea of make-believe—"let us suppose that what I'm going to tell actually happened"—nor the idea of faithfully reporting, Defoe-like, will work in his novels. He is one of the greatest candid liars in the language.

> When I said I had turkeys and so on, I lied.
>
> It is midnight. The rain is beating on the windows. [. . .] It was not midnight. It was not raining.
>
> The porcelain, the mirrors, the chromium, instilled a great peace within me. At least I suppose it was they. It wasn't a great peace in any case. (*M,* p. 127)
>
> The last word is not yet said between us. Yes, the last word is said.
>
> Yes, it was a plateau, Moll had not lied, or rather a great mound with gentle slopes. (*MD,* pp. 31, 130)

*H. Porter Abbott in "Beckett and Autobiography" says: "On the side of words, the poet is necessarily not on the side of truth" (in Friedman, Rossman, and Sherzer, *Beckett Translating/ Translating Beckett,* p. 123).

> I drowned, more than once, it wasn't I, . . . thumped on my head with wood and iron, it wasn't I, no wood, no iron. (*U*, p. 124)

These kinds of remarks are rare in novel writing, even in the novels we might expect to contain them, like *Tristram Shandy.* In that book all the lies are cunningly concealed, or saved till the end (the admission that the novel is a cock-and-bull story, for instance). But Beckett threatens to show that lying is an inevitable part of all uttered or written language. (Even in ordinary conversation the words "I tell a lie" are common.) Indeed, for Beckett it has a naturalness; we are hardly shocked at the direct about-turns in most of the above sentences. The lying mind is obviously the producer of this, too:

> But can one speak here of fresh and ancient cares? I think not. But it would be hard for me to prove it. What I can assert, without fear of—without fear, is that I gradually lost interest in knowing, among other things, what town I was in. (*M*, p. 68)

Mixed with the opportunity for a lie just cut short by the dash—we would easily believe whatever Beckett might have inserted there—is the concern with clarity and precision: "among other things" and "it would be hard for me to prove it" are purely gestures, meaning "leave no stone unturned, this is supposed to be a report." The concern to admit that things would be hard to prove has the air of faultless responsibility. And, absurd though it sounds, the lies that abound in the trilogy can be identified as lies only by virtue of the narrator's confessing them to be lies as soon as he has told them, or shortly afterward. Just as we feel there is undeniable veracity in the proverb of the Cretan Liar, so we do not feel exactly cheated by a liar as adroit as Beckett, even though, like the proverb, he unsettles our distinction of fact from fiction.

The written word is what seals legal agreements and conclusions: Beckett's prose conjures up a world in which the written word can be the ultimately *non*-committal medium. If Beckett does not always lie as outrightly as in some of the above-quoted sentences, his narrators' reports are often left open to review at any moment:

> A little dog followed him, a pomeranian, I think, but I don't think so. . . . The little dog followed wretchedly, after the fashion of pomeranians, stopping, turning in slow circles, giving up and then, a little further on, beginning all over again. (*M*, p. 12)

> [Sapo] left the house on the pretext that he worked better in the open air, no, without a word. (*MD,* p. 23)

> Lemuel remained for a long time plunged in thought, . . . motionless or if you prefer scratching his armpit. (*MD,* p. 116)

White lies, perhaps, but again they jolt our intake of information while maintaining the air of ostensible credibility. Notice how the speaker's incompetence to identify the dog, truthfully exposed by "I don't think so," is given an attempted patching up, as though to say, if it moved "after the fashion of pomeranians," then perhaps it was one, despite the uncertainty. But the added remark, "Constipation is a sign of good health in pomeranians" alerts us to the likelihood of a lie here, too, in the midst of the laborious giving of evidence. Never was the job of identifying something undertaken with so much assiduity and with so little result. Then there is the double lie in the Sapo sentence. Sapo is a liar, to use a pretext; yes, to lie in that way is no doubt what Sapo would do, given the contextual information about him and his ways. But "no," he went "without a word." This is also just as likely a course. By the lie we are being given more information: we know what he *would* do (make a pretext), what he tempted Beckett to say he would do, and, finally, what Beckett would have him do "in fact." But in such a prose the final fact, the end product of the process of review, has no more the ring of fact* as against fiction than has any that preceded it.

There is a sense that throughout these three fascinating novels, everything that surfaces could be a result of the narrator's faulty judgment.

> And perhaps it was A one day at one place, then C another at another, then a third the rock and I, and so on for the other components, the cows, the sky, the sea, the mountains. I can't believe it. No, I will not lie, I can easily conceive it.

> Cows were chewing in enormous fields, lying and standing in the evening silence. Perhaps I'm inventing a little, perhaps embellishing, but on the whole that's the way it was. They chew, swallow, then after a short pause effortlessly bring up the next mouthful. A neck muscle stirs and the jaws begin to grind again. But perhaps I'm remembering things. (*M,* pp. 8, 15)

---

*And, by analogy, the ring of truth. Cf. the lost truth in *Worstward Ho,* pp. 20 and 32.

The last sentence is the fuse to the implications of everything said there and henceforward in the trilogy. That drifting hold on the cliché "seeing things" alerts us, as Beckett's treatment of many clichés does, to the incendiary nature of some of them. "Seeing things" or "remembering things" means that in fact you neither see nor remember correctly. As here:

> An aeroplane passed overhead with a noise like thunder. It is a noise quite unlike thunder, one says thunder but one does not think it. (*MD*, p. 118)

So can language lie as it declares. No wonder a specialist in language, like a writer, cannot tell fact from fiction. In one sense, fiction is all that he has at his command. If he tells lies, their renunciations are trapped in the same medium, the words on paper. Nevertheless, there is no doubt of the extraordinary energy still being released in Beckett's writing at this stage. It is evident in his enjoyment of adding that word *embellishing* to a sentence that has already made its point. The image evoked of the pasture is at once bleak, commonplace, and faintly romantic—the "evening silence" belongs to the world of *Four Quartets,* whereas "enormous fields" in which cows do the predictable thing, "lie" and "stand," can only be boring. This given, the narrator then says, "Perhaps I'm inventing a little," which is fair enough; perhaps he is. But then comes yet another spurt, the squib, as it were, that explodes last: "perhaps embellishing." In speech this would sound parenthetic; an extra breath would be necessary to fit it in. And again, because of its arguable superfluity, it is absurd. The word *embellish* itself also has an uneasily genteel ring in English ears, suggestive of fake; and its etymology, if we notice it in passing, is preposterous in this context (Old French en + *bel,* "beautiful"). The hidden fire in such jokes as this is what also lurks in the face Beckett presents to the camera on the cover the Jupiter edition of *Molloy.* He is false enough to embellish, and responsible enough to alert us to that fact in a faintly insolent and amusing manner.

There is the same ring in a remark about a sheep butcher in *Molloy:*

> And if he was going away from the town that meant nothing either, for slaughterhouses are not confined to towns, no, they are everywhere, the country is full of them, every butcher has his slaughterhouse and the right to slaughter, according to his lights. (*M,* p. 80)

And in Malone's fatuous agenda:

> I think I shall be able to tell myself four stories, each one on a different theme. One about a man, another about a woman, a third about a thing, and finally one about an animal, a bird probably. (*MD,* p. 7)

Again there is specificity for the sake of it: "a bird probably" is tagged on, like a feeble explosion, to a list which is already absurd for the degree of organization applied to so vague a subject. The rush of specificity in the slaughterhouse passage likewise claims attention, but the clichés and hurry—"no, they are everywhere, the country is full of them" and the pun on *lights*—take the bottom out of the credibility and are perhaps new lies told to wreck the ostensible effort to get things clear. (For instance, the country is hardly likely to be "full of" slaughterhouses.)

One wonders how this air of pedantic responsibility, which covers the first two books in the trilogy, can be maintained where none of the promises is fulfilled. Beckett has the habitual academic fussiness—"What business has innocence here? What relation to the innumerable spirits of darkness? It's not clear."[3]—which makes us think his mode of writing in these novels has been conditioned or determined by the presence of a panel of interrogators, "they," "Basil and his gang,"[4] but the net effect of reading the prose is as much one of being bombarded with evasive devices as of scrupulousness. It is strange that speech, which is all the trilogy can be said to consist of, seems to blend the two contradictory intentions, the one of responsibility and the other of evasiveness or escape. Those tags, "a bird probably" and "perhaps embellishing" cannot be faulted on grounds of failing to enlarge the information. Nor can this:

> My weekly supply of lager, half a dozen quart bottles, was delivered every Saturday. I never touched them until the next day, *for lager must be left to settle after the least disturbance.* (*M,* p. 116, my italics)

But they are all unmistakably pieces of talk such as would be babbled out by someone who wants to evade a certain question, as are characteristic phrases that appear in all Beckett's prose: "that is to say," "in this connection," "but he was still young," "needless to say." Such babble fills the moment with new words, which it is hoped will seize the listener's attention long enough to banish or shelve the question really being asked. This is precisely what the embellishing and copious reporting does. There can be no doubt that Beckett is trying to make us suspect the commonly accepted notion that the more organized information is, and the more there is of it, the more truthful a picture of reality we will get. It is particularly true of nineteenth-century and realist novel-writing conventions—what Beckett in *Proust* called "the grotesque *fallacy* of a *realistic art*"[5]—that each new detail is adding a prop to a stage that we are going to think is real rather than a stage, because it is so faithful to what exists.

> I am even capable of having learnt what his profession is, I who am so interested in professions. And to think I try my best not to talk about myself. In a moment I shall talk about the cows, and the sky, if I can. (*M*, p. 13)

This is a typical Beckett mixture: the ironic and archaic "I who am so interested" recalls the ponderous information-giving of a George Eliot in bad form; it has a musty feel, which we suspect is ironic because it looks anachronistic compared with the reflexive remarks about narrative conduct he goes on to make. Molloy may indeed have been interested in professions, though it is doubtful on the evidence. But in any case, it is a useless and evasive ploy, and it advertises itself as one. The whole Moran story (*Molloy*, part 2), unique as it is in the trilogy for being a staged "novelette" with familiar objects, time sequence, and locale, is an object lesson in the ultimate mendaciousness of all attempts to provide truthful information, an "authentic picture," or a "true likeness" of the world. Every detail is in fact an evasion, as the treatment of this one pinpoints:

> I had no information as to his face. I assumed it was hirsute, craggy, and grimacing. Nothing justified my doing so. (*M*, p. 122)

At one point Moran moves toward diagnosing his own evasive tactics:

> For in describing this day I am once more he who suffered it, who crammed it full of futile anxious life, with no other purpose than his own stultification and the means of not doing what he had to do. And as then my thoughts would have nothing of Molloy, so tonight my pen. (*M*, p. 131)

Hence all the delay in departing, the elaborate confession scene with Father Ambrose, the gratuitous information—all of it ostensibly warrantable—about the lager. But in "visionary" passages like the one above, Beckett explores the problem, and challenges us to view the symptoms and the diagnosis together. It is as if a mental malady made telling the truth impossible, however determined the sufferer is to try.

Lies as "Performative Truths"

Disturbing conclusions might be inferred from the above picture of lying in Samuel Beckett's trilogy prose, and of contingent forms of not telling the truth.* It is difficult to call the principle of endless review of propositions lying; indeed, such a principle could be seen as an extra display of fidelity to fact. To say, "Those were the circumstances. No, they were otherwise" opens two avenues of reply. One might be to suggest erasing the original statement and leaving its qualification. Another would be to expand the qualification into a new statement. The trouble with a statement like "He left the house on the pretext that he worked better in the open air, no, without a word" is that in some ways, the qualification depends for its proper function on its difference from the original statement. In this example, the only reason why it does is that the sentence "he left without a word" would seem redundant or boring in comparison with what we are given. But in a case such as

> a small dog . . . a pomeranian I think, but I don't think so,

the net result of the review depends logically on the first, mistaken assumption. The truth and the lie must, as it were, cooperate. Another example of complete ontological incompetence (again concerning dogs),

> The dog was uniformly yellow, a mongrel, I suppose, or a pedigree, I can never tell the difference . . , (*M*, p. 36)

nevertheless manages to succeed as a declaration of information. The distinctive feature of such bet-hedging talk is again the excess of plausible detail employed in a seemingly honest portrayal of what happened. But no sooner is the information given than it is taken away again.

Why, it would be reasonable to ask, put it there in the first place? How can something be declared and denied at the same time? The

---

*See Sissela Bok, *Lying: Moral Choice in Public and Private Life,* for an excellent discussion of the subject.

answer, or one of the answers, is that every detail is in fact another declaration and can work to support the declaration that it denies. This may sound nonsensical, but it is difficult to refute the proposition that most language, once it is put into a structure of some kind, into a "connected statement,"* asserts something. It cannot actually negate anything. The closest you can get to negating something is not to say it, rather than to say and deny it. The very words *structure* and *linguistic construct* demonstrate the building process that takes place every time speech is uttered or writing written. In one particular sense—one very useful to a reading of Beckett's prose—the truth or untruth of an utterance, the question whether it is a lie or not, is subsidiary to the truth of its having been uttered—constructed—at all. And since it is subsidiary, it cannot easily enjoy the status of truth-value. Heidegger and Marx had the same point to make: truth is located in praxis rather than in intellectual systems. In the case of Beckett's prose, truth-status has been usurped by the enormous positive declaration that is the book or speech. If this proposition seems too absurd to take seriously, think of the positiveness that attends images of negation or denial in normal life. *Emphatic denials* and *unanimous no's* cannot easily be classed as nonaffirmative. Nor can Alban Berg's remark that Mahler's Sixth Symphony "says a definite no." The phenomenon has mysterious roots, and Beckett manages to tap them and make their effects noticeable where often they lie concealed by the unremitting normality of everyday life. His war against Habit is waged from unlikely positions.

In some ways Beckett's treatment of the problem is much simpler than one might expect. Not only are Beckett's trilogy novels like speeches, and therefore of a simpler structure than either a play (with its many voices, speeches, and time schemes) or a novel (with its many registers of utterance, from that of the demagogic "organizer" of the whole down to that of a minor character appearing only once); they also address the fundamental matter of speech and its ontological status. On occasions Beckett's fiction at this period reads more like essays—we have seen how academic and/or reflexive a great deal of his writing is. Perhaps it is fair to say that Beckett in the trilogy is always speaking precisely as academics speak: as though he is accountable to the truthmongers,

---

*Beckett has used this locution twice: he attributes it to Duthuit in *Proust and Three Dialogues,* p. 122 and repeats it in *The Unnamable,* p. 53.

whoever they are, whether a "dirty pack of fake maniacs"[6] or the ministers of God and justice.*

For the narrators of the trilogy, the basic linguistic truth to which it seems all other truths and falsehoods sacrifice their status is this:

> I have nothing to do, that is to say, nothing in particular. I have to speak, whatever that means.
>
> I emit sounds. If that's not enough for them, I can't help it. (*U,* p. 30, 70)

These are as much biographical statements on the part of Beckett as they are elements in a genre classified as fiction; and to say this is not to reduce them to psychological curios. It us undeniable, I think, that the tenor and tone of those two sentences from *The Unnamable* are indistinguishable from the tone and tenor of Beckett's public statements recorded in Bair's biography and elsewhere. "My work is a matter of fundamental sounds" is a famous comment of Beckett's (made to Alan Schneider), and he went on to say that their meaning was something critics could haggle over if they wanted. When in *The Unnamable* he said, "If that's not enough for *them,* I can't help it" it is quite likely that Beckett's public was meant to be a possible analogue for the gang of interrogators referred to as "them" throughout his works. Not only a public of critics, of course: beyond saying what he has said in his novels, it seems it was impossible for Beckett to help even a general reader of them toward the "real meaning" either.

"No, I must not try to think, simply utter,"[7] says the voice of *The Unnamable.* Contemporary theory and linguistics have suggested that we view utterance as a form of *action* (the "performative" or "illocutionary" aspect).[8] The value of new theory is often more a matter of what changes of perspective it has occasioned than of altering the contents of intellectual life itself. But the changed perspective on language and its performative aspect is useful to an appreciation of Beckett's novels. The above-quoted sentence could be re-written as

> No, I must not try to think, simply act,

which amounts to sane advice from a man whose career as an

It seems to me that, for Beckett, they are either one or the other. The spirits that exact from him all his work could not occupy any station between those extremes. Beckett make no ultimate decision as to which side they are on. It academic was terminated by his own choice. To many readers of his biography, it would seem that Beckett opted for a life of inaction—opted out, as it were—when he refused to continue at Trinity College, Dublin, teaching others "what he didn't know himself,"[9] and later refused academic posts in the United States. But a life of writing was what he chose, under the compulsion to utter. A self-alleged inability to do so—"I can't go on"—did not kill the compulsion: "I must go on, I'll go on." Beckett is in many ways seen as a writer whose work has been stalled by too much thinking, but the headlong compulsion to utter, "with a kind of fury,"[10] seems to invite a more primary, and simpler, interpretation than that. "A poet writes because he has to" is how Arthur Guirdham put it.[11]

Utterance is an action employed both in lying and in telling the truth. Like denial, lying is direct, active, and positive: to lie silently is virtually impossible because lying depends on a use of language which the reader or hearer takes in good faith. Actively speaking, in respect of praxis, lying is a truth-gesture, an incursion into the social fabric: only thus can it succeed. Silent concealment of a state of affairs is a generically different form of deception, for it does not offer new information with the claim of truth; it merely avoids showing the old. Folk wisdom supports this view of lying: those with the most to say are the liars, those with least the wise:

> And I shall not abandon this subject, to which I shall probably never have occasion to return, with such a storm blowing up, without making this curious observation, that it often happened to me, *before I gave up speaking for good,* to think I had said too little when in fact I had said too much, and in fact to have said too little when I thought I had said too much. I mean that on reflection, in the long run rather, my verbal profusion turned out to be penury, and inversely. (*M,* p. 36, my italics)

This passage, riddled with crooked axes, shows an almost burdensome awareness in the author of the risks attending any utterance whatsoever. Lies are all too easily told. In this passage alone, the whole thing is not in fact made clear—although the word *fact* is ventured—but it is a potent enough introduction to the subject to make the inklings multiply. As usual, there is a certain amount

---

would be unwise to conclude from the evidence of *Not I* or *How It Is* or *The Unnamable* that they are demons.

*Such "primary" interpretations can be found in Jung's essays "Psychology and Literature" and "On the Relation of Analytical Psychology to Poetry" (in *The Spirit In Man, Art and Literature,* pp. 65–105).

of information: the narrator has stopped speaking altogether, for some reason, at a point after the recognition about verbal penury but before the moment of narration. A period of inertia of this kind is not unusual in Beckett's speakers. Recall Molloy finding "the necessary words and accents" to beg, or the narrator's "way of assimilating the vowels and omitting the consonants" in *The End.*[12] Like the bodily disabilities of the Beckett heroes, the refusal to speak, or the forgetting how to, is most likely a symptom, in this case about the truth-status of speech. It is a symptom articulated in the thought that

> Whatever [is] said was never enough and always too much.[13]

The narrator's sense of responsibility about giving an account of himself before the judges stands him in good stead here. There is no doubt that he is breaching the wall of evasiveness which the narrative of *Molloy* as a whole has been building up. This is why Beckett cannot merely be seen as a liar and fabricator.

It is an underlying notion of truth, or, if not of truth, of some reckonable power, which causes in part that tendency to an infinite review of declarations: there is something to which his linguistic gestures, his white lies about Sapo and the pomeranian for instance, do *not* approximate. As *The Unnamable* has it, "Our concern is with someone, or something, that is not there" (p. 122). In another phrase, "in the frenzy of utterance" (compare the "fury" mentioned earlier), there is "a concern with truth,"[14] and this makes everything hazardous. Perhaps the frenzy and fury derive from there. There is a feeling of hazard in the passage from *Molloy* about speaking quoted above; the narrator fears a "storm blowing up." Also, "on reflection" is reviewed and left as "in the long run, rather," which indicates that "on reflection" was too safe a bet to stick with, partly because reflection is something he wants to avoid—"Try not to think, simply utter"—and also because the solidified, ready-made phrase "on reflection" is linguistically tempting, almost as unpremeditated and easy to insert as a breath, and therefore probably meaningless:

> I know those little phrases, . . . Once you let them in, they pollute the whole of speech. Nothing is more real than nothing. (*MD,* p. 22)

This, coupled with the likelihood that thinking in sequence is beyond the capabilities of the man Molloy anyway, makes the whole bid to modify "on reflection" a joke as well as a diagnosis of the ills of speech itself.

But this prose cannot easily be tied down. It is easy to argue that the sentence "I mean that on reflection, in the long run rather, my verbal profusion turned out to be penury, and inversely" is as evasive and imprecise a series of hitches and jolts as one is ever likely to come across, and also to argue that it only just saves itself by the adroit sparing of even greater fuss in its neat ending, "and inversely." Three declarations, none of them sitting very well with the others, are made: "I mean" (which itself seems a review of a previous thought); "on reflection"; and "in the long run"—what *does* he mean if he changes tack twice in midsentence?—and they are all supposed to relate to what follows. The reason why I cannot dismiss them as a smokescreen or words merely intended to bamboozle us is that as in the previous examples of "reviewing" techniques, it looks here as if what could have been crossed out is consciously left in place. Phrases such as "or rather" and the formerly frequent "nay," used to preface a change of direction in speech and prose, are not unique to Beckett's writing: in a great deal of utterance there is a tendency *not* to delete first thoughts after the advent of second thoughts; and this says something about language and the independence it seems to acquire once it has been released into the air or onto paper. It is uncancelable, much as we might wish to cancel it and frequently attempt to.

But Beckett is unusually aware of the consequences of this for anyone who "in the frenzy of utterance" has "a concern with the truth." If there is anything in the idea that language once uttered claims its own existence and defies absolute or immediate deletion, then the ontological status of lying, as it is actually *done,* turns out to be disturbingly high. If a lie is a form of action, and if actions really speak louder than words when legal evidence is in question, then where is the truth of a case to be found? Or where does it lie? is perhaps the juster question.

> *I simply believe I can say nothing that is not true,* I mean that has not happened, it's not the same thing but no matter. Yes, that's what I like about me, at least one of the things, that I can say Up the Republic! for example, or Sweetheart! for example, without having to wonder if I should not rather have cut my tongue out, or said something else. Yes, no reflection is needed, before or after, I have only to open my mouth for it to testify to the old story, my old story. (*MD,* p. 77, my italics)

> I must lend myself to this story a little longer. There may possibly be some truth in it. (*U,* p. 37)

> He began to talk. He was right. Who is not right? I left him. (*M,* p. 133)

> But it is gone clean out of my head, my little private idea. No matter, I have just had another. Perhaps it is the same one back again, ideas are so alike when you get to know them. (*MD,* p. 64)

The implication is outrageous, the unease unmistakably evident. The mischief of the lie is that it can convince. "I *tell* myself so many things," says Malone, realizing that when he does so he is filling his mind with material—thought structures, images, stories—that has no reason not to be valid, even though we are used to a process of sifting through possibilities to weed out the invalid from the valid. There is a grim undertone in the affable-sounding "ideas are so alike, when you get to know them"; that is, one idea is substitutable for another, and yet the ultimate significance of their having been conceived is left unchanged. We are also put in mind, by that phrase "when you get to know them," of how rarely we do get to know any of our ideas. There is a kind of anguish in the remark. A defense, or deflector, is put up against each of these four assertions, within the tissue of the assertion itself. In the first passage there is an assumed flippancy, a light mood, darkening at the edges when "the old story, my old story" creeps in. There is the academic's fussiness again in "at least one of the things," accuracy for the record. But generally there is forced lightness. Likewise, a careless tone deflects the import of the lines from *The Unnamable,* and testy rhetoric influences the *Molloy* line.

Forced lightness also characterises the shock, administered in the same unnervingly casual way, in Moran's narrative:

> Molloy, or Mollose, was no stranger to me.

The change of name is given no explanation. It stares out of the page, arbitrary and without referent.* But it is only an extension onto the level of the single word (a group of letters) of what is happening in the trilogy prose (groups of words) all the time: any

---

*Angela Moorjani (in Friedman, Rossman, and Sherzer, *Beckett Translating/ Translating Beckett,* p. 151) has suggested that *Mollose* is a coalescence of Molloy and Lousse, which is plausible. But it does not explain why Moran, who knows nothing about Molloy, should thus allude to Molloy's affair with Lousse.

syntactic whole, whether or not qualified by "That's all a pack of lies, I feel,"[15] gathers to itself an unshakable status. This is what prompts the speaker of the third extract above to say in a helpless rhetorical wonder at what seems immutable: "He began to talk. He was right. Who is not right? I left him." It is a powerful chain of inferences, and he dares not doubt a single one. Since the substance of the "talk" is left unclear—as it so often is—we suspect that it is also unimportant. But "he was right," whatever it was that issued from his mouth. And on top of that comes the thought that of those who talk, none, presumably, can be wrong. There is no way of telling. "Who is not right?" It seems that talk is sufficient. Molloy, Mollose, even Moloch—what name is not right? And yet, just as the forced lightness of one passage makes us at heart uneasy, the four separate sentences and rhetorical question in this line give us pause.

What we are being alerted to in these passages, and many others in the same vein in the trilogy, is the reality of what is normally assumed to be fiction, and the fictiveness of what is assumed to be fact. *Mollose* appears more fictive than Molloy, since Molloy's name has become a known quantity, whereas *Mollose* appears only once, unexplained beyond possible identity with Molloy. And partly because *Mollose* is not explained or apologised for, it challenges us to accept it into the sphere of the given without question. This interchange of fact and fiction is something we are not usually aware of. This is why there is a sense, even in Beckett's writing at these points, of bewilderment. *First Love* had suggested this already, with another unexplained word:

> I heard the word fibrome, or brone, I don't know which, never knew what it meant, . . . The things one recalls! and records! (*CSP,* p. 14)

In the early prose the same interchange was a source of enjoyment. The lead of language was followed in *Watt,* for example, with a degree of merriment and abandon that should make us doubt Deirdre Bair's view of the novel as a document of schizoid depression.[16] But in the trilogy the hues are darker, even though the laughter is not gone. The "little phrases" that were so enjoyed by the Beckett describing Lady McCann's knowledge of the road or the fineness of the nights around Mr. Knott's nearest railway station,[17] now "*pollute* the whole of speech"; and in the trilogy, speech has replaced the narrative of the earlier novels. The fact that language can build itself up into formidable tales and structures, seemingly independent of any prior reality, and can convince the speaker that they nevertheless represent "his old story," has become a threat. In the midst of Malone's blustering comes a frightening distinction, slipped in sideways:

> I can say nothing that is not true, I mean that has not happened, it's not the same thing but no matter. (*MD*, p. 77)

Why is it not the same thing? If something happened, can it be said not to have been fact? And if something did not happen, can it be said to be true? If the easy advent of a lie, or of Mollose, is anything to judge by, the answer is yes. "Nothing is more real than nothing."[18]

Truth and Silence

This is Molloy, in expansive frame of mind, expanding his concept of things:

> And now it was the name I sought, in my memory, . . . with the intention, as soon as I had found it, of stopping, and saying to a passer-by, doffing my hat, I beg your pardon, Sir, this is X, is it not? X being the name of my town. And this name that I sought, I felt sure that it began with a B or with a P, but in spite of this clue, or perhaps because of its falsity, the other letters continued to escape me. I had been living so far from words so long, you understand, that it was enough for me to see my town, since we're talking of my town, to be unable, you understand. It's too difficult to say, for me. And even my sense of identity was wrapped in a namelessness often hard to penetrate, as we have just seen, I think. And so on for all the other things which made merry with my senses. Yes, even then, when already all was fading, waves and particles, *there could be no things but nameless things, no names but thingless names.* I say that now, but after all what do I know now about them, now when the icy words hail down upon me, the icy meanings, and the world dies too, foully named. *All I know is what the words know.* . . . And truly it little matters what I say, this or that or any other thing. Saying is inventing. (*M*, p. 33, my italics)

And to invent is to lie, as has become clear. But such things as Exelmans!, "Watt snites,"* Mollose, or this phrase:

> the paraclete perhaps, psittaceously named[19]

*Watt, reappearing in *Mercier and Camier* (1974), says the Constable was "dying for a snite" (p. 113).

definitely veer toward the category of "thingless names." Whether because the names are "invented" or simply beyond the reader's ken, their mere occurrence, like *First Love*'s "fibrome," is their raison d'être, not what they name. The intention of such tactics is to make that clear and unmistakable. Once that is established, it is easier to see the entire narrative in a similar light. "Saying *is* inventing." And yet, far more than a passing nonsense word or unfathomable lexis, a speech text as long as *Malone Dies* has significance and objective existence. It has become an object, a book, generally available.

But in one sense the text itself is an enormous extended version of the thingless name or lie: "And truly it little matters what I say, this or that or any other thing"—this could be translated as: And truly I may lie, for all the difference it will make to readers of me. "Ideas are so alike, when you get to know them." The word *truly* is an odd sign in this argument, but it is there for a reason. The long passage from *Molloy* above is another fine example of Beckett giving an account of himself to the judges: the passage is a digression from the "story"—"To hell with it anyway," he finishes, "Where was I?"—and to a large extent it analyzes, or attempts to analyze, why he neither tells the truth (because he cannot) nor keeps quiet (because he must not). It is full of terms with vying truth-values—"*Truly* it little matters", "I *know*", "perhaps because of its falsity"—and these are probably nearer the key to what fiction is for Beckett than is anything else in the passage. Of the things, and names, he says, "But after all what do I *know* now about then, now when the icy words hail down upon me, the icy meanings, and the world dies too, foully named." For the speaker here, naming does not contribute to knowledge and order, as most of us think most of the time. Once named, the world dies. It is a sobering thought, and it opens up, as does the remark that there are "no things but nameless things," the possibility of a world in which the existence of things, properly understood, can only happen in silence, undiscussed, unnamed, unreported. The image of frozen rain attached to meaning and word as they relate to the world is extraordinary, the very opposite of what Watt experienced when in naming an object he "made for it a pillow of old words" and was to some degree comforted. The narrator of the passage cannot any longer read, write, or speak fluently, and this cannot be fortuitous, given the "namelessness" in which his identity has become "wrapped," and given that the existence of things can be pure only if it is nameless as well. One wonders what the connection is: whether because he has lost the ability to speak (name) and read (assimilate names) he can no longer perceive a world in which speech and objects are in harmony—a world that does not die named—or whether the life of named things was so much an exposure to icy wind that he abandoned linguistic faculties the better to appreciate objects in their "true" state, as one does music, "the idea in itself, unaware of the worlds of phenomena" (Cf. *Proust,* pp. 91–93)

But if truth resides only in the nameless thing, then it is inaccessible. The term *truth* can then enter a linguistic structure only as a metaphor or "parasemantic" gesture indicating a direction rather than a value. The narrator (or narrators) of the trilogy have a habit of trying to criticize all the language that has been uttered, and the criticisms bring with them, inevitably, a sense of value. All the words are seen as symptoms by their speaker:

> When I said I had turkeys and so on, I lied.

If saying is inventing, and if anything said must be true, then he would have no need to say this. He corrects the information to the claim that he had some hens. When he says he lied, he means it. And similarly, when he says, "Truly it does not matter what I say," he means that, too. Another sense of value is always reaching into the discourse, from a level one degree higher than the apparent one.

In the first two volumes of the trilogy, this state of split knowledge persists and could be thought a serious confusion by a bewildered reader. But there do seem to be two identifiable species of knowledge being annexed all the time. One is related to the firmness of the bond between words and fact—"all I know is what the words know"—and to a faith in words themselves as a guarantee of truth: "I must lend myself to this story a little longer, there may possibly be some truth in it"—this means, more or less, that if enough is uttered, some of it will be bound to "testify to the old story, my old story." The other knowledge is that of the nameless thing: by definition unspeakable. Unspeakable perhaps in both senses, for it is arguable from another perspective that where words end, inhumanity begins. But this is to anticipate.

In a parallel process, truth too, though not an absolutely "parasemantic" gesticulation, has become a cheaper commodity as the first two novels progress. Side by side with the compulsion to give evidence to the trial, there is an insolence and roguery that seeks to justify talking about anything at all, however arbitrary. The longer Molloy and Malone blunder on, the more credible and creditable their linguistic edifices will be. The moments of deep puzzlement, like the *Molloy* passage quoted on page 78, do not detain the romancer for long. Two notions of truth are dabbled with, just as two knowledges are, and each weakens the other. The narrator's admission that he had turkeys could be just as true as that he said he had hens. He cannot come down on either side, and ruffles our perceptions of both sides:

> But this evening, this morning, I have drunk a little more than usual and tomorrow I may be of a different mind. (*M*, p. 142)

> If . . . I speak of the stars it is by mistake. (*M*, p. 1)

And it is perhaps because of the tension maintained between the two that the narrators can keep us interested for two-hundred-odd pages. It is as though the two truths, what happened and what the narrator said happened, are floating without moorings and thus ontologically equal, searching for or even unconsciously subserving some new principle.

Conscience: *The Unnamable*

In *Molloy* and *Malone Dies,* as so far in this discussion, the moral dimension of lying has been virtually ignored. There is no reason why it should not be. Although, according to Aristotle, lying is a "mean and culpable" thing[20] (and an act which encourages euphemism to spare someone who imputes a lie the need to use *lie* itself), its rightness or wrongness is a shiftable boundary depending entirely on the situation. While hesitating to call someone a liar in public, people never tire of justifying the lie told to deflect a murderer from his quarry. We do not trust the evenhandedness of God sufficiently to tell the truth and let the murderer murder. We prefer to take the truth into our own hands, rather as Molloy, Moran, and Malone do in the first two volumes of the trilogy.

However ambiguous the morality of lying may be,[21] and much as Beckett enjoys the idea of lying through his teeth and getting away with it, there is an increasingly serious reservation about it as the trilogy progresses. Revelry in linguistic objects already had a dubious side in *Watt,* just as the repose in material objects in *Watt* and earlier works was seen to be an attribute of Habit the Deadener. The trilogy is philosophically serious every time one of the narrators comes to view a particular lie or invention and takes the time to discuss it. In this passage there is a moral seriousness, or a seriousness in some way connected with conscience, that surfaces temporarily but vanishes almost immediately:

> I was unable to get up. That is to say I did get up finally to be sure, I simply had to, but by dint of what exertions! Unable, unable, it's easy to *talk* about being unable, whereas *in reality* nothing is more difficult. (*M,* p. 149, my italics)

This is a joke, of course; but next time round the same thought-trap may be real. There is a lie again, first of all, "I was unable to get up," then "that is to say I did get up," and under the lightness of tone in the analysis of it all is the recognition of how easy it is to talk, and how difficult it is to identify reality.

By the time of *The Unnamable,* Beckett has begun to express clearly the shortcomings of a reality constructed by talk.

> We are all innocent, enough. Innocent of what, no-one knows, of wanting to know, of wanting to be able, of all this noise about nothing, of this long sin against the silence that enfolds us. (*U,* p. 93)

Silence is the domain of the "nameless things," of the man who has ceased to be able to speak words intelligibly, "for I always say either too much or too little, which is a terrible thing for a man with a passion for truth like mine."[22] Speech which, besides towering up into novels, "foully names" the world, is a sin against that silent world. So Beckett would seem to be saying. One of the constantly occurring themes in Beckett's work and life is the idea of guilt at having been born, a guilt impossible to deal with because it is not, at first glance anyway, induced by voluntary action. There can be no "I wish I hadn't" emotion responsibly maintained in this guilt, a guilt like original sin to which man is condemned. Speech, like birth, is a scarcely avoidable human attribute. To refine speech into novels and plays as Beckett has done is to face the unhappy fact of working with a medium that one considers is sinning against a far greater silence. Beckett's later plays, with the opportunity drama gives for actual silence, seem to cope, practically, better with the notion that speech is a kind of sin. But the trilogy, Beckett at his most garrulous, presents difficulties.

In difficulties the trilogy certainly is. That is one reason why the idea of producing tale upon tale, stretch upon stretch of language, is repugnant and problematic to the narrator even as he narrates them: hence the digressions and self-criticism. In the first two books the garrulity is kept within reasonable bounds by the legalistic, academic conventions of address and by the sane, reflective interludes:

> Not one person in a hundred knows how to be silent and listen, no, nor even to conceive what such a thing means. Yet only then can you detect, beyond the fatuous clamour, the silence of which the universe is made. (*M,* p. 130)

> Anger led me sometimes to slight excesses of language. I could not regret them. It seemed to me that all language was an excess of language. (*M,* p. 125)

The implications of these statements of course oppose all impulses to garrulity, though Beckett does not spare talk to describe what the silence means. One consolation to the writer who suspects that speech is a sin to which man is born condemned is that silence can come into its own only in counterpoint, as it were, to speech or noise. The appreciation of silence is deeply founded in the trilogy, and alternatives to it become less and less palatable as the work grinds—or hastens, as you will—to a close in *The Unnamable,* the longest paragraph of fiction ever written.

> The search for the means to put an end to things, an end to speech, is what enables the discourse to continue.

> I know no more questions and they keep on pouring out of my mouth. I think I know what it is, it's to prevent the discourse coming to an end, this futile discourse which is not credited to me and brings me not a syllable nearer silence. (*U,* pp. 15, 23)

In the first two novels, the questions that pour from the narrator's mouth might have been transcribed, and answers invented and similarly written down But by now,

> I am on my guard. I shall not answer them any more, I shall not pretend any more to answer them. Perhaps I shall be obliged, in order not to peter out, to invent another fairy-tale, yet another, with heads, trunk, arms, legs, and all that follows, let loose in the changeless round of imperfect shadow and dubious light. But I hope and trust not. (*U,* p. 23)

By 1966 "the changeless round of imperfect shadow and dubious light" had become the major locus for the characters of a very different, much less garrulous, prose *(All Strange Away, Imagination Dead Imagine, The Lost Ones).* But this passage already shows an enormous change from the first two volumes of the trilogy. The sentence about "petering out" is typical of the whole novel in that it is difficult to avoid both a biographical and a fictional reading of it. Beckett's writing life was to avoid "petering out" by his writing more and more laconic works; and *The Unnamable* does manage one more "fairy-tale," though without the arms and legs: the protagonist imprisoned in a jar, an image well known from the plays, makes an appearance toward the end of the novel. But the fact that Beckett or the narrator "hopes and trusts" more tales will *not* materialize is for the sake of silence.

One of the first observations of a serious nature about silence, and, interestingly, one of the first ever jar images in Beckett's work, comes in the first part of *Molloy,* referring to the "silence of which the universe is made":

> It was a night of listening, a night given to the faint soughing and sighing stirring at night in little pleasure-gardens, the shy sabbath of leaves and petals in the air that eddies there as it does not in other places, where there is less constraint, and as it does not during the day, when there is more vigilance, and then something else that is not clear, being neither the air nor what it moves, perhaps the far unchanging noise the earth makes and which other noises cover, but not for long. For they do not account for the noise you hear when you really listen, when all seems hushed. And there was another noise, that of my life become the life of this garden as it rode the earth of deeps and wildernesses. Yes, there were times when I forgot not only who I was, but that I was, forgot to be. Then I was no longer that sealed jar to which I owed my being so well preserved. . . . But that did not happen to me often, mostly I stayed in my jar which knew neither seasons nor gardens. (*M,* pp. 51–52)

It is interesting how, for Beckett, silence is something to be listened to as well as being the absence of noise. The silence involved in most music* is a familiar thing, and it offers us a lead into the significance of Beckett's paradoxical reference to a far unchanging noise, or *hear*able silence. "Nothing is more real than nothing" has a new meaning with respect to sound. Silence seems to be conceivable as a thing, just as speech is. Simone Weil describes the state of prayer as one in which "there is a silence, a silence which is not the absence of sound but which is the object of a positive sensation, more positive than that of sound."[23] But nor-

*Cf. Beckett's French title for the works written immediately after *The Unnamable—Textes pour Rien: pour rien* = bar's rest.

mally, the sense datum of audibility must be present to guarantee existence, just as tangibility was shown to do in the first chapter.

In *The Unnamable,* the vastly extended and more serious consideration of silence—its being made a goal, indeed—releases a new and fresh flow of energy and insight. It is as though in this burst dam of speech, performed in the full knowledge that silence is an aim and the torrent of words an obstruction or even a sin, the problem of the two ontologically equal "truths" begins to be solved as the principle that they are subserving gains shape. Notwithstanding the amorphousness of *The Unnamable* by comparison with the first two novels, there is a resolution of emotion and intention that we do not find earlier:

> This voice that speaks, knowing that it lies, . . . too old perhaps and too abased ever to succeed in saying words that would be its last, knowing itself useless and its uselessness in vain, not listening to itself but to the silence that it breaks and whence perhaps one day will come stealing the long clear sigh of advent and farewell, is it one? (*U,* p. 23)

The prose rings with an authority beyond the wit of Molloy, Malone, or Moran. With the pace of an adagio and a rhythm much akin, the prose confronts the lying voice full-face, the trickery of Malone and the pedantry of Moran completely absent. The voice no longer *wonders* about fiction and fact. It ignores the entire question; and *The Unnamable* as a whole ignores, again with a huge aplomb, the question of distinguishing autobiography from literature. As in the great speeches in the Theban plays or in *Macbeth,* genre suddenly seems an irrelevance. If tragedy materializes out of a conflict between members or terms in a relationship, the voice of *The Unnamable* is struggling against the command to given a spoken account, in order to achieve silence, a silence longed for by a human condemned to speech.

In the text of *The Unnamable,* the word *lie* and the phrase *all lies* are as ubiquitous as foam on a rough sea. Reference to lying is far more frequent and pronounced than in any previous work of Beckett's, including *Molloy* and *Malone Dies.* It is likely that the heightened consciousness of lying—and of having lied—in the final part of the trilogy is owing to a heightened, or newly emerged, awareness of what might have been earlier concealed by the lies. While in *Molloy* a lie was told in order to add another segment to an ingenious edifice and to assert itself as a piece of linguistic stuff, in *The Unnamable* the voice is so haunted by lying that it can no longer indulge it without fear. The lackadaisical, evasive Molloy's

"For I weary of these inventions, and others beckon to me" (*M,* p. 72) is lost in the outpouring of *The Unnamable*'s guilt on discovering that all along, the narrator has been evading with inventions nothing less than himself:

> All these Murphys, Molloys and Malones do not fool me. They have made me waste my time, suffer for nothing, speak of them when, in order to stop speaking, I should have spoken of me, and of me alone. (p. 19)

A page later:

> Mean words, and needless, from the mean old spirit I invented love, music, the smell of the flowering currant, to escape from me.

The tone is apocalyptic. The time has come, after all the madness of fiction and fact, to speak barefacedly in the hope that, afterwards, the rarely heard moments of universal silence will become longer and take over the speaker's life. In this prose the great dramatic silences are easier to imagine.

Perhaps the third term, subsuming the truths of fact and fiction that conflict in the web of Beckett's storytelling, is not what is true or not true, but what is in the deepest sense chosen. Evasion itself might have given the earlier narrators of the trilogy, and given us, a clue. Evasiveness on its own—especially as on its own it does not indicate exactly what is being evaded—should always alert us to the possible failure of will that brought it about. When the will of the speaker is disengaged, it seems to me that any language employed by him is going to follow only its own courses rather than occupy its normal terrain, which is a struggle between following its own courses and following a directive of the speaker:

> one *says* thunder, but one does not think it. (*MD,* p. 118)

> It's easy to talk about being unable whereas in reality nothing is more difficult. (*M,* p. 149)

These, as we have seen, are pre-*Unnamable* insights. But they are the two occasions in the first two novels where the fictionalizing (unintentional) is directly investigated and criticized. In each case, a lie has been told directly before: in the first case "An aeroplane passed over with the noise of thunder," and in the second "I was unable to get up." In each case, speech or talk is identified as the liar, independently of the talker. But the voice of *The Unnamable,* far from half-proudly admitting an embellishment here and there as Molloy does, "speaks, knowing that it lies," and seems determined, in its desperate end-in-view of silence, to will itself into not lying any more.*

But side by side with the tougher, more direct, desperate speech of *The Unnamable* there is still the sense of the trial, and of the speaker justifying himself. In many ways, the trial atmosphere is continued and intensified in direct proportion to the general urgency. The convicted person, standing accused and required to give an account of himself, turns on his imagined interrogators and involves them too in his terrible expression of guilt at having written so much fiction, so many lies, and at not having attended properly to what really needed expressing. The interrogators are implied here in the passive voice.

> I couldn't speak of me, I was never told I had to speak of me, I invented my memories. (p. 63)

He makes a desperate attempt to delegate responsibility to the interrogators themselves for having put him in such a position:

> I have no language but theirs, no, perhaps I'll say it, even with their language, so as to go silent, if that confers the right to go silent. (p. 42)

> rest is one of their words, think is another. (p. 51)

The speaker, alerted to a reality hitherto masked, is wide awake, knows his "eyes are open, because of the tears that pour from them unceasingly," and knows too that his responsibility is undeniable here, unlike in *Molloy* and *Malone Dies,* where responsibility was shirked because the thorough *manner* could guarantee credibility most of the time. Here, the speaker has no mask, and the register shifts uneasily from fearful defiance toward "them," the interrogators, to a divination that he may even have fabricated the trial scenario and the questioners in order to accommodate his native defensiveness:

> Basil and his gang? *Inexistent, invented to explain I forget what.* Ah yes, all lies, God and Man, nature and the light of day, the heart's outpourings, and the means of understanding, all invented, basely, by

---

*Coleridge relates consciously the perception of truth with the engagement of the will: "In all inevitable truths . . . I feel my will active: I seem to *will* the Truth, as well as to perceive it. Think of this!—" (*Notebooks,* vol. 1, par. 1717).

> me alone, to put off the hour when I must speak of me. (p. 20, my italics)

It is some of the finest prose, in terms of sound and impetus, that Beckett ever wrote. No word or usage dates the passage, and the phrasing is such that it appears Beckett has heard the "music" of the prose before finding the words to put in it. The devastating verbal net catches the speaker, or Beckett, irretrievably. Nothing has been spared suspicion, even "the means of understanding," which I take to mean the processes of mental articulation that people go through in order to arrive at a practical conception of something from "raw materials" inconceivably various and disconnected, "waves and particles" in the words of the formerly speechless Molloy.[24] It is symptomatic that he should forget what it is his evasions were devised to explain; but it is fairly clear from the tragic outcome that they were devised to explain a failing will, a lacuna, rather than anything definitive. It is probable that the Molloys, Malones, Saposcats and the rest, although figments and inventions, seemed to have more reality and life on paper than "talking of me" would have had, given the narrator's lack of strength to fight against the self-perpetuating nature of language and the predictability of stories.

This flood of recognition determines the shape of the whole novel. It is a headlong rush to say and be done, to "go silent" in the end. Out of a sneakingly betrayed regard for silence earlier on in the trilogy has come now the realization that, in order to achieve it, the root cause must be sought of all the speech that kept it out of reach. Storytelling and fiction, the speaker realized, were ultimately shaky foundations. This resolution is acknowledged in the title of Beckett's next full-length work, *How It Is,* which attempts to bypass the categories of fiction altogether. The following exposure, from *Molloy,* of the untrustworthiness of novelistic convention as opposed to the dramatic (where the past tense is a less basic element) is to have widespread repercussions by the time of *The Unnamable,* which is a dramatic novel par excellence.

> What I assert, deny, question, in the present, I still can. But mostly I shall use the various tenses of the past. For mostly I do not know, it is perhaps no longer so, it is too soon to know, I simply do not know, perhaps shall never know. (*M,* p. 113)

The Unnamable is much more strongly grounded in the present tense than are the other novels, and there are fewer "stories" to tempt the narrator to use the past tense. "What I assert, deny, question, in the present, I still can" reveals the need, even as early as here in the trilogy, to achieve a speech in which review and questioning have a natural place, and where the distance between the moment of narration and the moment of the narrated allowed Molloy to speak fluently of being unable to speak fluently. In *The Unnamable,* partly because it is mostly in the present tense, the principle of review does seem more natural; there is none of the flat-out contradiction of "When I said I had turkeys and so on, I lied," because nothing has actually been claimed at all. Turkeys can less easily ensconce themselves in a prose of the present tense. Moreover, there are definite ends in view in *The Unnamable,* to "speak of me" and to "go silent," which was not the case in the first two books written "in various tenses of the past." This is probably why the plays start to become more important to the "Beckett canon" from 1953 onward, when *The Unnamable* was finished. The present tense is a kind of crossroads from the past tense to the future: and *The Unnamable* looks to the future in more ways than the purely grammatical. When something is willed, consciously wanted, as it is in *The Unnamable,* the means of bringing it about suggest themselves straightaway. It is as though the trilogy had been searching or waiting for this recognition and found it in the concentrated agon of its third part, which is at once resolute about its own purpose and diagnostic of all that was not resolute in *Molloy* and *Malone Dies.* The book is none the more comforting for its recognitions: a true tragedy, it cannot rest with what it succeeds in stating. It does not touch the subject of whether the intention to go silent can be fulfilled. More questions, unanswered as yet, arise from the words "I'll speak of me when I speak no more." Perhaps you cannot speak your way to silence after all; or if you can, it is less straightforward than even the narrator of *The Unnamable* expected.

Lying and Self-Consciousness

Some of the conclusions reached by Owen Barfield concerning the consciousness of the Romantic and post-Romantic periods draw fascinating connections between lying, language, and the consciousness of self. Barfield sees the separation of man and nature, and the corresponding feeling of emptiness, as the event represented by the Fall of Man, and re-echoed historically in Cartesianism. This might explain why the sense of guilt is so suddenly intensified in *The Unnamable,* a book in which the ghost of original sin is always so near. Barfield further conjectures that the effects of the Fall continue to be apparent so long as man does not choose to engage his willpower to overcome egotism. In the world picture of post-Cartesian rationalism, nature is not a manifestation of man at all; it is "an object, a finished work."[25] Seeing nature in this way will obviously lock man in a one-sided and therefore egotistical confinement of the brain: the "finished work" of the world has nothing to do with us, if this reading of reality is taken seriously. Thus *The Unnamable:*

> Perhaps that's what I am, the thing that divides the world in two, on the one side the outside, on the other the inside, . . . on the one hand the mind, on the other the world, I don't belong to either. (*U,* p. 100)

Barfield concludes, in a sentence that does much to explain the anomalies in Beckett's trilogy, "it is easy to see how it is that this new relation to nature [the rationalistic] has made possible lying, deceit and error—none of which are possible for beings whose outer world always and immediately corresponds with his inner experience."[26]

Barfield also outlines an etiology of present-day self-consciousness which reaches the heart of Beckett's writings. It is worth quoting in full:

> The very small child has, properly speaking, no self-consciousness at all. He cannot say "I". But then, through the operation of his physical senses, he gradually comes to realise: on the one hand there is something that is "I", and on the other, there is something out there in space which is "not-I". At this stage he still feels the *words* which he speaks to be emanating wholly from himself, the "I"-division. But, *sooner or later, because words, too, have this sensual sub-stratum, he begins to feel detached even from them.* They are instruments which he picks up, uses, and drops again. He begins to discover that, even when used in quite ordinary, prosaic, logical forms, *they can be made to prove the most contradictory things—can be made to prove almost anything.* . . . He will become vaguely confused by the variety and disharmony of all the different systems of ideas (each apparently quite convincing when taken by itself), . . . and, with more or less awareness of what he is doing, he will transfer the words from the "I" to the "not-I" division of his consciousness, just as Hamlet did when he cried out "Words, words, words!" in that mood of loneliness and despair. And at last comes the experience—possibly a deep and painful one—that *not merely words but thought itself, abstract thought—"reason"—must be*

transferred in the same way, for in its inmost nature it is wholly dependent on words.[27]

The speaker of Beckett's trilogy has most of these experiences—in particular those which I have italicized in the interests of readers more concerned with Beckett than with Barfield—and it is fair to say that the emergency of *The Unnamable* is due precisely to them.

In the first chapter of this book material objects, far from being a consolation to the islanded consciousness, turned out to intensify the sense of estrangement. Linguistic objects, on the other hand, though less tightly bound to the sense-world, and though amusing for their masquerade as real in the face of their obvious disparity from their referents, still taught a pleasure that, in denying a relation to the world, also denied any veracity in the speaker's relationships with others, and made lies as pleasurable to tell as truths. It put even human relationships into the "not-I" division of consciousness. (Is that not the very center of Beckett's play *Not I?*) If words continue unregenerately to occupy the "not-I" realm, they can indeed be "made to prove almost anything." ("I simply believe I can say nothing that is not true.")

The problem with both kinds of objects was that their systems located reality either in the material on the one hand and in the abstractly conceptual on the other, but never in the activity of thinking and imagining itself, in which the two are involved. But the "mental fight,"[28] as Blake called it, is not over. If not only words, but thought and reason also come to be transferred in modern man from the "I" to the "not-I," then pure silence is not necessarily the thing to seek, for reason is "wholly dependent on words." "Thingless names" and "nameless things" may be worth being conscious of, but they alone, and consciousness of them alone, do not bring any further the process of that consciousness's development.

4

The You That Is Not You (*How It Is*)

In the prewar prose and the first two books of the trilogy, narrators and readers alike start to feel that to produce language is an epistemological act, one that defines knowledge and truths as whatever is represented once the words have been uttered. What determined their utterance was left out of account. By a twist of narrative practice lies became truth-agents, their sheer existence as text seeming more convincing than the relatively uninteresting and usually short statements that identified the linguistic edifices as lies. In *The Unnamable,* however, the implications of making these edifices begin to rise to the surface. If the mendacious "stories" end up longer and more interesting than the denials—and the fact that they do is the mainstay of Beckett's prose pre-1960—then the identification of the true and the false becomes impossible, and leads to the anguish that is probably the only attribute of *The Unnamable* over which critics are unanimous. The division or conflict is well expressed by Hoffman in *Samuel Beckett Now:* "To talk is the only guarantee of identity" is one side of it—the belief that words, whatever words they are, are footholds for knowledge. On the other side is his description of the novel as "an hysteria of can't and must and will."[1] Although the narrator talks, he is guaranteed no identity at all: he is in hysteria, one of the plainest signs of nonidentity. It is in fact only a certain kind of talk that will guarantee identity: the talk for which the ego of the talker takes responsibility.

Hoffman is right to bring up the crucial modal verbs *can/must/will,* which end the trilogy and end a period in Beckett's writing career. The invocation of them at the end of the trilogy is a summing up, a statement of the problem in which, perhaps, the "germ of a solution" can be found. The verbs are more recognizably of a class in German* because they can all share the infinitive form. *Können, müssen, wollen* offer an image of the three aspects of a human being: the capability of the physical body (*können*); the moral capacity (*müssen*); and the will or volition (*wollen*). *Müssen* has two secondary aspects: the "must" of destiny, on the one hand, and the "must" determined by the ego on the other. The ego links this latter "must" with the third verb, *wollen,* but it is a higher ego that says of itself: "I must" instead of "I want to." Thus the statement "I must go on, I can't go on, I [will] go on" at the end of *The Unnamable* is one of the truest and clearest epistemological starting points that Beckett's work up to that time had achieved, even though it came at the end of the trilogy rather than started it.

It is important to see these words as an epistemological statement, as well as a statement of an emotion and a dramatic gesture. What is crucial to it as a key to a theory of knowledge is that it regards the I or ego as essentially constitutive of knowledge. It does not seek to isolate truth from perception of it as a materialist epistemology does. To talk, merely, may not afford a guarantee of identity. But to say "I" does. The problem with the Beckett trilogy is that the first person keeps being used even when no responsibility is being taken for numerous lies: "I wonder if I am not yet again talking about myself. Shall I be incapable, in the end, of lying on any other subject?"[2] In *The Unnamable,* which is more noticeably in the first person than are *Molloy* or *Malone Dies,* one experiences the threat to the ego in the silent maxim "to talk is the guarantee of identity." To use the first person implies a responsibility of will. "I can't go on, I'll go on." It is significant how in many (not all) of the lying episodes in the earlier prose and the trilogy's first two parts, a third person—Arsene, Moran, Sapo, Macmann,—was substituted for the first person, when, according to the voice of *The Unnamable,* I "should have been speaking of me and of me alone." One cannot keep using the first person and yet fail to "speak of me" without bearing the consequences.

These considerations should be brought to bear on *How It Is* in which, after an eight-year period, Beckett "went on" in prose. The work was in a sense foreseen at the end of the sixth of the *Texts for Nothing:*

> I have high hopes, a little story with living creatures coming and going

---

*And Beckett sometimes uses them in English in a similar manner. Cf. *Texts for Nothing,* XIII: 'who can the greater, can the less' (*CSP,* p. 113).

> on a habitable earth crammed with the dead, . . . with night and day coming and going above. (*CSP,* p. 92)

In *How It Is* there are elements of the earlier Beckett prose—the humor of the trilogy, for example—and foreshadowings of the prose of the late sixties, seventies, and eighties also. But the overall impression gained is that the book is Beckett's nearest to sui generis, that he was trying something he had not tried before and would not try again. In this book he speaks more of "himself alone" as he had resolved to do, and at the same time includes his image in one of corporate humanity, a sort of Dantesque vision embracing thousands revolving in a prostrate circular procession, face down in a sea of mud.* There is a tighter structure to this book than to any in the trilogy, and there is a also a clearer approach to spiritual reality in it, which is announced on the first page: "tell me again, finish telling me *invocation*" (my italics). The scene and events are more obviously symbolic than those in the trilogy, and there are far fewer objects. The way the book is written is more conducive, therefore, to pure thought, or thought involving nonmaterial objects. The avoidance of punctuation, without parallel in Beckett's prose, obliges the reader to perform an unusually active kind of thinking in assigning grammatical status to the various parts of speech that appear ambiguous or unclear until that thinking has taken place. For example, in the phrase "I am given a dream like someone having tasted of love of a little woman within my reach" (p. 14) it is not immediately clear whether it is love per se that has been tasted, or that of the woman, or both. The phrases form themselves slowly under the power of thinking and listening for the cadence, out of the apparently amorphous mass of words, as filings arrange themselves out of chaos under the influence of a magnet. I do not agree with Kenner that in reading or understanding the book "all thought of punctuation becomes unnecessary,"[3] unless he means that we supply it instinctively. Studying parts of the novel amounts to a certain kind of exercise in meditation. That the very effort of will Beckett is making in this work is mirrored in the demands made on the reader's will is an interesting development. *The Unnamable,* for all its reputation as one of the most

---

*Cf. *Inferno,* canto 7, in which the souls of the damned toil through mud; and Coleridge's "Allegoric Vision": "a string of blind men, the last of whom caught at the skirt of the one before him, he of the next, and so on till they were all out of sight. . . . The string of blind men went on forever without any beginning" (*Miscellanies, Aesthetic and Literary,* p. 220).

wildly unconventional of all Beckett's works ("perilously close to the unreadable"),[4] makes fewer demands than does *How It Is*. Although stamina is needed to cope with a 120-page paragraph, *The Unnamable* is conventionally punctuated for the most part, whereas the meaning in *How It Is* is as it were "unearthed" from the mud of unclear grammatical relations. (Sometimes the mass will not yield to the marshaling force of the reader's attention and remains obscure.*)

How far all these strengths are owing to the renewal and clarification of will at the end of *The Unnamable* is one of the purposes of this chapter to investigate. Its other aim is to argue that the process of thinking through to the end the issue of self-consciousness and will has been an agent in the achievement of a purer thought; because the higher ego of man, since it is precisely not a thing but insistently something to reckon with, comes close to being a paradigm of nonsensory knowledge.

Metafiction and the Attrition of Poetry

Two modes of will must be distinguished in the text of *How It Is:* the outwardly declared will motive, which fails dismally as if in knowledge of its own superficiality, and a more sustained inward discipline, which reveals itself in one respect by the lesser number of evasive ploys and linguistic edifices claiming truth but not supplying it: "words have their utility the mud is mute" and "a word from me and I am again" are practically the only hints of that tendency in the whole book. One other mention of nagging doubt as to what is invention and what is actual memory occurs, reminiscent of the trilogy: "samples whatever comes remembered imagined no knowing."[5] But the effective organization in *How It Is* is stronger than that of any work preceding it. The text is divided into periods or segments, each with its own cadence as if to prevent the headlong rush and endless passages of irrelevance that were risked in the trilogy. These bursts of speech are organized very consciously into three parts, which is at once a source of meaningless busyness for the superficially stated will to organization and a truly effective form for a subject that threatens chaos at every moment. There is some confusion for readers of *How It Is* as to which elements of form are of service and which are not. It is

---

*For example, the last paragraph on p. 113, in which several phrases seem to be unintentionally ambiguous.

resolved to some extent in the fact that in this novel there is a real distinction between author and narrator. The author succeeds, the whole novel considered, whereas the narrator sometimes, often indeed, fails even though he purports to be writing the novel. This is clear evidence of the novel's metafictional character.

When the intentions of the narrator are consciously asserted, they fail to be consistently fulfilled. The organization starts out as a promising grip for the will:

> how it was I quote before Pim with Pim after Pim how it is I say it as I hear it (p. 7)

> progress properly (p. 24)

> end of part one leaving only part two leaving only part three and last (p. 36)

> end of part one before Pim that's how it was before Pim (p. 54)

But it ends up accounting as much for the failure to stick to intentions as for success in fulfilling them:

> for when number 814336 describes number 814337 to number 814335 and number 814335 to number 814337 for example he is merely in fact describing himself to two lifelong acquaintances (p. 131)

> fleeting impression I quote that in trying to present in three parts or episodes an affair which all things considered involves four one is in danger of being incomplete (p. 142)

The organization is too conscious to be useful but becomes a source for jocular amusement. The burst of numerical representation in part 3, of which the above example is only a fifteenth, is a case in point. In an effort to contain the flow of creativity or the outpouring of a life—"we're talking of my life," he says repeatedly—the measures of containment have themselves become laughable. Such a remark as

> the objects against the palms the tin the opener these details in preference to nothing (p. 37)

tempts us to reply that something, something more, would be better, if there is room for a preference to be expressed at all. And when, on the same page, as if in anticipation or reply, we find

> who knows . . . the last prawns these details for the sake of something

we are not really satisfied. "For the sake of something" and "in preference to nothing" cancel each other out and indicate a general ennui. The old defensiveness, once located in lies, is reappearing as exaggerated conciseness or pedantry. This accounts for the insistence that *something,* in this apparent sea of nothingness, is always being talked about, as in "we're speaking of my life," "my nails," "the opener," and so forth. There is the impression that if this conscious control is not kept up, the material will fly in all directions and become unrenderable. But in the absence of material, the will has nothing to hold, in which case its outward manifestations of constraint must always be superfluous. There is at once a sense of superfluity and of continuing resolution in the repeated phrase "something wrong there" every few pages throughout the novel. One of the most amusing examples of its role is its climactic appearance, for about the hundredth time, transformed by its humor into something more than superfluity:

> Bom to the abandoned not me Bom you Bom we Bom but me Bom you Pim I to the abandoned not me Pim you Pim we Pim but me Bom you Pim something very wrong there (p. 124)

The author succeeds, precisely where the narrator is mired in "all the doing suffering failing bungling."[6]

The above passage illustrates another gulf lying between the stated will and its fulfilment. The division into Before, With, and After Pim comes to mean less and less as the "program" proceeds and Pim, Bom, and Bem, not to mention Krim, Kram, and Krem, become confused rather than distinguished:

> m at the end and one syllable the rest indifferent ignorance not realising that Bem and Bom could only be one and the same (p. 67)

> Pim quick after Pim before he vanishes never was only me me Pim (p. 113)

> can't go on we're talking of me not Pim Pim is finished he has finished me now part three not Pim my voice not his saying thrice these words can't go on and Pim that Pim never was and Bom whose coming I await to finish be finished have finished me too that Bom will never be no

> Pim no Bom and this voice quaqua of us all never was only one voice my voice never any other. (p. 113)

The organization is denied validity even while it is being undertaken in these passages. In the last of them, the original intention of "part three after Pim" actually becomes "part three *not* Pim." The will and ego, realizing the futility of the conscious planning, reengage with the task of "talking of me,"[7] the primary activity. It should be stressed how consistently the voice of *How It Is* follows *The Unnamable*'s crucial innovation of throwing to the winds any distinction between autobiography and fiction. *How It Is,* and many of the works that follow, is both and yet neither.

Another untrumpeted strength of this fiction is its detached, throwaway humor, which offsets the bleakness of the scene and the difficulties facing the narrator and the reader (not to mention the writer: Beckett spoke of "wrongness, but necessary wrongness" in the "slow, painful" course of writing the novel, whose "direction [was] all wrong," though he was "powerless to change it").[8] If *How It Is* is a hell, it is still possible for the narrator to see and show the funny side:

> with the gesture of one dealing cards and also to be observed among certain sowers of seed I throw away the empty tins they fall without a sound (p. 11)

> I am given a dream like someone having tasted of love of a little woman within my reach . . . or failing kindred meat* a llama emergency dream an alpaca the history I know my God the natural (p. 14)

> When the great needs fail the need to move on the need to shit and vomit and the other great needs all my great categories of being (p. 15)

> a fart fraught with meaning issuing through the mouth (p. 29)

> nothing now but to eat ten twelve episodes open the tin put away the tool raise the tin slowly to the nose irreproachable freshness (p. 39)

> Some reflections none the less while waiting for things to improve on the fragility of euphoria among the different orders of the animal kingdom beginning with the sponges (p. 43)

---

*Cf. *All Strange Away:* "hint of jugular and cords suggesting perhaps past her best and thence on down to other meat" (*CSP,* p. 125).

> I can't make out the words the mud muffles or perhaps a foreign tongue perhaps he's singing a lied in the original perhaps a foreigner (p. 62)

In Beckett's prose there are few examples better than *How It Is* of how he works "with impotence, ignorance" to make us laugh.* It is a "minimalist" humor, indulged in "while waiting for things to improve," reversing many of the normal expectations of humour. "A little less is all one begs" or "imagination on the decline having attained the bottom"[9] show how lightness and smartness of wit save the negativity from being morbid or tiresome. A feature of the jocose minimalism of *How It Is* is, paradoxically, its obligingness. The stylistic excellence implies the fact that the narrator *and* author have spared no effort to make an unnecessary point well, as in "with the gesture of one dealing cards and also to be observed among certain sowers of seed." The split-second perception of this, and the image itself, makes us laugh out loud. Like the "freshness" of the tinned fish, the style of these quips is "irreproachable," and Beckett consciously evokes this to hint to the reader how unbearable it would be to be presented with these images to take seriously. The incongruity of comparing the mud-soaked narrator with card players or "certain sowers of seed" is counterpointed by the elegance of the phrasing itself. And "perhaps he's singing a lied in the original" is typical of Beckett's way of leaving no stone unturned for a plausible explanation and at the same time giving absurd evidence of broadmindedness and a wide-ranging culture. The phrase "in the original" and the choice of "lied" ring of the cognoscenti's jargon, even more out of place in the world of *How It Is* than it would be in *Molloy,* whose hero is also deeply educated in the European humanities. In *How It Is* the narrator has several occasions to return to culture: "The humanities I had my God and with that flashes of geography"

The names chosen in the book are another example of "minimal" humor—they are "fundamental sounds" par excellence, far removed from the idiom of human names. As in *The Unnamable,* it is indeterminable whether they are Christian names or surnames. Pim in particular is an essentially insignificant sound, and the names that derive from it, all ending in *m*—the easiest of all sounds to produce, even opening the mouth is not necessary—feel placeness and "beingless." The one syllable, characteristic of the lan-

*Compare the examples given by John Pilling in *Frescoes of the Skull,* p. 78, n. 3.

guage of babies* and clowns, makes us laugh, especially when the tone of the context deserves more dignified names for the protagonists. All the beings in the "down here" hell of *How It Is* conform to the rule of "m" at the end, one syllable, but even those up above in the remembered world are affected—the protagonist's wife, Pam Prim, and his dog, Skom Skum. Beckett liked the single syllable and *m* formulation, having devised it in *The Unnamable* (with less effect than in *How It Is*), and used it again in one of his later plays, *What Where* (1982).

The fact that the self-declared structure or organization of *How It Is* is only imperfectly fulfilled and adhered to affects the quality of what it is the narrator is trying to tell, which is the story of his life prior to entering the mud world. In the case of Beckett's prose, the life that is being summoned, later revealed in essence in the eighties prose, is arguably that of the isolated self of the artist. This is different from a description of Beckett's actual life (see pages 61–63), although events from the latter may coincide with the fiction. In the case of the lyric poet or contemplative writer, events and scenes that were unquestionably located in the author's life experiences are bound with and merged with universal symbols which take us as far as possible away from the personal, or autobiographical, subjectivity.** Eliot refers to the "alchemical process" by which personal states are transformed into symbol and thus connected to a universal "field" or circuit of meaning. And Owen Barfield, following Shelley, claims more: "Men do not *invent* those relations between separate external objects, and between objects and feelings, which it is the function of poetry to reveal. These relations exist independently, not indeed of thought, but of any individual thinker."[10] In the trilogy, the lyric visions were interludes in the tales of wandering tramps and prisoners who were relating principally their journeys as old men: what happened to the protagonists of *Watt, Molloy,* and *Malone Dies* in the "narrative present" represented a good portion of the text. Of the lyrical visions coming from the past, or existing temporarily in the present, as in the garden scene in *Molloy,*[11] one could say, as Malone says of Sapo's reflections, "these stations were short-lived," the

---

*Cf. also *Text 3*'s 'Bibby Bibby . . . Yum Yum' (*CSP,* p. 79); and George Russell (AE), *The Candle of Vision* (London: Macmillan, 1918), chap. 14, "The Language of the Gods."

**See H. Porter Abbott, "Beckett and Autobiography" in Friedman, Rossman, and Sherzer, *Beckett Translating/Translating Beckett.*

protagonist "was off again, on his wanderings, passing from light to shadow, from shadow to light, unheedingly."[12]

In a world of mud in *How It is,* the possibilities for events relating to the narrator in the present are quickly, though thoroughly, exhausted in the meeting and "training" of Pim and the minimal adventures associated with the sack and fish tins. The scenes from the past are therefore a focus for the creative potentiality of the author. In *How It Is* the journey or wandering still occurs, but it is radically altered in form and is even more atavistic, as if bound by destiny: circular and processionary, rather than linear, solitary, and meandering. The case is not of a life being remembered from old age, as it is in *Malone Dies* or *Molloy,* but of "LIFE ABOVE . . . IN THE LIGHT" remembered from "down here" in the dark, arguably from the region of the dead. Vivian Mercier quotes *The Unnamable:* "Then it will be all over with the Murphys, Merciers, Molloys, Morans and Malones, unless it goes on beyond the grave," and adds, "In *How It Is,* perhaps."[13] The journey does not take the narrator away from the one scenario (mud) into any other scenes. This is one reason why the twenty-two memories and visions become so poignant and play such a significant part in the book. They do not predominate in quantity, constituting approximately a fifteenth of the total work. But in the operation of the novel on the reader's consciousness, they seem to occupy a larger proportion than that, in part because of their status as pieces of imaginative language, resonating and radiating meanings, in part also because a lot of the rest of the book is repetitive, seeming thus to shrink in significance. The numerical exercises—"dear figures," says the narrator half-ironically—and the ceaseless documentation of crawling admit their futility as gestures rather than, as earlier in Beckett's prose, attempt to validate themselves with mendacious eloquence in the manner of Watt, Moran, or Malone. Notice how, when a real effect is intended, *How It Is* invokes numbers but absolutely avoids writing them down:

> a slowness of which figures alone however arbitrary can give a feeble idea (p. 136)

But such an imaginative and effective formulation, though more in evidence in *How It Is* than earlier, is still rare in comparison with the repetitive pedantry of, say, pages 127–34. Just as certainly as some remarks call derision down on futile gesturing, so the lyrical visions assert themselves in contrast as meaningful. Almost alone amongst Beckett critics in commenting on this is Frederik Smith, in his essay "A Land of Sanctuary."[14]

These visions are scarcely recoverable from the mud in the narrator's realm. But this does not so much diminish as increase their value:

> the sack my life that I never let go here I let it go needing both hands as when I journey that hangs together all these sudden blazes in the head as empty and dark as the heart can desire *then suddenly like a handful of shavings aflame the spectacle then* (p. 38, my italics)

That is how the visions appear, coming and going as quickly as the burning of wood shavings. During the incandescence, any ostensible impoverishment of the means of expression is shown to be far from real.

> We are on the veranda smothered in verbena the scented sun dapples the red tiles yes I assure you*
>
> The huge head hatted with birds and flowers is bowed down over my curls the eyes burn with severe love I offer her mine pale upcast to the sky whence cometh our help and which I know perhaps even then with time shall pass away
>
> in a word bolt upright on a cushion on my knees whelmed in a nightshirt I pray according to her instructions
>
> that's not all she closes her eyes and drones a snatch of the so-called Apostles' Creed I steal a look at her lips
>
> she stops her eyes burn down on me again I cast up mine in haste and repeat awry
>
> the air thrills with the hum of insects
>
> that's all it goes out like a lamp blown out
>
> the space of a moment the passing moment that's all my past little rat at my heels *the rest false* (p. 17, my italics)

The last verset, not usually included in this often quoted (and often

---

*Cf. Beckett's poem "Enueg II" (1930), in which the phrase "doch doch I assure thee" occurs twice (*Collected Poems, 1930–78,* p. 13).

misquoted*) passage is crucial to an understanding of *How It Is*. The wording of the whole scene is deceptively simple, but some of the tonal inflections in the words chosen produce an effect not dissimilar to that created by a correlative use of color or of notes in the musical scale. Indeed, it is color and music that distinguish the visions of the past—such as the one above—from the langage of the rest of the book: only in these passages does any color other than black appear at all. All the lyrical visions are rich in the colors of nature especially. The "huge head hatted with birds and flowers" is a startling yet simple formulation, eliciting awe without our being immediately conscious of it: already, with the words "huge head" the faces of the reader and narrator are metaphorically upturned, so that "pale upcast" is a confirmation of something already prepared. The "burning eyes" are again framed with the oddly juxtaposed but truthful words: "severe love." And there are religious overtones in the hugeness of the head, and the "burning" of the eyes, which connects with the later description of the visions as brief and transitory, like the burning of shavings. In this sense the visions are small theophanies, burning being a traditional symbol of theophany. These religious or ecstatic tones, as adumbrated by "the air thrills** with the hum of insects," are so strong that they are complemented rather than debunked by the demonstration of how little the saying of prayers means to the child. The embarrass-

---

*In what follows it should be borne in mind that not all critics quote the words as they stand in the published version of *How It Is* of 1964, either because early drafts borrowed from Beckett were used (in Fletcher's *Samuel Beckett's Novels*); or because they were translated from French (in Kenner's *Samuel Beckett: A Critical Study*); or because they are wrongly arranged (in Mercier's *Beckett/Beckett*).

**Compare the use of *thrill* in *The Return of the Native:* "the heath thrilling silently in the sun." Affinities between Beckett and Hardy run deep. Compare *More Pricks*'s story "A Wet Night," whose title is of Hardy's poem (irresistibly Beckettian):

> A Wet Night
>
> I pace along, the rainshafts riddling me
> Mile after mile out by the moorland way,
> And up the hill, and through the ewe-leaze gray
> Into the lane, and round the corner tree;
>
> Where as my clothing clams me, mire-bestarred,
> And the enfeebled light dies out of day,
> Leaving the liquid shades to reign, I say
> "This is a hardship to be calendared!"

ment evident in "according to her instructions," "that's not all," "drones a snatch," "so-called Apostles' Creed" indicate the irreconcilability of, on the one hand, fixed tradition and rote learning, and on the other, the aesthetic of religious intimation itself, to which the "scented sun dappling the red tiles" is far more important than a "droned snatch" or (to borrow from *Watt*) a "pillow of old words." The "snatch" and the "pillow" begin to function as objects, suggesting—in their existence as separate things—man's separateness from the world, whereas the aesthetic intimation effects a living union of the self with "the contemplated."

What distinguishes the words in this passage is that the relationships drawn between them are fresh and new. The words themselves are simple, well-known words. It is interesting to note how this kind of language contrasts with Beckett's practice elsewhere in *How It Is* of estranging us by the baffling introduction of such words as *bo, ebonite, deasil* (often to appear later in the sixties prose), *oakum, thebaid* and *sparsim*. In the veranda passage, it is the fresh relations drawn between almost homely words that enact the religious/aesthetic experience itself, which is stealthy—in a benign sense—and indistinct. The experience is brought home to the reader as transcendent but not airily transcendental. In this sense we can understand H. L. Baldwin's comment that "the hiddenness of God in the material world is reflected in the hiddenness of the transcendent in Beckett's writing."[15] Stronger than litanies or droning churchiness is "I offer her mine pale upcast to the sky." He offers "his" not necessarily only to the eyes looking down on him. "Mine" is here curiously indistinct in its reference, and just as much so in context as when isolated here. It seems to refer to the eyes, taking the previous phrase into account. But it could just as easily suggest the face—pale and upcast are attributes of faces as well as eyes—and also something rather more general, *that*

Yet sires of mine now perished and forgot
When worse beset, ere roads were shapen here,
And night and storm were foes indeed to fear
Times numberless have trudged across this spot
In sturdy muteness on their strenuous lot,
And taking all such toils as trifles mere.

And it is well known that Belacqua read *Tess of the D'Urbervilles* (*More Pricks Than Kicks,* p. 171).

*which is mine.** This is only a "transgrammatical" suggestion, it is not stated. Beckett's usage of it here also suggests something else: that the narrator can give or offer in devotion only what is already *his* ("mine") to give. The grain of Beckett's feeling in this whole passage is against the profuseness that is everywhere a threat when sentiment is involved. (see chap. 2, pp. 49–50)

Upcast is yet another instance of Beckett renovating common words and rotating clichés. *Downcast* is suggested negatively, as both a mood inappropriate to the devotional act and as a piece of stale language; *upcast* is as fresh and virginal and innocent to the language as the child is to the mother, whose eyes, burning, suggest a revelation of divine love. Similarly, *whelmed,* an old word for *wrapped,* gathers to itself the suggestion of *overwhelmed*—which the child is, both by the divine intimation and by the frustration of learning the litany—and also takes us back into the past, where small children are whelmed, not wrapped. It is a short associative step from there to the wraps in Christ's cradle.** And with remarkable lyricism again, the child's innocence *and* prescience are combined in a phrase which expresses with these things the immense age of the narrator in the narrative present:

> to the sky whence cometh our help and which I know perhaps even then with time shall pass away

This bringing together of age and youth with such impressive firmness and plangency is arguably as genuine an "intimation of immortality" as anything in Wordsworth's poem. The child has an ageless knowledge—

> *The ancient without end* we're talking of *me*[16]

—described from a point outside time, perhaps from a purgatorial region, "the rest false." The biblical strain "whence cometh"*** is no more a piece of antichurch savagery than is the case with the

---

*Cf. Bob Dylan's "I'll Keep It with Mine" in which *mine* refers only loosely to a preceding subject, if at all (*Writings and Drawings* [London: Grafton, 1984], p. 355).

**The narrator is likened to Christ at the end of *How It Is,* "the arms spread . . . like a cross . . . LIKE A CROSS no answer yes or no yes" (p. 159). Also cf. *Company,* p. 77.

***The phrase "the sky, whence cometh our help" appeared in *The Expelled* (*CSP,* p. 24).

other religious institutions discussed in the passage. The biblical reference in this case, rather, is used to suggest how helpless one is, when young, in face of an archaic language that one's elders have declared to be profound. One understands it aesthetically rather than cognitively or semantically. Any possibility of mere jibing is taken away by the solemn phrase which follows, referring to the sky, and possibly secondarily to the "help," and evoking biblical English without aping it: "which I know perhaps even then with time shall pass away."

Of the visions, Beckett later says (in part 2):

> I lose the nine-tenths it starts so sudden comes so faint goes so fast ends so soon I'm on it in a flash it's over (p. 89)

"Like a lamp blown out": this failure of the memory would seem to be out of the will's control, even though the author says he is engaged in "talking of me," and the visions are the best sign that this is true. The narrator does not try to deny the problem or turn it into something else. Like many characteristics of *How It Is,* it is stated as a problem:

> I was young all that all those words chevrons golden vertices every word always as I hear it in me that was without quaqua* on all sides and murmur to the mud when the panting stops barely audible bits and scraps (p. 53)

This statement amongst many others bears witness to the narrator's longing for insight, for more than the "midget grammar" and the "bits and scraps"** that he repeatedly calls his visions of the past. This kind of expression is what *More Pricks Than Kicks* gave no sign of, a language in which lyricism and simplicity are foremost. It might be seen as the language of unified feeling as opposed to the "tonal" language of refracted or divided feeling, of which irony is the clearest form in Beckett. Owen Barfield suggests that a language of unified feeling indicates a sense that one's thoughts are one's own, but that irony indicates that the thoughts uttered are nevertheless not one's own.[17] This latter state of consciousness, which he attributes especially to the literature of the modern age, corresponds to the root meaning of *irony:* distance (here, between the sayer and the said).

---

*Cf. *Mercier and Camier,* p. 54: "they pee not, neither do they *cack.*" *Quaqua* is a pun on that word. Here *quaqua* refers to mud (shit?) and utterance per se.

**This phrase occurs in *Texts for Nothing,* texts 3 and 6.

There are in *How It Is* brief recurrences of the kind of irony that cannot easily coexist with the simpler language of the visions:

> a few mouldy old reliables azure that never dies morning with evening in its train . . . one or two usual flowers (p. 104)

Such a piece of jocular "literary criticism" grafted onto a text like *How It Is* opens up a separate register of expression from that of the scenario and the journey. Azure never dies in two senses in this novel: it has been a staple in English poetry since Milton and Cowley, and it is probably no coincidence that the *Oxford English Dictionary,* in documenting the fortunes of *azure,* refers us to Klopstock—a character markedly conspicuous in *How It Is* (p. 47)—via a quotation from Carlyle: "Is not Klopstock, . . . with his azure purity, . . . a man of taste?" (Misc. 1.36). The narrator of *How It Is* is nothing if not a man of taste: "the humanities I had my God and with that flashes of geography". The tone of the literary-critical graft and the trick by which *azure* is granted "eternal life"* make us laugh, as well as show, in the same way as Mallarmé showed, the dangers attending the literary evocation of anything at all. The risk is that the colors and forms of nature will become meaningless talismans, unable to evoke because they have been overused. Beckett wrote in his first published writing (literary criticism again): "[Dante and Joyce] both saw how worn out and threadbare was the conventional language of cunning literary artificers; both rejected an approximation to universal language."[18] But to protest too much against cliché is to betray to the listener its nearness—as in *Texts for Nothing* 2's genteel understatement, "Superlatives have lost most of their charm"—and the need to put it at arm's length. But for most of the time in *How It Is,* such a threat is not present. Moreover, the "mouldy old reliables" *are* employed to great effect, in the manner so ably commented on by Frederik Smith with respect to the later prose, in many of *How It Is*'s visions: that of the veranda, that describing the walks out on the hill, that of the boy seeing the sunlight through his jumper as he lies next to a wall (pp. 94, 98), that of the "mauve evening," to name only four. Real though the risk is that these images may become clichéd, and alert though Beckett is, in the "metafictional" voice, to this danger, they do not have such an effect in *How It Is:* partly because all trace of sentimentality is avoided, partly also

---

**Azure* also lasts well in Shelley's *Prometheus Unbound,* appearing at least fifteen times.

because Beckett does not usually express, in the few lines following such an image, an immediate doubt that they may appear stale or moldy. He is aware that although *azure* as a staple of poetry may be going stale, the reality of azure, its quality as a phenomenon, remains. Indeed, it only dies in poetry when the literary artificer has forgotten what it actually means.

In the following passage, the "bits and scraps" to which the narrator's memories are reduced are again made painfully apparent.

> those murmurs fallen in the mud from our mouths innumerable and ascending to where there is an ear a mind to understand a means of noting a care for us the wish to note the curiosity to understand and an ear to hear even ill these scraps of other scraps of an antique rigmarole (p. 147)

As well as perfect symmetry of thought, there is almost an "absence of tone" here, which is another characteristic of the "language of unified feeling" mentioned above. It is a tone undisturbed by destructive passion or sentimentalism, and it avoids invective where, for Beckett, invective is often an immediately tempting attitude to adopt. There is an emergence of will in this control—more genuine than any of the willed control of externals—that has not been a feature of Beckett's writing before *How It Is*. The tone of "these scraps of other scraps of an antique rigmarole" is entirely new—in the early prose the composure was not adequate to such a subject (pressing and recalcitrant as it has always been for Beckett, as is clear from the Tal Coat section of *Three Dialogues* about expression); and in the trilogy, exasperated fuss would have been the main response.

Particularly interesting are the words "antique rigmarole": it is a loaded phrase, admittedly, implying a qualified attitude. But it does not *un*load its implications onto the reader as "mouldy old reliables" or "a few usual flowers" do. "Antique rigmarole" is in this sense *not* a literary critical comment like the former phrases and such others as "something wrong there" or "correct" or, indeed, "nothing to correct there." The emotion, though qualified, is not refracted into different registers. Frederik Smith, writing in 1987, has given the only convincing account of why Beckett does not simply debunk the lyrical, as he is supposed to have done according to the majority of commentators. The argument of chapter 1 of the present book is implied in one of his concluding remarks: "Once the referential function of language has been exposed as a sham, the lyrical is put on an equal footing with the less than lyrical." His views on the lyrical make a new and welcome direction in Beckett criticism: "while unoriginal, these [poetic] words and phrases are most emphatically *not* used ironically, for they arrive trailing their golden pasts, and the metaphors are fresh enough to be a welcome relief from the deserts of uninflected prose in which they blossom."[19]

The question is raised, from the recognition that "bits and scraps" is still the best that the narrator can manage, whether such a limitation can be overcome, whether anything more than such traces is possible, or whether in fact the condition of the narrator—perhaps in a purgatorial realm of the dead, perhaps between death and a new birth)*—determines the fragmentary mode in which the nonphysical element of the narrator can perceive his former physical existence:

> I remembered my days an handbreadth my life as nothing man a vapour (p. 88)

It seems that *How It Is* leaves those three related questions half answered by words like these. The later prose increasingly completes the response.

Wholeness and the Possibility of a Higher Ego

In *How It Is,* the sense of infinitudes of time is evoked consciously as never before in Beckett's fiction. This becomes an essential theme later in Beckett's prose, where its connection with will and self-consciousness is clarified more. But in *How It Is* the idea of eternity, like that of deliberate organization and utterance, is new, incomplete, and therefore not fully present to the reader. The "vast stretches/tracts of time," reiterated continually, is one of the novel's leitmotifs:

> bah I've lashings of time centuries of time (p. 19)

But what makes the intended orderliness incomplete is that very insistence. Just as the insistence that "we're talking of my life" or the "holes we're talking of the holes" seems an overemphasis, so

---

*G. C. Barnard involves reincarnation in his interpretation of *How It Is* (*Samuel Beckett: A New Approach,* pp. 68, 70–85). See also chapter 11 of the present study.

eternity—if it is going to be expressed at all—might be better expressed without deliberate or labored reference to eternity itself. But the consciousness of eternity does surface in more satisfying ways in *How It Is*. And as before, where a universal idea was expressed in terms that could be related to the personal life of the narrator or author without being personal, here, too, the satisfactory expression of eternal universals, or of the mind's agelessness, is located in things other than abstractions and leitmotifs:

> others had always known me *here in my last place* they talk to me of themselves, of me perhaps too in the end of fleeting joys and of sorrows of *empires that are born and die as though nothing had happened* (p. 13, my italics)

> that age will be over all the ages (p. 26)

> the ancient without end we're talking of me (p. 68)

Not only is the agelessness implied, but also comprehended:

> the people above whining about not living strange at such a time such a bubble in the head all dead now others for whom it is not a life and what follows very strange *namely that I understand them*

> always understood everything except for example history and geography everything and forgave nothing never could never disapproved anything really not even cruelty to animals never loved anything (p. 46, my italics)

These two statements come close to expressing the solar plexus, as it were, of *How It Is* and have wide relevance to Beckett's work before and after. They provoke an unconventional response, at the same time they defy the conventions of unconventionality represented by Modernism. The first section implies that the mind of the narrator has lasted longer than a "life up there" in the "above." It expresses real perplexity as to how those up there, normal mortals, can worry about death: "strange at such a time." But even stranger is that, from his position, the narrator can understand as well as acknowledge the strangeness. It is made clearer still as he goes on, without irony, to say that he understood everything, except things like history and geography. In other words, he understood the essential and failed to understand the "separatist" or agglomerative thought processes that the school history of Beckett's youth, and the study of geography, inculcate. Another way of putting this is to say that at all times the narrator's understanding was holistic, it saw essences, completeness or wholes, and was offended by parts arbitrarily* brought together and talked about as though they were wholes.

This way of expressing things accounts for the at-first-glance inhuman end to the quoted passage, the seemingly destructive "never forgave . . . never disapproved . . . never loved anything." This is not to say it is not a tragic statement: it is, in all its implications as well as in the fact that love was not possible. Beckett was already aware of this when he was drafting *How It Is:* "horribly difficult new work in French. The hole I have got myself into is as 'dumb of all light' as the fifth canto of Hell and by God no love," he wrote to Jake Schwartz. But each word—*forgave, disapproved, loved*—bears two meanings. Not to forgive may not be destructive, since forgiveness without awareness of the essence is mere forgetting, a not bothering even to recognize or comprehend an offense before considering it void. Disapproval, being entirely dependent on its motive, is morally ambiguous, and the fact that the narrator says he "never loved anything" may mean more than that he never developed the ability to love;** it may mean something completely different, in fact. A holistic consciousness may not be able to take or give love as taught by the separatist consciousness. This possibility is stressed over and over again by the young and old Beckett, from the first *transition* stories to the last short novels. What is beginning to be recognized in *How It Is* is that the mind which has unearthed it indeed understands everything, perhaps because it has a more than usual ability to perceive, perhaps because it is at a different point of development from our own. At least this is what should be suggested before anything obscure in Beckett's novel is dismissed, particularly when it is as obviously serious as the above passage appears to be. Academic disciplines per se are *not* repudiated by the narrator in this part of *How It Is.* But they are viewed with the sense of proportion that an ageless mind with "centuries of time, lashings of time" inevitably has.

Again, as from a great distance, the Beckett-persona remembers his wanderings in Germany:

---

*The distinction is more clearly brought out in the German word *willkürlich* (arbitrary) whose etymology suggests that what is arbitrary is by no means fortuitous; on the contrary, it is *perversely willed* out of what is whole in its natural state.

**Though that, in relation to Beckett himself, is likely. See Richard Ellmann's *James Joyce,* pp. 661–62, concerning Beckett's relationship with Lucia Joyce.

> . . . Potsdam where Klopstock lived a space and laboured though buried in Altona the shadow he casts
>
> at evening with his pale face to the huge sun or his back I forget it's not said the great shadow he casts towards his native east the humanities I had my God and with that flashes of geography (p. 47)

Where the wholeness of anything *was* afforded this mind by its education, the tribute is there in the aesthetic frame it is given in these lyrical visions of memory. Beckett's interest in German Romanticism* is acknowledged in the words "huge sun" ("huge" again changes the proportions of the outside world into those they have in the imagination at the moment of perception, just as it did in the veranda scene) and "the great shadow he casts," even in "lived and labored a space." "The humanities" pays a better tribute to the wholeness Beckett is looking for than do history and geography, some of its separate disciplines. The creative impulses—art—unites them so that they really work toward an education of the feelings, the mind and the will in harmony. Only then is love of anything possible. So little of that kind of education was done, says the previously quoted passage, that love was virtually ruled out. It is noticeable how education is always referred to in *How It Is* in terms of its single separate disciplines—mathematics, arithmetic, astronomy, physics, natural history, geography: "they have marked me, that's the main thing" (p. 45). This whole dimension seems to have been missed by Hélène Baldwin in one of her concluding remarks on *Samuel Beckett's Real Silence:* "there is no love in these works."[20] The reasons why this might be so are far more important than the fact, if indeed it is one. Such a view fails to appreciate the loving detail with which the works have been written.

Sapo's education in *Malone Dies,* described in more straightforward terms than *How It Is* can manage, was of a separatist kind and led to the emptying rather than to the filling of a soul. Sapo, repulsive as he has become by the time Malone/Beckett comes to write of him, had once been Beckett himself. (Beckett agreed that the "gulls' eyes" passage referred to himself and "got a bit out of

---

*Cf. Beckett's direct translations in *Text 3:* "wanderyears" for *Wanderjahre,* "nix" for *nichts* (*CSP,* p. 79); his play *Nacht und Träume;* and the quotations from *Dichterliebe* ("Ich grolle nicht") and Goethe's 'Mignon' ('Nur wer die Sehnsucht kennt, weiβ was ich leide') in Beckett's 1976–82 notebook (RUL MS. 2901), as specific instances of an altogether pervasive influence. See also footnotes to pages 102, 123, 144, 160, 201.

hand."[21]) The description of Sapo is a perfect gloss on the view of education implicit in *How It Is:*

> Sapo loved nature, took an interest in animals and plants and willingly raised his eyes to the sky* day and night. But he did not know *how* to look at all these things, the looks he rained upon them taught him nothing about them. . . . He did not associate the crocus with the spring nor the Chrysanthemum with Michaelmas. The sun, the moon, the planets and the stars did not fill him with wonder. He was sometimes tempted by the knowledge of these strange things, sometimes beautiful, that he would have about him all his life. But from his ignorance of them he drew a kind of joy, as from all that went to swell the murmur, you are a simpleton. But he loved the flight of the hawk and could distinguish it from all others. He would stand rapt, gazing at the long pernings, the quivering poise, the wings lifted for the plummet drop, the wild reascent, fascinated by such extremes of need, of pride, of patience, and solitude . . . then he was sorry he could make no meaning of the babel raging in his head, the doubts, desires, imaginings and dreads. And a little less well endowed with strength and courage he too would have abandoned and despaired of ever knowing what manner of being he was, and how he was going to live, and lived vanquished, blindly, in a mad world, in the midst of strangers. (*MD,* pp. 20–22)

These phenomena are the ones which the narrator of *How It Is* is trying to dredge up "for future restoration,"[22] in Wordsworth's phrase, as though the persona has finally discovered what they were for—the seasons, the colors of the sky, the habits of animals, the stars, sun, and moon. The feeling for birds, the profound identification with the being of the hawk, one of the few things Sapo *could* understand, reappears on page 38 of *How It Is:*

> I saw one blessed day at the pitch of heaven's azure towering between its great black still spread wings the snowy body of I know not what frigate-bird the screaming albatross of the southern seas

Azure is in no danger of being a "mouldy old reliable" here.

The view of education expressed in *How It Is* matters because, insofar as the novel is a compendium of autobiographical lyric, the involvement or integration of the will in education is a crucial factor in what that education is to produce in an artist's work. At the root of the declaration "never forgave . . . never loved any-

*The precise phrase "raised my eyes to the sky" occurs in *The Expelled* (*CSP,* p. 24).

thing" is some failing in education. The intellect alone, if trained without the feelings and the will influencing it, will fail to make such connections between the inner and outer world as Sapo, thus trained, failed to make. Again the distinction is between agglomerative "objectizing" and the intuition that removes all sense of subject separate from object. Sapo may not have been aware of the offense represented by a divisive education against the unity of consciousness and the environment, but there is an uneasiness in him; he is even "sorry"; his heart, reduced to this condition, asserts itself, in a kind of yearning, over the intellect and produces that sensation of rejoicing in ignorance; this in turn goes "to swell the murmur, you are a simpleton." Like Sapo, the simpleton or fool may be rich in intuitive knowledge: Beckett calls his state the "amabilis insania," the "holder Wahnsinn" (*Proust,* p. 91), and in an essay on the autobiographical in Beckett, H. Porter Abbott is reminded of Wordworth's *Preface:* "I have often applied to idiots, in my own mind, that sublime expression of Scripture, that 'their life is hidden with God."[23] But the simpleton lacks intellectual machinery and has come to seem to the world (itself becoming more and more separatist) incomprehensible and out of place; and crucially, his opinions are not seen as true, because they are unsupported by empirical evidence. But this outward incapacity that cripples the fool is something that an integrating education prevents while it maintains at the same time the inward intuition that has, for example, such profound understanding of the hawk and the albatross. The custom of associating "the crocus with the spring and the Chrysanthemum with Michaelmas" is likewise not arbitrary and depends on intuition. The education associated with the humanities that Beckett links with its essential *aesthetic* aspect—the sunset, the tomb, Klopstock's shadow to the east—is an education that would foster such a connection (if not explore its origins) and realize more fully in the self a union of will, thought, and feeling. In Beckett's fiction, the marked failure of will has often been commented on, not only by critics but also by Beckett himself.

There are more indirect references to this problem of the ego in some of the other vision scenes in *How It Is,* notably the following, which, having already occurred once in Beckett's story *The End,* reappears twice in *How It Is* and once again in *Cascando.*[24]

> sea beneath the moon harbour mouth after the sun the moon always light day and night little heap in the stern it's me all those I see are me all ages the current carries me out the awaited ebb I'm looking for an isle home at last drop never move again a little turn at evening to

the seashore seawards then back drop sleep wake in the silence eyes that dare open stay open live old dream on crabs kelp (*How It Is,* p. 94)

It will be noticed how much the visions that have already been discussed and quoted refer to the individual self, at least in terms of their autobiographical content. This beautiful passage is representative of a great conflict in Beckett's work. The conflict is between the inevitable separateness of a conscious subject and the selflessness it feels it needs to return to in the age in which the works are written. We have mentioned the loss of merely personal self involved in the lyrical "alchemy" of transforming memories into poetry; and to achieve that is already to overcome the egoism that by its nature tries to deny unity. But the problem still remains of how to maintain the sense of "I" that separates *I* from *he* or *she* or *it*, and, at the same time, to remain aware of what man must do in order to fulfil his capability and contact those universals which are alone responsible for pulling him up from whatever "mud" he is in. In a word, the problem is how to avoid "seedy solipsism" on the one hand, and how to avoid drowning in a sea of amorphous "Oneness" on the other, both of which things rob Beckett's man of his ego, his identity, and, finally, his will, too.

One way of moving toward a solution is shown in the apprehension of vast stretches of time in this novel; another is the suggestion that *something universal is the basis for making a remark about the personal,* and not vice versa. This is the sort of balance that is being looked for. But the boat scene is especially interesting because it illustrates perfectly the abandonment of self to the care of a universal force.* Rather than trying to appropriate the universal, it shows surrender to it. It is a tender evocation, fraught with danger, and because of this, the symbol is very moving. "I'm looking for an isle home at last"—not coincidentally reminding us of Yeats's "Innisfree" poem—is one side of the balance, the side of the "I" that distinguishes itself as unique. But at the same time, the self is multiplied, dissolved, and entrusted to something much larger:

all those I see are me all ages the current carries me out the awaited ebb . . . a little turn at evening to the seashore seawards then back drop sleep wake (ibid., my italics)

The fact that the sea may swallow and obliterate the little heap in

*Cf. also *The Prelude*'s boat scene and Shelley's "My soul is an enchanted boat," (*Prometheus Unbound* 2, v. 72).

the stern is precisely symbolic of the way in which the soul has to discard its self-interestedness and not care about what may happen to it. The tenderness is true just because it is not guaranteed. In order to achieve this state and this evocation, there has clearly been a relinquishment of self-will also: the image of the boat borne on the current is also the essential image of surrender.

This question receives only a slow and painful working out. But part of its solution is the realization that the state described by the boat scene, though will-less, still has to be *chosen.* A higher part of the ego, individual but not pursuing individual self-interest, makes the choice. The act of entrusting the self to universal forces is supremely difficult to perform and therefore requires strength of will to choose as well. "The old ego dies hard," said Beckett in his *Proust* essay (p. 21), "such as it was, a minister of dullness, it was also an agent of security." The "new ego" presaged by that comment is making itself felt in the boat scenes, in all its danger and enchantment, and Beckett's early essay also says something prophetic about the state of will-lessness just described:

> The Proustian stasis is contemplative, a pure act of understanding, will-less, the "amabilis insania" and the "holder Wahnsinn" (p. 91).

It is clear, then, how Sapo's simpleton's intuition is related to the development of a higher personality. Beckett's *Proust* essay also declares:

> will, being utilitarian, a servant of intelligence and habit, is not a condition of the artistic experience. (p. 90)

The conclusion to be drawn is crucial. The artistic experience depends on eliminating the lower will determined by habit and intelligence (the will Coleridge terms "egoistic" or "personal will"); but the higher will, or higher ego, which strives to realize the potential of a human personality and yet to ignore the pettily personal, cannot live without contact with the artistic experience or intuition from which it draws much of its strength. This is why the creation as well as the appreciation of artworks cannot be divorced from the individuality of the artist, nor yet be so limitingly tied to the incidentals of his personality as to make all artworks seem mere autobiographies.

Complementing this search for a higher ego in *How It Is* is the search for higher knowledge also: the new manner of addressing the objective as against the subjective. The title bears blatant witness to this. "How it is" is not merely "how I see it." Whereas before, in *The Unnamable* particularly, there was a sense of "me and only me," some of which carries over into the later novels, *I* and *they* are now located firmly in the scenario as well as in the language (where "they" lurked mysteriously in *The Unnamable,* "think is one of their words, rest another"). The numerical tangle at the end of *How It Is,* if nothing else, is successful in describing the multiplicity of souls caught up in the endless circular procession "down here." The trilogy, copious as it was on detail compared to *How It Is,* dealt only with one person, and when others entered, they related solely to the wandering narrator and gained their being only from their relation to him. Whether the same can be said of *How It Is* is doubtful. Even if, as at some points the novel suggests, all the other people in the gigantic circle are purely imaginary, they have a place in the text—and in the imagination—that is firm and unshifting, firm enough for strong denial to be necessary when the time comes to deny (here, it is at the end: in the trilogy, denials were issued every few pages).

The narrator is surrounded if not by real people, then by the imagination of numerous people in the same state as himself. What is crucial is that they do not exist for the sake of the narrator: any one of them could *be* the narrator. They move in a circle, the symbol of completeness and infinity, suggesting the common being and consciousness of all who turned in it, "a thousand thousand nameless solitaries" (p. 125): imaginative involvement of oneself with others is the basis of all objective moral thinking.* Whereas the narrators of the trilogy really were on their own, the vision of the thousands-strong procession through the ghostly landscape of *How It Is* resembles the *Divine Comedy* or *Piers Plowman* because of the sheer numbers involved as well as the seriousness of their destiny and the otherworldliness of the scene. In many ways the idea that subjectivity is an illusion has never been put to us better by Beckett before. "No world left to me now but mine," says the narrator, making us remember for a moment the solipsism of the trilogy; but "very pretty** *only not like that it doesn't happen like that*" (p. 35, my italics). The world of everyone else is as important as his own if the novel is really to address the matter of how *it* is.

The relationship between the objective and the eternal has been

---

*For example, see Sissela Bok, *Lying: Moral Choice in Private and Public Life,* p. 93.

**Cf. *From an Abandoned Work:* "very pretty really the whole thing" (*CSP,* p. 130).

alluded to earlier. There is no better way of distancing the self from illusive subjectivity than to emphasise its smallness in the great procession of cosmic events, as happens here:

> and the day so near its end at last *if it is not compact of a thousand days* good old question terrible always for the head and *universally apropos which is a great beauty* (p. 44, my italics)

This connection between eternity and objective reality is perhaps what is mysteriously being referred to in that recurrent insistence that the narrator is *not* devising it, that it is coming from somewhere else:

> how it was *I quote* . . . three parts *I say it as I hear it* (p. 7)
>
> I say it as I hear it *every word always* (p. 46)
>
> here then at last *I quote on* part three
>
> the speech I've been given do I use it freely *it's not said* (p. 111, my italics)

In such a strange narrative, uncompromising and bleak as many of its features are, the tone of scrupulous fidelity to something other than fancy sounds an authoritative note. Whereas in *The Unnamable* the suggestion was that the interrogators were forcing the narrator to shift responsibility for his actions and utterances onto a *fabled* source, here the sources strike us as more likely to be authentic. This stance suggests the attitude of the mystic, whose utterances are not claimed as his, but rather as the results of investigation into things some others cannot see.* It is the nature of the case that proof is impossible, but some of the utterances in *How it Is* approximate very closely in this respect to the language of mystics. That *can* be empirically described, for it is a matter of *how* the material is presented as well as of *what* it is. There is a plainness and ingenuousness which seem to go with the lack of need to explain the whys and wherefores of the source, or to defend its existence: Jakob Böhme, the seventeenth-century German mystic, prefaced his *Mysterium Pansophicum* with the words "All very earnestly and faithfully given from knowledge of the Great Mystery, the 8th May 1620."[25] In some senses this stance is a kind of

*See also G. C. Barnard's *Samuel Beckett: A New Approach,* p. 64, concerning the phenomenal and noumenal.

liberation from the torment of giving an account, which was one of the great difficulties the narrator encountered in Beckett's trilogy. There is an interrogator too in *How It Is*—Krim—but Krim is much more shadowy than "Basil and his gang" and appears only toward the end. Fletcher in fact sees him as no more than a witness, and G. C. Barnard says Krim is a phantom, the same as all the beings in *How It Is* whose names begin with K.[26] But the presence of an interrogator still shows that many of the problems in *The Unnamable* are yet to be solved. The theme of interrogation is not exhausted: it persists in the plays right up to *Catastrophe* (1982).

Despite this, the objectivity in *How It Is* is preserved, notably in that telling reversal which follows the atrocities with the tin opener and begins with the tentative reflection "what the fuck does it matter who suffers faint waver here faint tremor" (p. 144) and then leads to the conclusion that

> to this third part now ending at last a fourth should normally be appended in which would be seen among a thousand and one other things not at all to be seen in the present formulation this thing
>
> Instead of me sticking the opener into Pim's arse Bom sticking it into mine
>
> and instead of Pim's cries his song and extorted voice be heard indistinguishably similar mine
>
> the two couples that in which I figured in the north as tormentor and that in which I figure in the south as victim compose the same spectacle exactly (p. 142)

The circle of sufferers is made complete by this turning point. The subject has become an object, and the words "indistinguishably similar" are repeatedly applicable. For everything the narrator does, he gets it done back to him; whatever he says, he hears it said to him; whatever he wished on someone else is wished on him. The scenes of cruelty in *How It Is*, when compared with those in the previous novels, show clearly the advance in objectivity gained in *How It Is*. The cruelties in *Watt, Molloy,* and *The Unnamable* were one-way acts, unavenged even in imagination.

Light and Spiritual Substance

> even such relation as that of colour to the light of heaven, and as the light itself bears to the knowledge which it awakens.[27]

The "invocation" of *How It Is* is nowhere better instanced than in its repeated expression of a desire for the light. Light symbolizes knowledge and love on the one hand and spiritual reality on the other, and persuades us as few other things can that both "hands" belong to the same being. Light is the symbol for what pervades everything, it is nowhere concealed. Thus we say that to "throw light" on something is to know more of its being and its truth. Likening light to a king, Novalis illuminatingly remarks of it: "Seine Gegenwart allein / offenbart die Wunderlichkeiten / des irdischen Bereichs" (His presence alone can reveal the marvels of the earthly realm).[28] It is easy to see when the narrator of *How It Is* is animated by this desire; likewise, when the dark takes over and smothers it:

> the voice quaqua on all sides then within the little vault empty closed eight planes bone-white if there were a light a tiny flame all would be white ten words fifteen words like a fume of sighs when the panting stops then the storm the breath token of life part three and last it must be nearly ended (p. 140)

It would be difficult to assert what this passage is really about. It suggests manifold desires but is written, again, in an undivided tone. Perspectives are not tilted by irony or laughter. The equivalent of the "sealed jar" in *Molloy* (p. 52) and the dustbins and urns of the plays reappears here in the form of the "little vault," which in turn dominates six texts in the later prose and signifies imprisonment in the I-consciousness, the inability to unify with what is outside and should be interpenetrating what is inside. In John Pilling's words, "Hell is not so much other people as oneself: the truly infernal experience is to be im*mur*ed in one's own consciousness with one's own illusory companions."[29] Hence the longing for light *inside* the vault as well as outside. The bone-white surface is eminently able to receive and distribute light, but is in darkness. (There must once have been light in it for its color to have been known.) I-consciousness is located in the skull, therefore *bone-white** is a deliberate choice of word. The voice of longing speaks again in the very middle of a despairing outburst:

> my life a voice without quaqua on all sides words scraps then nothing then again more words more scraps the same ill-spoken ill-heard then nothing vast stretches of time then in me in the little vault bone-white

*Cf. *All Strange Away,* where *bone-white* appears again (*CSP,* p. 124).

> if there were a light bits and scraps ten seconds fifteen seconds ill-heard ill-murmured ill-heard ill-recorded my whole life a gibberish garbled sixfold* (p. 140)
>
> then within when the panting stops ten seconds fifteen seconds in the little chamber all bone-white if there were a light oakum of old words ill-heard ill-murmured that murmur those murmurs
>
> fallen in the mud from our mouths innumerable and ascending (p. 144)

Even ten seconds of the divine light of wisdom or of truth in the prison of consciousness would suffice to transform the "bits and scraps," the "gibberish garbled sixfold." The light is needed to transform *consciousness:* light as such is always mentioned in connection with illuminating the skull, vault of consciousness. Nothing is less inviting to light than mud over the eyes, however. That is why it is fair to suppose that the longing soul in question—it is a soul: its body is largely metaphoric and its scene wholly so—is in a hell, or at a point at which the evils of existence are becoming apparent to him during a sojourn outside it.

The only light to reply to the repeated calls is the inner light of the burning shavings (p. 38) which shines every time a memory or an imagination becomes strong enough to conquer the darkness for a moment. At such moments, the fact that light and an imagination of memory coincide indicates how light is a fitting symbol for spiritual rather than sense-perceptible reality:** for there is a difference between the original experience that has been remembered, that is, the sense-perception of the sun on the tiles (p. 16), and the reliving of it a long time afteward, the *presence* of it in the

---

*Cf. Blake's "Sixfold Emanation," the error of mortality:

> Say first! what mov'd Milton, who walk'd about in Eternity
> One hundred years, pond'ring the intricate mazes of Providence,
> Unhappy tho' in Heav'n—he obeyed, he murmur'd not, he was silent
> Viewing his Sixfold Emanation scatter'd thro' the deep
> In torment—
>
> (*Complete Writings,* p. 481)

**In connection with El Greco, Blake, Proust, and Huxley, as well as with the experiences of his own protagonist Phaedrus, Robert M. Pirsig writes of the "*dharmakaya* Light," or "white Light", and of the frequent use of electric lamps to suggest it in fiction, film, theatre, and cartoons. He links this light to "the undefined auspiciousness" present when a "Dynamic" potential supervenes on a situation till then determined by habit. (R.M. Pirsig, *Lila: An Inquiry into Morals* [London: Black Swan, 1992], pp. 393–97.) Such images and suggestions permeate Beckett's prose and stage works.

imagination when all that the senses are offered is opaque darkness and mud. In these moments of intuition the language of unrefracted feeling, a certain calm, rightly coincides with the longed-for burst of light:

> the scented sun dapples the red tiles yes I assure you
>
> my mother's face I see it from below it's like nothing I ever saw (p. 16)
>
> your life above YOUR LIFE pause my life ABOVE long pause above IN THE in the LIGHT pause light (p. 79)
>
> Krim imagines I am drawing what then faces places loved forgotten (p. 92)
>
> one [world] perhaps there is one perhaps somewhere merciful enough to shelter such frolics where no one ever abandons anyone and no one ever waits for anyone and never two bodies touch (p. 156)

This kind of tone, evident in the tender cadences in those extracts, is associated with love and its manifestations in *How It Is,* nearly always passed off as a loveless work. The first words of all in Novalis's *Hymnen an die Nacht* bear out a natural affinity between love and perception—the perception of light in its fullest signification: "Welcher Lebendige / Sinnbegabte / Liebt nicht vor allen / Wunderscheinungen / des verbreiteten Raums um ihn / das allerfreuliche Licht[?]" (What living being, gifted with feeling, does not love the all-joyful light before all the wonders spread out around him in the regions of space?)[30]

It may be true that, as we have seen, the narrator of *How It Is* "never loved anything" while he was in the physical existence which he remembers and which makes love seem such a hollow concept. But from his present vantage, love becomes possible "in memoriam," in "illuminated" imaginative activity. It is significant that Sapo, a persona for whom the words "never loved anything" are apt, "*loved* the flight of the hawk," nevertheless. He loved it because of his interest in it, not because of a hazy emotion about it; he allowed it to enter his consciousness unprejudiced by any attempts to judge it.* In *How It Is* the bird returns, as the alba-

---

*See my discussion of Moran's observations of plants and animals and his bees, in 'Giving Up the Ghost Be Born at Last: Three Novels and Four Nouvelles," in Pilling's *The Cambridge Beckett Companion.*

tross* in one of the imaginative bursts of light within the narrator's consciousness. It follows also that those points during physical existence which are recalled outside it were probably those in which the person was closest to the spiritual reality, or, to put it another way, when the wall of the jar or vault gave way, or when the light shone within it. It is noticeable and interesting—not to say dramatic, considering *How It Is*'s extremely monotonous basic scenery—how many visions of *life* appear in the mind of the narrator when the shavings burn and the desire for light is for "ten fifteen seconds" satisfied: mother, lover, sunlight, sky, flowers, the movement of the sea—these are elemental experiences that concern movement more than stasis, and show energy, color,** growth, and transformation of matter rather than "dead" matter itself.

The ancient and traditional impersonation of knowledge and truth as an enamouring female (Sophia, Isis, Beatrice) makes sense in connection with the undeflected *desire* for truth, the effect it has on language, the images of life, growth, and colour that it summons up. The phrases "it matters" or "does not matter" are significantly employed in this book:

> It's impossible it's not said *it doesn't matter it does it did that's superb a thing that matters* (p. 84, my italics)

In the phrase "it matters" there is the suggestion of materiality mixed simultaneously with the insistence on a pure idea. The two sit ill together; yet it is perfectly normal for something that has no material basis to matter to someone. The insistence on concept appears more clearly in such an ordering as "what matters is . . .," in which the *object* is given syntactic second place and its mattering the first: the verb *matter* can be understood without an object. But its etymological/historical meaning links it with matter. "That's superb a thing that matters" is not said without a tinge of irony, a tongue in the cheek. It is another way of saying that what matters (= is significant) does not matter (= is immaterial). Perhaps in this respect Beckett approaches what he calls not a satisfaction

*The albatross in Coleridge's *Rime of the Ancient Mariner* is comparably symbolic of the imagination.
**Goethe wrote, in his *Farbenlehre:* "Die Farben sind Taten des Lichts, Taten und Leiden," (Colors are the deeds of light, its deeds and sufferings). Quoted in Nisbet, *Goethe and the Scientific Tradition,* p. 16.

but an ablation of desire* for matter itself, whereas in the prewar prose something of that desire (or illusion) was still there (see chap. 1, pp. 27–31). Sixteen pages earlier in *How It Is* we find

> an oriental my dream he has renounced I too will renounce I will have no more desires. (p. 62)

None, perhaps, except the one desire expressed in:

> in the little chamber all bone-white if there were a light

In the early prose desire always centred on matter as objects. As a result of the torment of *The Unnamable* and a long period in which Beckett wrote no prose, in *How It Is* desire is transferred to the light, to what *matters but is not matter.* This is a literally incalculable change. Ruby Cohn notes in *Back to Beckett* how, in the brutal middle section of *How It Is,* tenderness is offered to matter, to an object (the sack), while an atrocity is practiced on other humans. This is another symptom of the "nightmare thingness"[31] described in chapter 1. Too much involvement with material things leads to a closing-off of the heart. The middle section of *How It Is* is, tellingly, the last of its kind in Beckett's prose canon.

In *How It Is* there are two other symbols of the move away from materialism and of the author's awareness of its dangers. One is the repeated stress on the movement of the procession from West to East (pp. 45, 155, 156). In the East materialism never entered into philosophy as it did in the West. That the narrator alludes to an oriental in connection with renouncing desires makes some sense in the light of Anthony Santomasso's comment on the Goetheanum (a building designed by Rudolf Steiner on Gnostic principles): "Ideally, forms, colours and sounds were to be drawn into reciprocal rhythms and fluctuations impelling one to move from west to east, from the sphere of the physical world toward the sphere of spiritual revelation, the apsidal stage."[32]

The other symbol is the ocean of mud itself. If thought of as a "land-scape," it bears a marked resemblance to William Blake's allegorical illustrations of materialism. One of them depicts Urizen struggling through the sea of materialism; another, particularly striking in connection with *How It Is,* immortals falling from the

---

**Proust,* p. 18: "the wisdom of the architect that is also the wisdom of all the sages from Brahma to Leopardi, the wisdom that consists not in the satisfaction but in the ablation of desire."

region of light in the top part of the picture into the dark waters of materialism below.[33] Beckett's mud is very soft, approaching wateriness, and his protagonist is spiritually very alert, in spite of his "minimalistic" insistence, largely humorous, on impotence and failure.

What makes the approach to the spiritual so hard to grasp in *How It Is* and in the trilogy is that at the same time as the narrator's consciousness deals with the spiritual, it is nevertheless maintaining a consistently firm grip on the physical world. This is in fact an enormous advantage, because it helps avoid a vague or poorly conceived "mysticism" or abstraction from sense perception. Beckett is always conscious of the physical body, even when he is speaking of the activities of the imagination. This is why he pays such attention to the interior of the skull, the supposed "seat" of imagination. Beckett's interest in the skull parallels Hamlet's in the skulls unearthed in the graveyard. Owen Barfield, tracing the effects of the Romantic movement, comments on the relationship between consciousness itself and the decay of nervous tissue that takes place during thinking and death: "The *undertone* of the conscious I is the opposite of its materialistic doubtful murmur. The English doubter is referring to the spiritual whenever he writes of death."[34] Barfield's words are eerily apt to Beckett here, especially the phrase "doubtful murmur" as it is applied to the "materialistic" consciousness of the physical world.

None of this interpretation is intended to make *How It Is* seem straightforward and easy to approach. Such a problematic work can only invite responses that posit and provoke more questions. It marks the beginning of what Beckett was to specialize in more and more: the involvement of the reader in the *process* of creation or live thinking. The last and greatest problem for the dedicated reader is the final page of *How It Is* where all the attempts to reach a state of knowledge are declared to be "all balls" not once but many times. It is as though the whole book need not have been written, or no attempt made to understand it. The gesture is again of defensiveness at the last stand: to deny vigorously any serious intention deflects judgmental antagonism. It also illustrates more than a little of the sense of failure the narrator experiences when, in the mode of "critic," he views his array of "bits and scraps" and compares them with what he might have created had he been given, or seen, the light. The recantation seems destructive and desolating, but it is not placed so as to obliterate the work itself. It occurs at the end, for one thing; had it been the preface, or been integrated with the search or journey undertaken, it is unlikely that the novel's effect would have amounted to anything at all. If we find ourselves reading *How It Is* more than once, then it is clear that the denial has failed to convince us. Like many of Beckett's books, this one lives in spite of, not because of, its self-destructive elements. There is also a memorable counterweight to the recantation, which makes a more forceful impression on repeated readings of *How It Is:* the words "the rest false" concluding the veranda scene in part 1 (p. 17). The words suggest, on one level, that everything in the book that is not concerned with imaginative reality (spiritual substance) is as much "balls" as the end of the book claims all that precedes it is. The raging at the end is impotent; it cannot convince us that the work has not been worth reading for its trials and errors as well as for its insights.

So what has the will, so determinedly awakened at the end of *The Unnamable* and at the start of *How It Is,* achieved? One achievement is the preparation of a test for the validity of the poetic: what I have called the *attrition of poetry,* carried out by the metafictional voice of *How It Is,* commenting, often caustically, on the methods of evocation used to conduct the central business of the work. Such a concern to test the poetic means is not only an expression of skepticism but an indication that significant works of imagination can on no account afford to use suspect methods. This is a project which had its beginnings in the 1920s (see pp. 49–51). It is nothing less than the truth of the poetic that this test is undertaken to establish.

In *How It Is,* the attrition of poetry has been accompanied by a move away from materialism, away from dependence on objects. And with the loosening of the hold on objects there coincides an increasing sense of objectivity: open-minded pursuit of the truth. The will of the author and the will of the narrator—aspects of a self-consciousness that are assuredly distinguishable but by no means separable from one another—have united in exploring the relation between imaginative intuition and the calls of the higher ego to transcend self-interest. Beckett is moving toward saying that the former can work with the latter. Self-realization on this level is perhaps the strongest example that is not abstract of what truth actually amounts to. "Once the moment of *metanoia* is past," says Owen Barfield, "the most inflexible and lasting choices of the will are those which originate in response to neither emotion, exhortation nor command but because of knowledge."[35] The view of imagination in *How It Is* outlined here suggests that its powers must be respected as knowledge rather than as personal taste or whim, if they are to contribute to the lastingness of human choices.* Along with Blake, Shelley, and Coleridge, Wordsworth had the same point to make in his declaration: "Poetry is the breath and finer spirit of all knowledge."[36] Beckett too was to spare no effort in illustrating what can happen if imagination is outlawed completely from human self-consciousness.

---

*The links between imagination, knowledge, and the development of personality traced here are explored fully in the works of Rudolf Steiner. Gottfried Büttner, in his book *Samuel Beckett's Novel* "Watt", draws attention to the relevance of anthroposophical spiritual science to *Watt* and Beckett's works in general, and is the first anthroposophist, to my knowledge, to write on and become a friend of Beckett. His book on *Watt* is the most convincing interpretation of that novel and of Beckett's aesthetic that I have yet come across, but the strength of his interpretation is almost equaled by the scantness of his respect for literary criticism, in which he sees no more than "fixed vocabulary and nailed-down concepts" (p. 37). This is a markedly one-sided view for someone who stresses (after Steiner) the need for developing the faculties of perception in order that a spiritual dimension may become known. There is a parallel need for developing the faculties of transmission of such perceptions. Beckett's works invite not only a gnosiological but also a close reading. The close reading will inevitably be "fixed and nailed down" if it ignores the gnosiological (a word which Beckett suggested to Büttner was preferable to epistemological); but equally, the gnosiological reading, if it is not close, will tend to resist understanding and remain unappreciative of the contribution style makes to content—a contribution indispensable in any discussion of knowledge and poetics.

Part 3
A Fancy Prison (1966–1976)

5
Fancy and Imagination in the Rotunda (*All Strange Away*)

The works discussed in this part form a cycle, from *All Strange Away* (begun in 1963) through to *For to End Yet Again* (published in 1976). None of them can be said to be complete or freestanding, except *All Strange Away*, in either the form of the texts or their manner of publication. Beckett described them to Brian Finney and others as residual "both from larger original wholes and from the whole body of previous work." Like the *Texts for Nothing*, their titles (*Residua, Fizzles*) and their haphazard presentation to various publishers suggest a strong impulse to self-deprecation. The fact that the later collection of texts from the sixties and seventies (*For to End Yet Again and Other Fizzles*) attempts, in Beckett's words "to break wind noiselessly" shows that in Beckett's remark to Schneider about "fundamental sounds" there is a "joke intended" after all, and almost certainly more of the same deprecation. And as one moves from the exterior of the sixties texts to what is "within," the sense of incompleteness persists. But emptiness is twofold: *empty* means either containing nothing, or ready for everything.

Experiments in reducing language to its barest elements have been the topic of countless studies of Samuel Beckett, which are all in their own ways right in pointing to his dearth of resources at this period and a kind of despair in the face of a language so tired that traditional metaphor, rhetoric, and even normal grammar cannot be effective anymore. In this sense the short works fulfill the process initiated by *How It Is*. In Beckett criticism there is a tendency to admire experimentation and reduction for their own sake; but I think it is difficult to assent to the idea that *Ping*, for example, adequately rewards the labor needed to winkle out its withered kernels. In recognition of Beckett's minimalism, is it not enough to recall Shelley's words from "On Life": "How vain it is to think that words can penetrate the mystery of our being! Rightly used they can make evident our ignorance to ourselves, and this is much."[1]

A "poetics of indigence" or a "syntax of weakness" is probably, as Beckett himself surmised, a function of ignorance rather than of knowledge: Shelley and Beckett are both suggesting that language helps us to perceive what *is* true only by ruling out what is not. In the question is to be found the germ of a solution; more readily, at least, than in the statement of a hypothetical solution. Thus, to deal with ignorance, as Beckett does in these texts, need not be a barren exercise. but it does not help us much toward an understanding of the works to read a comment like "The *têtes-mortes* (*Residua*) trace the difficulty of writing fiction, which becomes synonymous with expressing being in the void."*[2] Modernist orthodoxy notwithstanding, it is by no means a gain for a work of art that it should trace the difficulty involved in making it. Insofar as that tracing is visible in Beckett's sixties texts, it is a failure rather than the success which many critics are determined to account it. Moreover, *how* it "becomes" synonymous with expressing being in the void is not made clear, and what the void is does not receive any explanation either. It is a doomed enterprise to try to make the lack expressed in these texts into a virtue. Beckett was obviously doubtful enough of them, on the whole, to speak of them dismissively, which he does not do of all his works, notably the trilogy and *Waiting for Godot*. It is, in short, justifiable for the reader to react to the short texts in much the way Beckett reacted as maker. This chapter and the next will offer some possible reasons for the texts' incompleteness or lack, will try to give a meaningful interpretation of "the void," and will suggest that the texts' only coherence is their function all together as a cyclic history of consciousness.

In many ways these texts represent in the art of Beckett what études and studies represent in the oeuvre of a major composer. They are little "pieces" of language; they draw attention to their style, they recall certain periods in Beckett's writing career hitherto, and they are testing grounds for new styles. Many of the *Fizzles* remind us stylistically of works we know: they seem like

*The same concern with the fiction writer's "artistic predicament" and the same annexation of the term *being* to cover a multitude of sins also characterises David Read's essay on *Company* and *Ill Seen Ill Said* (*Modern Fiction Studies* 29, no. 1 (1983), pp. 120, 123.)

fragments, tidied up and presented almost like archaeological specimens. In "Horn Came Always," for instance, the presence of an agent with a notebook, the unwillingness of the narrator to face reality—"I had come to bear everything bar being seen"—and the contemplation of his physical ruination, not to mention the tone and syntax (irritable and pedantic), reminds us of Moran. "I gave up before Birth" and "Afar a Bird" recall the nervous hair- and ego-splitting of *Texts for Nothing* 3 and 4. "Closed Space" is possibly the idea for *The Lost Ones:* much the same tone obtains and much the same scene, a scene perhaps inherited from *The Unnamable*'s arena.

Whether these are curiosities from Beckett's "trunk" of papers or contemporary recapitulations on old styles, the effect of small exercises remains. Indeed, to see them as just that is one of the only two points of view that makes sense of their apparent lack of content. The other point of view, addressed by this chapter, will be set forth in the context of the Romantics' distinction between Fancy and Imagination, and its application to the texts' illustrations of human experience.

All Strange Away

All Strange Away does have some claim to independence and completeness as a new beginning, departing as completely as it does from *How It Is,* which was finished some four years before (Carlton Lake suggests in 1960.[3]) It is the source work for all the texts of the sixties and early seventies that are concerned with imprisonment in a chamber. It is also the only complete work amongst them in that it conceives the entire world of all the texts in one go. The world of *Imagination Dead Imagine, Ping, Lessness, The Lost Ones,* and *For to End Yet Again* is a world which Barbara Hardy feels is "breaking down because humankind can't bear so little character, so little action, so little time and so little space."[4] Hardy's words (playing on Eliot's "human kind cannot bear very much reality") are apt in that there is a pervasive feeling that nothing is there—"that white speck lost in whiteness"—but take no account of the fact that the trilogy has very little in the way of character, action, time, and space either, and succeeds perfectly well without breaking down.

Barbara Hardy's "classical" expectations of narrative may appear to be elementary criteria that modernist and postmodernist writing has seen itself as destined to supersede, but much depends on the level at which one is thinking this. It may be that Hardy misapplies a principle in her consideration of the sixties texts, since character and action here are not on the level of the physical, potentially social world as they are, for example, in *Molloy*. But actually the short texts contain, as we shall see, far greater spans of time and space than does almost any conventional fiction. The problem is not one of being given too little time and space but, if anything, too much. The infinitudes are not, however, those of science fiction, which attempt to provide humankind with the sensation of reality without the inconvenience of reality itself; they are spans of imagination, uniting the forces and objects of the physical world with the faculties of pure thought. It is in this regard that the texts depart from being mere exercises in style. The question of levels of reality is one that Beckett was really interested in and becoming more lucid about as his texts developed out of each other and moved into the 1980s (the subject of Chapters 8–11). The idea of destroying reality—"Beckett's lifelong search for that impossible shape that will capture in its own destruction life's ultimate shapelessness"[5]—is largely an irrelevant invention of post-Modern dogma.

One of *All Strange Away*'s peculiarities, one of the first impressions it offers is the disarray of its tone and style. Although in terms of scenario it is the origin of *Ping,* that model of stylistic homogeneity, this work shows a remarkable variation:

> That's better, now he's better, and so sits and never stirs, clutching it to him where it gapes, till it all perishes and rots off of him and hangs off of him in black flitters.
>
> . . . no, not that again . . . try that.
>
> So on other four possibilities when begin again.
>
> Dread then in rotunda now with longing and sweet relief but so faint and weak no more than weak tremors of a hothouse leaf. (*CSP,* pp. 118–26)*

The first sentence, rich in verbs and conjunctions, even garrulous with its repetition of the colloquial, Irish-sounding "off of him"

---

*All page references to the texts discussed in this chapter, except where otherwise indicated, are to the *Collected Shorter Prose, 1945–1980*.

and "flitters,"* could be from the trilogy. There is even the familiar coat, "clutched where it gapes," reminding the narrator of "after the war" (*CSP,* p. 118)—of the trilogy, in other words. But an unwillingness to rest with that world and that language surfaces in the violent or testy "not that again" of the second extract—"A place [?] that again [?] Never [.] another question"—and shows us that the narrator wishes to make a break with the foregoing prose. That break is linguistically achieved by the words in the third example, whose aim is to exclude rigorously any word not essential to the import. Verbs are omitted—verbs describing affective states most assiduously—as are most determinants of time. The sentence could have read "*And* so on *for the* other four possibilities *until at last you* begin again." But in the attempt to objectify and shorten involved in composing telegrams (to which Beckett's reductive process is similar) there is also a loss in terms of human inflection. (Hence the particular incongruity of the telegram as conveyor of news eliciting happiness or grief.)

Beckett achieves the same effect in:

> eyes burnt ashen blue lashes gone lifetime of unseeing glaring, jammed open, one lightning wince per minute on earth, try that. (p. 118)

But it is interesting to see how that very sentence betrays itself at the last moment: "jammed open, one lightning wince per minute on earth" has departed from the toneless mold of "so on other four possibilities" and engaged the reader's emotions, just like the fourth example in the group above. The mysterious "tremors of a hothouse leaf"—echoed again later as "tremors of a leaf indoors"—are summoned to describe the hopes and fears of the prisoners in *All Strange Away*'s rotunda. Dread, longing, and relief, all specified in the text, are some of the emotions distinctive of tragedy. In such language the telegrammatic intention, or—in John Pilling's words—the "vehement rigour,"[6] of the sixties generation of texts lapses to offer a hint of the "infinite suggestibility" which he also identifies as a quality of the three early seventies *Still* texts. But between these two poles there are many intermediate zones to which *All Strange Away* introduces us.

The disarray of tone—various styles startlingly presented together—suggests the narrator's unease in this new environment. Such interjections as "aha," "details later," "try that," "no not

*The piano tuners in *Watt,* arguably Dubliners, say the piano's "strings are in flitters" (p. 69).

again," "get all this clearer later" indicate defensiveness, provisionality, and a real discomfort with a method which generates the old need for excuses and pretexts. Even the "rigour" of "so on other four possibilities when begin again" is not quite a success: one feels it has been an attempt to make concise the pseudo-exhaustive language of *Watt* and the trilogy and to discipline the opaque straggle of unpunctuated words in *How It Is* by merely extracting words like unwanted teeth, leaving gaps instead of recasting the whole mode of utterance.

Yet this recasting *has* been done occasionally, at points where the writing is at its most compelling:

> The glaring eyes now clearer still in that flashes of vision few and far now rive their unseeingness.
>
> Imagination dead imagine all strange away.
>
> even on the very sill of black and at long last the murmur too faint for mortal ear
>
> long black hair when light strewn over face
>
> Murmurs sometimes as great a space apart as from on earth a winter to a summer day and coming on that great silence, she's not here, for instance or if in better spirits Fancy is her only hope, too faint for mortal ear (pp. 120–22)

The effect is either mysterious and musical as in the title phrase and the reference to the hothouse leaf, or "leaf indoors on earth in winter to survive until spring," and in the words, once again otherworldly, "from on earth a winter to a summer day and coming on that great silence"; otherwise it is powerfully synesthetic, as in "rive their unseeingness" and "on the very sill of black," in which two cases the material world of physical manifestation is put in the direct service of pure thought, *unseeingness* and *black* being qualities, *rive* and *sill* being tied to the solid and the physical.* The economy of this language is indisputable, but we do not find ourselves admiring the "minimalism" or "reduction" of these sentences so much as their traditionally metaphoric force and beauty.

---

*Cf. *King Lear* 3.2.56: "close pent-up guilts, rive your concealing continents," which offers a similar sense of storm and stress. Compare also "flashes of vision" with Lear's storm, and, in turn, the storm mentioned by name at the end of *Imagination Dead Imagine* (*CSP*, p. 147).

As so often with Beckett, the powerful or striking thrusts of metaphor and cadence are associated with particular subjects, emotions, and levels of consciousness. These are what this cycle of texts explores, and it is here that the Romantics' definitions of consciousness become important.

Although all Beckett's novels are works of imagination, none before *All Strange Away* comes near to making imagination into the protagonist of a myth. The whole question of imagination has been developing in the prose subsequent to the *Proust* essay and is still often under the surface in *How It Is*—"imagination on the decline having attained the bottom". But the whole string of texts arising from and associated with *All Strange Away—Imagination Dead Imagine, Ping, Lessness, The Lost Ones, For to End Yet Again*—is tied exclusively to the first three words of *All Strange Away:*

> Imagination dead imagine.

The imagination as it has been traditionally espoused in poetry, and against which *How It Is* inveighed ("mouldy old reliables," "a few usual flowers"), is subjected to the severest possible review in these six short texts, which for clarity can be termed the "Rotunda texts" or "Imagination Dead" texts. They are carrying out a particular task, different from that of *Enough,* the three *Stills, As the Story Was Told,* and *Heard in the Dark* and *One Evening* (two later "shorts" which appear to be drafts of *Company* and *Ill Seen Ill Said*). The different purpose of the Rotunda texts is "announced" in *All Strange Away,* and only worked out gradually during the chain.

These texts' special purpose is, broadly speaking, to put to the test the proposition that the Imagination—as described and used by literary tradition (particularly poetry)—is dead and unusable, indeed, to inquire whether that assumption is correct. For, given the death of imagination hinted at in the *Texts for Nothing* and *How It Is* (but only confirmed at the start of *All Strange Away*), how is the compulsion to utter to be viewed? If imagination is dead, what is it possible to write after *How It Is*? The only practical answer is a survey of the supposed mortuary. The deeper Beckett goes into his survey, however, the more infernal and potentially evil the consequences become. The texts serve at once as the trial of a broadly "Modernist" axiom and a journey through purgatory into hell. The result, achieved concurrently by other sixties texts (and again later by those in the eighties), is a renewed interest in an imagination which has actually proved impossible to regard as dead.

There are assuredly compelling reasons why Beckett was led to assume it was dead. If the bizarre quip in *How It Is*—"imagination on the decline having atttained the bottom"—is an indication of Beckett's mistrust of the idea, then *All Strange Away*'s allusions refine his skepticism into a suspicion of false, cerebral imaginations:

> Imagine lifetime, gems, evenings with Emma and the flights by night, no not that again.

The reference to "lifetime" (as opposed to the "present" of purgatory or "suspended animation") reminds us of *How It Is*'s "life up there in the light," and the "gems" mentioned here are arguably the same as the visions of life that occasionally appeared to the narrator on his journey through the mud, but the visions are even more suspiciously cast by the word "gems" (reminding us perhaps of the tawdry "poetic gems" of William McGonagall). The pointed specification of Emma intimates that Emma Bovary might have been the epitome of vain dreaming, the falsest form of imagination possible, the one Dr. Johnson warned against when he proclaimed its "dangerous prevalence."[7] The visions from "life above," "in the light" (where the light was natural, not artificial), which were a possible source of insight for the occupier of the "dark little chamber all bonewhite," were all put at arm's length at the summing up of *How It Is,* mistrusted as pieces of sentimentality, just as Bovary's "flights by night" are banished in the even starker opening of the Rotunda cycle.

But having mistrusted and to some extent debunked received meanings of the concept *imagination,* Beckett cannot throw it out. On the contrary, *All Strange Away* confronts the word again head-on, as if opening a trial:

> Imagination dead imagine. A place, that again. Never another question. A place, someone in it, that again. Crawl out of the frowsy deathbed and drag it to a place to die in. . . . Five foot square, six high, no way in, none out, try for him there. (p. 117)

In these few phrases the whole cycle of six texts is engendered: character, action, time, and space are here sorted out with one dismissive gesture ("a place, someone in it, that again"), the last two words denoting, as well as weariness, exasperation and impatience to get rid of the outer world of fiction and proceed to the core; the level of this prose does not require props. The initial command shows that if anything follows in response to the imperative "imagine," the resulting statement will, at first sight, achieve the impossible. If imagination is actually dead, how can any imagining be done? The preposterous nature of some of the detail in *All Strange Away* and the texts that follow can be accounted for if we admit that fiction without imagination is an extreme paradox. It may be possible for some nonfiction to be imaginative (the treatises of Paracelsus or Jakob Böhme, for example), but it is almost inconceivable for fiction to be intentionally nonimaginative. Such a fiction would be a purgatory for the writer determined to write it, as it would be for the reader, since both would be in a land where the desire to imagine subsists but no environment or opportunity is available to fulfill or satisfy it, just as in the mystics' region between death and rebirth the soul must experience, say, physical appetites with nothing in the way of objects to fulfil the desires.[8] This is why the imagination, or more accurately, the *consciousness* of the Beckettian narrator in the Rotunda texts, lacking its proper subjects, ravenously feeds on husks of meaning, measurements, coordinates, mathematical calculations, and the charting of perfunctory bodily movements, or, when it is exhausted by these, thinks of alternatives to what has been posited, like a badly programmed computer:

> But a, b, c and d now where any pair of right-angled diameters meet circumference meaning tighter fit for Emma with loss if folded as before of nearly one foot from crown to arse and of more than one from arse to knees and of nearly one from knees to feet though she still might be mathematically speaking more than seven foot long and merely a question of refolding in such a way that if head on left cheek at new a and feet and new c then arse no longer at new d but somewhere between it and new c and knees no longer at new b but somewhere between and new a with segments angled more acutely that is head almost touching knees and feet almost touching arse, all that most clear. Rotunda then three foot diameter and three from ground to vertex, full glare, head on left cheek at a no longer new, when suddenly clear these dimensions faulty and small woman scarce five foot fully extended making rotunda two foot diameter and two from ground to vertex, full glare, face on left cheek at a and long segment that is from crown to arse now necessarily along diagonal too hastily assigned to middle with result face on left cheek with crown against wall at a and no longer feet but *arse* against wall at c there being no alternative and knees against wall at ab a few inches from face and feet against wall bc a few

> inches from arse there being no alternatives and in this way the body tripled or trebled up and wedged in the only possible way in one half of the available room leaving the other empty, aha. (p. 124)

When the wearied and wearisome consciousness finally runs out, it gives up entirely and inserts the word *diagram* to rescue the reader from boredom and to leave him or her the responsibility of deciphering the mass of words: words have become the least suitable of all means of expression. Such is one consequence of trying to imagine a world without imagination.

Another is the sudden growth of a powerfully imaginative—in the sense of metaphysical—myth, which is anything but boring. By a paradoxical feat, Beckett manages to bring his mortuary of imagination alive from within:

> crawl out of the frowsy deathbed and drag it to a place to die in.

The reference of "it" is tellingly multivalent: possibly to the bed; possibly to the imagination itself; possibly to the "someone in" the "place." On the face of it, it looks as though the principal meaning is this: "crawl out of the frowsy deathbed[,] and drag it [the deathbed] to a place [for me] to die in." But even in this version it is not clear whether the bed itself is "frowsy," nor is the issuer of the imperative "crawl out" identified. If the bed is frowsy, as the grammar indicates, then he who has crawled out of it is likewise frowsy. He at once occupies the bed and commands it to be vacated. The words are so obliquely placed that the identity of the speaker, the imagination, the occupier of the bed, and "it" are all conflated, though still distinguishable. The aim of the text being to imagine imagination dead, one task is to accomplish the killing, to find a "place" where the burial can be performed. The authorial consciousness (I, me), which issues the command "Crawl . . . ," claims also to be imagination (like Malone on *his* deathbed). This is why suicidal phantoms also gather over this stillborn sentence.

The "place for it to die in" is "not far to seek." By the text's fifth line the imagination is already installed there, with no way in or out, in the rotunda or chamber. The symbol is extremely powerful and although it has appeared before (*Molloy, The Unnamable, Endgame, Play*), its meaning is never so clear as it is this cycle of prose works, set apart from all the others because the imagination is consciously outlawed and the rotunda has become a prison. Devoid of human attribute or characteristic, the prison represents the consciousness of man conjectured to be lacking the capacity of true imagination. The walls are colorless, "all white flaking plaster or the like," the floor is "like bleached dirt." The light is artificial, unstable, and hellish, coming from "no visible source" and accompanied by uncomfortably high temperatures punctuated by sudden lapses into corresponding darkness and cold. *The Lost Ones* hints that the rapid fluctuations of light and temperature—light occurring at 25° C and dark at 5° C—are the indications of day and night as seen with a different time perspective, from after death. For the highest temperature is that of a summer's day, while the lowest is that of an average winter night: *All Strange Away* mutters of the span of time between summer and winter "on earth" somehow corresponding to a much shorter period in the rotunda. Consciousness alive and imagination dead make an inhospitable home for man, who is still there on the scene whatever atrophies he may have undergone. The inhospitableness is forced home even more strongly by the presence of a couple in most of the texts, who it is suggested were once in love—in another state of which the supreme province is the imagination.

> memories of past felicity no save one faint with faint ripple of sorrow of a lying side by side. (*All Strange Away,* p. 126)

> eye black and white half closed long lashes imploring that much memory almost never. (*Ping,* p. 151)

Several forms of consciousness have entered the discussion up to this point under the name of imagination: authorial enterprise (Malone); vain or idle dreaming (Emma Bovary); consciousness able to fabricate or extend itself, pure and simple; imagination as it appears in the initial sentence of *All Strange Away;* and the same word as I have used it above in "the capacity of true imagination." The effect of this group of texts depends entirely on our being able to distinguish the differing senses of the word and, occasionally, on our holding them together all at the same time without confusing them.

A few hints apart (Emma and the capitalized word *Fancy*), Beckett is not interested in giving us a *history* of the imagination as it has been employed in criticism and philosophy. His purpose is to create an evocation, a picture, a scenario, with a particular effect. But it is an effect in the background of which stands much of past thinking about imagination, and an effect which is also one of the few serious statements in contemporary literature of what the future fortunes of imagination might be. The disturbing nature of

Beckett's art at this period is no less of a warning than were Blake's prophetic poems, which themselves revolved around the subject of imagination.

The context in which Beckett's "Rotunda" myth makes most sense is the Romantics' distinction between fancy and imagination. In the period of Pope and Johnson no consistent distinction was made (*Oxford English Dictionary,* s.v. *fancy:* "In early use synonymous with imagination . . . 1712, Addison, *Spectator* 411 p 2, 'The pleasures of Imagination or Fancy, which I shall use promiscuously.'" Neither does *Rasselas* 44 distinguish between the two words. "There is no man whose imagination does not sometimes predominate over his reason" says nothing measurably different from "all power of fancy over reason" in the same paragraph). Hazlitt gropes toward a distinction;[9] Wordsworth seems often to blur the issue again while being as an artist the example upon which Coleridge was then to build his own detailed distinction between them.[10]

Peter Murphy, though otherwise helpful in touching on the relevance of Coleridge's distinction to *All Strange Away,* surrenders arms somewhat by declaring that "Coleridge's ideas here are notoriously elusive and probably confused."[11] He does not spell out what the confusion is, even given the resource of Barfield's *What Coleridge Thought,* a book written to clarify Coleridge's unfinished but potentially coherent *Biographia Literaria*. Because confusion has so often been attributed to Coleridge without due inquiry, any application of his concepts to Beckett's work requires a clear outline of the facts concerning fancy and imagination in Coleridge. It is possible to define imagination as divergent in kind from fancy or as one with it in kind but differing in degree; different in kind because at certain times so different in effect; but sometimes visible as a degree of the same kind. The kind that includes fancy and imagination (as degrees) is "the ascending series that manifests the seminal principle of mind or intelligence"[12] or "the *antecedent unity* in all natural variety." Fancy is still lower in the series.

For Coleridge, the imagination (in man the secondary imagination, which serves the primary, the "living power and prime agent of all human perception" or "very power of growth and production") does the transformative metaphorical work of the poet, "dissolves, diffuses, dissipates in order to re-create." Fancy, on the other hand, "has no other counters to play with but fixities and definites" (very much the basis of the binary operation of computers, the fixed counters 0 and 1). Fancy is an *aggregative* faculty; it arranges units but does not create them or change them.

Imagination "modifies" the units themselves. In doing so it shows itself to be more distinctly one in kind with the primary imagination than it is with fancy, because imagination can change the nature of the materials which fancy has to "take or leave ready-made." Fancy is the organizer—not the origin—of memories, keeping them accessible. Imagination is the origin of those memories, and it is imagination that determines their value. As with the ascending series mentioned above, value judgments are necessarily involved in a distinction between the two terms fancy and imagination. While a difference in kind can accommodate, though it need not stipulate, a value judgment, a difference in degree must usually involve a hierarchical aspect. William Blake brings out the same distinction and similar value judgments in his mythology of the daughters of memory and the daughters of inspiration, in which memory equals Coleridge's fancy and inspiration Coleridge's imagination.* And Beckett's *Proust* essay mentions voluntary memory "the uniform memory of intelligence," and involuntary memory, which "in its flames . . . has consumed Habit and all its works."[13]

But imagination in art (as against criticism and philosophy) is necessarily human, mortal, and by implication involved with things; when imagination dies in Beckett, all natural objects and phenomena disappear, and then the words that stand for nothing (even *texts* that stand *for nothing!*) either take their place—"a white speck lost in whiteness"—or they neutralize themselves: the coinage "bleached dirt" contaminates the proverbial cleanness of bleach and bleaches the earthily rich color of dirt, leaving nothing. Fancy, with its power to arrange units, is the tool of imagination in the world. Grammatical rules are a symbol or extension of fancy. Or, to quote Barfield, the one "kind" that includes fancy and imagination as degrees is "the intelligence present both in nature and in man, from which may be deduced not only poetic fruitage [imagination] but all forms of consciousness [including fancy] and indeed of life." Coleridge confirms this:

> Genius must have talent just as in like manner imagination must have fancy. In short, the highest intellectual powers can only act [manifest

**The Marriage of Heaven and Hell* and numerous other of Blake's writings make it absolutely clear that Coleridge was not alone in making the distinction between imagination and fancy. Many of the two poets' theoretical distinctions are identical.

> themselves in the human world] through a corresponding energy of the lower.[14]

Their mutual necessity established, Coleridge still insists that fancy, if allowed to predominate unduly in any situation, is a danger. Barfield points to Coleridge's revealing vocabulary in connection with fancy: "fancy is always the ape, too often the adulterator and counterfeit of our memory" if it is not in a correct relationship with imagination. It "plays" with fixities and definites, described as "counters." Whilst being clear, not confused, about the reciprocity of fancy and imagination, Coleridge leaves no doubt at all as to his view of fancy when it operates alone. It is then "dead," "mechanical," "artificial," an "ape," an "adulterator."

In proportion as it becomes a danger, Coleridge's fancy becomes relevant to Beckett's purgatorio in the Rotunda. To quote Barfield again:

> In the first place, then, fancy has its proper place in the genesis of consciousness as a whole and, particularly, in the conversion of perceptions into memories. But it is easily debased. In its debased form it is, as *passive* fancy, more or less identical with precisely those characteristics of human perception which it is the function of imagination (by modifying perception) to overcome, namely: "the film of familiarity* and selfish solicitude", in consequence of which "we have eyes, yet see not, ears that hear not", or more shortly, "the lethargy of custom". The mind is *in thrall to the lethargy of custom when it feeds solely on images which it has itself taken no active part in producing*. But there is more to it than this. For the debasement of *active* fancy carries this process further. Where the mind deliberately chooses to feed only upon such images, there you have the debasement of active fancy; there, the lethargy of custom becomes the deliberate practice of reducing *"the conceivable" to the "bounds of the picturable"* at which Coleridge never tired of pointing his warning finger.[15]

The relevance of Coleridge's description (and Barfield's interpretation) of fancy to *All Strange Away* could hardly be clearer. The provisional, speculative, and idly permutative language which generates the bulk of the text is clearly an example of fancy running away with itself, left on its own by the dying imagination to sustain itself solely on "images which it has had no part in producing," on alternative arrangements of known units, coordinates, fixities, and definites.

---

*Shelley uses this phrase in exactly the same context in *A Defence of Poetry* (*Essays and Letters*, p. 37).

Peter Murphy quotes Coleridge to the effect that fancy is "always the ape and too often the adulterator and counterfeit of our memory" and is right to link fancy with the sexual fantasies in *All Strange Away;* but in doing so he contradicts another statement he makes in the same paragraph, to the effect that the authorial voice—whose fantasies they are—is keyed to the imagination, and the couple in the rotunda to fancy. Murphy, I believe, misrepresents Coleridge's distinction. Having asserted but failed to delineate Coleridge's "confusion," he claims that "Beckett is concerned with what could be called the fundamental Imagination, that which follows after the death of the conventional 'living Power.'" But the "living Power" as Coleridge conceived it is not susceptible to becoming conventional or stale. And there is nothing anterior to it—it is itself primary, fundamental. The word *conventional* is actually far more applicable to the fixities and definites of the fancy. I think Murphy has not distinguished between *tradition,* which is alive and which the "living power" of Coleridge's aesthetic energizes, and *convention,* which is dead and mechanical. Far from positing a "radically new" conception of imagination and jettisoning the traditional "living Power," *All Strange Away* ruthlessly documents the ravenous machinations of fancy alone, which are only occasionally alleviated by some final gasps of the imagination. Everything is provisional ("try that," "try for him there"):

> sleep if maintained with cacodemons making waking in light and dark if this maintained sweet relief (p. 127)

Here is the origin of *The Lost Ones*'s recurring phrase "if this notion is maintained." Fancy, the merely notional, presents no immediate problem; it is merely a matter of holding something up or letting it go. If fancy rules, life in the rotunda is a matter of "entertaining" notions, both in the adjectival and active senses. But mere entertainment is no nearer to art than idle speculation is to knowledge.

The effect of *All Strange Away* and the associated prose works is to conjecture or to "fancy"—not really to imagine—a world without imagination, in order to test the assumption that the imagination as it has been consecutively represented in literary and artistic tradition is worn out, effectively dead. In *How It Is* the ontological struggle between light and dark and the doubt about imagined scenes probably led to the enterprise of *All Strange Away,* a work later condensed aphoristically in *Imagination Dead Imagine:*

> Islands, waters, azure, verdure, one glimpse and vanished endlessly, omit. (p. 145)

The trial of the axiom has a twofold outcome. One result is that the text's interest does not really reside in the idle speculation and confused tone which dominate most of the text, and which literally seek to take all that is strange, all "modified" perceptions, away from the world of consciousness. The rigor of this and subsequent works, whenever it is employed in the service of an overactive, imagination-starved fancy, results in a delusion and cannot sustain much more than that overrated notion of neatness. To borrow a pseudo-value from consumer society, *Lessness* and *Ping* are "designer texts"; but a pseudo-value it certainly remains in the Beckett context—there indeed is "danger . . . in the neatness of identifications."[16] The other result of the trial is that the striking rhetorical and metaphoric feats in *All Strange Away* come to seem not the products of a dead imagination so much as occasional scraps of imaginative perception stealing into the text as though without permission: intermittent references to the tragic emotions, to winter and summer, to leaves, sunlight and moonlight are clearly enough cousins of *Imagination Dead Imagine*'s "azure" and "verdure"—themselves, as we saw in chapter 3, of long literary lineage. That the tests should end with this result frustrates what was originally a plan to prove that imagination is dead and gone. Beckett wrote in his first piece of published criticism, "Dante . . . Bruno. Vico . . Joyce," that the first- and last-named writers "both saw how worn out and threadbare was the conventional language of cunning literary artificers. . . . Both rejected an approximation to a universal language."[17] But the present texts reveal that imagination is neither a matter of convention nor of artifice, both of which, together with cunning, correspond much more to fancy. But imagination does have a universal language—perhaps Dante and Joyce "rejected an approximation" to it because they were actually capable of achieving it—and it is this that Beckett also begins to demonstrate in the later seventies and eighties prose works.

Another indirect but clearly discernible protest against the inhumanity of a consciousness forced to surrender to speculation alone is the laughter of exasperation with which the narrator, after building the colossal structure of his rambling conjectures on the crouched body, finally divulges the absurd conclusion to which they commit him:

> there being no alternatives and in this way the body tripled or trebled up and wedged in the only possible way in one half of the available room leaving the other empty, aha. (p. 126)

With a sense of comic timing he shows his computer program to be exhausted at last, his resources wearied by dealing with images—if they can be called images—which "he has no part in producing" (fancy). The same laughter, relief, and break of oppressive tension occurs as the narrator of *The Lost Ones*'s climbers' code completes his fantasy of fancy, with a winning demonstration that a very long sentence can keep its clarity even without punctuation and still be a talismanic example of stylistic elegance:

> An intelligence would be tempted to see in these the next vanquished and continuing in its stride to inquire of those still perpetually in motion that they all soon or late one after another be as those who sometimes pause and of these that they finally be as the sedentary and of the sedentary that they be in the end as the vanquished and of the two hundred vanquished thus obtained that all in due course each in his turn be well and truly vanquished for good and all each frozen in his place and attitude. (*The Lost Ones,* p. 164)

The nails are banged into the coffin here with extraordinary adeptness. The exasperated laughter engendered by these and similar extracts is as essentially human as the "floor of bleached dirt," the hellish light, and the uncomfortable temperatures are inhuman. The humor and humanity are in the relationship between author and reader rather than between narrator and subject. The inhabitants of the cylinder know nothing of stylistic elegance. And in this humor, as in the lyricism of the extracts on page 141, the effort exerted by the narrator's consciousness to exclude imagination cannot succeed, because the artist, or "seer," once he is in the process of creation, is connected to something larger than his merely personal sphere or "personally biased will," which Coleridge and Barfield both identify as a characteristic of fancy. That larger entity, the universally human, corresponds to Coleridge's imagination.*

---

*And, for the philosophically inclined, to Coleridge's reason. He defines it thus (I have italicized what seems relevant to *All Strange Away* and the related texts): "(i) Reason, and the proper objects of reason, are wholly alien from sensation. Reason is supersensual, and its antagonist is appetite, and *the objects of appetite the lust of the flesh.*
(ii) Reason and its objects do not appertain to the world of the senses, inward or

The fact that the best examples of expressive writing in *All Strange Away* remind us of the Elizabethans (and in *The Lost Ones* of Dante) is no accident. There is a tradition which a poet compulsively handles and occupies in the creative process when the imagination is present. It is important to distinguish this from convention, from those "mouldy old reliables" that were suspected in *How It Is.* This compulsion was seen to depend on an exertion of will in the first place: such was the conclusion of *The Unnamable.* But during *How It Is,* especially in the boat scenes discussed in chapter 4, the hint is increasingly given that to experience a "miraculous *re*discovery" of the living power, the will has to be as *disengaged* from desire as the little body in the boat is from its end-in-view, the "isle home at last." In the Rotunda texts of the sixties, the vision of imaginative reality, where it occurs, is always spoken of as an aperçu, a glimpse, vouchsafed rather than summoned. In *Imagination Dead Imagine,* interestingly, both the traditional imagination (which is "dying") and the supposedly new aperçu (which the text is illustrating) are just momentary: the "islands, waters, azure, verdure" are given just "one glimpse" before they vanish; but the rotunda, too, has no more than a couple of "sightings," both a "matter of chance" (neither willed in any way consciously), and both minute in comparison to the eternities yawning on either side of the moment of perception.

To return to *All Strange Away,* its turning point or *peripeteia* is in sight after the "diagram." A shock awaits the narrator, who, having created hell without knowing it, is suddenly compelled to imagine it for himself:

---

outward; that is, they partake not of sense or fancy. Reason is supersensuous, and *here its antagonist is the lust of the eye.*
(iii) Reason and its objects are not things of reflection, association, discursion, *discourse* in the old sense of the word as *opposed to intuition. . . .* Reason does not necessarily exclude the finite, either in time or in space, but it includes them *eminenter.* Thus the prime mover of the material universe is affirmed to contain all motion as its cause, but not to be, or suffer, motion itself.
(iv) We have seen in (iii) that *it stands in antagonism to all mere particulars,* but here it stands in *antagonism to all mere individual interests,* as so many selves to the personal will as seeking its objects, in the manifestation of itself for itself, . . . whether this be realised with adjuncts, as in the lust of the flesh and in the lust of the eye, or without adjuncts, as in egoistic ambition. The fourth antagonist, then, of reason is the *lust of the will . . .*

It is evident, then, that the reason as the irradiative power, and *the representation of the infinite* judges the understanding as the *faculty of the infinite,* and cannot without error be judged by it." ("An Essay on Faith," in *Aids to Reflection,* pp. 345–46). Compare, as a contrast, Wordsworth's spontaneous equation of imagination and reason in *The Prelude* (1805), 13.11.170–76.

> still hungering for missing lashes burning down* for commissure of lids at least when like say without hesitation hell gaping they part and the black eye appears, leave now this face for a moment . . . that black eye still yawning
>
> black right eye like maintain hell gaping any length then seethe of lid to cover
>
> normal neck with hint of jugular and cords and black bottomless eye . . . in sleep demons not yet imagined all dark unappeasable turmoil. (pp. 127–28)

The horror of this sight kills the desire for further conjecture altogether: it is now fancy that is dead, imagination having woken up again with a terrifying face. Fancy is now the loser, as is reiterated in the "murmur": "the dying fall of an amateur soliloquy." The tension of the inhuman conjecture is relaxed, broken as it were, by the sudden realization that to speculate on man in an environment divorced from his own is a perversion that dehumanizes man and turns his eye, Blake's "door of perception," into a bottomless pit. At this shock, the narrator's tenuous grammar dissolves altogether and all rigor disappears. That final phrase "all dark unappeasable turmoil," is such a loosening of syntax as to imitate precisely fear's loosening of the bowels. The horrific picture of the eye, the sense that the turmoil is an "unappeasable" monster, suggests the presence of something evil which is ready to strike. But once fancy, "the lust of the eye," is dead, or "murmured dead," the possible evil of surviving on it alone is expiated, and the work ends with a long sentence of extraordinary calm and beauty.

The question of good and evil, which is not much in evidence in the early novels and the trilogy but is incipient in *How It Is,* begins to be raised more clearly in the sixties texts and thereafter; and I do not think it is any accident, either, that this emphasis should start to be made concurrently with an investigation into fancy and imagination. Owen Barfield's comment on Coleridge goes some way to establishing a connection between, on the one hand, good and evil, and on the other, fancy and imagination.

> Imagination is, and fancy is not, "the very power of growth and production", and we have seen how it is this power which . . . works at all stages of the process at first of nature and then of consciousness. . . . It would seem then that fancy is part of the process; and there is much

*Cf. *How It Is,* "Her eyes burn down on me again" (p. 17).

> in Coleridge to suggest that it is. But in that case why should fancy be so very decidedly *not* a power of growth and production? The process is the whole process that constitutes nature and man; so that, if fancy is no part of the process, its provenance must lie somewhere outside of nature and of man; and again there is a good deal in Coleridge to suggest that it does. There *is* ambiguity then; but it could be argued that it is an inevitable one, and we shall be less inclined to fix the blame on Coleridge's system if we reflect that there is a similar ineluctable ambiguity about the cosmic status of evil. The specific relation he detected between fancy and death* points up such a parallel without pressing it. Matter itself (which is the *violent* "outness" of objects—outness congealed into absolute and idolatrous detachment) is evil as entailing the agonies of death and bereavement, but beneficent as enabling the maximum individualisation of detached spirits—and, therewith, the birth of freedom and love.[18]

Both issues—fancy and imagination and good and evil—demand such fine distinctions as are made in this passage. An understanding of Beckett's Rotunda texts likewise requires nothing less.

---

*See chap. 4, page 125, where the "decay of nervous tissue during thinking" is arguably fancy.

6

Exits for Amateurs of Myth (*Imagination Dead Imagine, The Lost Ones, Lessness, For to End Yet Again*)

Imagination Dead Imagine

The texts that follow *All Strange Away—Imagination Dead Imagine, The Lost Ones, Lessness,* and *For To End Yet Again*—are related to it not only by subject matter but also by title. *Imagination Dead Imagine* echoes the title of the source work, in that to take all that is strange away from the world is to leave it without imagination; as Heidegger said of art, "the more essentially the work opens itself, the more luminous becomes the fact that it is rather than is not. The more essentially this thrust comes into the open region, the more *strange* and solitary the work becomes . . . At bottom, the ordinary is not ordinary. It is extraordinary."[1] The French title of *Lessness, Sans,* indicates a world *without* strangeness or imagination, without, in other words, the strangeness that results from the operation of the "modifying power" of imagination. And it is a fair supposition that the Lost Ones are lost because the strangeness and interest of imagination have deserted them—are, as it were, "all away."

Where *All Strange Away* was the rough-and-ready focus of all the sixties Rotunda texts, its closest relative, *Imagination Dead Imagine,* is a beautifully crafted stylistic tour de force. Not quite a quarter of the length of *All Strange Away, Imagination Dead Imagine* has lost the confusing tonal multiplicity, as well as the nervousness of its predecessor. In *Imagination Dead Imagine,* we are in no such doubt about parts of speech as we were with "black right eye like maintain hell gaping." There is no panic in the work; its calm endures even the one important change of tone from that of the scientific textbook—"the extremes alone are stable as is stressed by the vibration to be observed when a pause occurs at some intermediate stage"—to that of the lyric:

> no question now of ever finding that white speck lost in whiteness, to see if they lie still in the stress of that storm, or in the black dark for good, or the great whiteness unchanging, and if not what they are doing. (pp. 146–47)

We can hardly help but be reminded of Shakespeare, since the misted mirror is used to prove that the couple is alive (echoing Lear with the hanged Cordelia), and of the German Romantics in the wry inversion of the phrase "Sturm und Drang" in the "stress of that storm." The pun on "still" also suggests greater subtlety in treating time than there ever is in *All Strange Away.* In the latter the phrase "a lifetime on earth" recurs in order to indicate duration, its directness recalling *How It Is*'s "bah I've lashings of time centuries of time"; in *Imagination Dead Imagine,* time indicators are characteristically found in subordinate clauses, quietly added:

> The extremes . . . are perfectly stable, which . . . may seem strange, in the beginning.

> Piercing pale blue the effect is striking, in the beginning, for one who remembers having been struck by the contrary.

The treatment of the couple is also refined. In *All Strange Away,* the lack of imagination shows how fancy, left on its own in consciousness, deprives sexuality of its aesthetic dimension, reducing it to the voyeuristic and crudely physical—"imagine him kissing, licking, sucking, fucking and buggering all this stuff." It is precisely after the horror of encountering the black eye that the narrator sees "all this prying" as "pointless," and this realization is yet another suggestion of the evil influence of fancy. In *Imagination Dead Imagine,* by contrast, the blue-eyed couple murmurs "Ah, no more" and longs for sleep. One might say that they wait, without fancy or imagination, whereas the narrator, more clearly identified as *not* one of the couple than in *All Strange Away,* indulges fancy—"imagination dead imagine. Pah, no difficulty there"—and finds imagination coming back to life, and stealing in on his narrative, by the end. One of the most striking things about *Imagination Dead Imagine* is its serene tone, its calm distinctions between norm and exception, a quality evident again in *The Lost Ones,* with more ornament admittedly, but with some of the same key phrases ("this at first sight is strange," "commonly," "in the beginning," etc.) Indeed, it might be said, as it certainly could not be of *Ping*, that in *The Lost Ones* more reductionist tactics would have paid off. The slightly testy "pah, no difficulty there" at the beginning of *Imagination Dead Imagine* (reminiscent of *All Strange Away*'s impatience) almost at once gives way to serenity and levelness.

Ruby Cohn says that in *Imagination Dead Imagine* and the associated texts there is a "move from death or nonbeing to life" suggested by the text's last word, "doing."[2] But the move would be more accurately described as one from a life of speculation and conjecture to a realization that imagination is an inexorable force in life and that it is the essential attribute of man as distinct from animals. This is also the meaning of the mysterious words in *The Lost Ones,* another "imagination-dead" world:

> None looks within himself where none can be. (p. 167)

This is why in the Rotunda any other activity—what there is of it—is inert, as in *Imagination Dead Imagine* and *All Strange Away,* or else unthinking, as in *The Lost Ones.*

The Lost Ones: Imagination Found

Although textual evidence suggests that *The Lost Ones* was conceived late in the period in which the Rotunda texts were composed,* its world and its events seem to occupy a time preceding that of *All Strange Away.* The Rotunda texts form a cyclic whole: to dispute their dates of composition is to a great extent to chase one's own tail. But it is plausible and useful to suppose that the cycle of texts covers a period of narrated time, and that, just as noon is the point of ending and beginning of an hour on the clock,** so *The Lost Ones* corresponds to a period of genesis in the cycle. Just as the clock's cycle never ends but can be joined at any time, so it is with *The Lost Ones, All Strange Away, Imagination Dead Imagine, Ping, Lessness,* and *For to End Yet Again.*

The stage for *The Lost Ones* seems to be set in "Closed Space"

---

*Work on it began in October 1965. (Carlton Lake, *No Symbols Where None Intended,* p. 133)

**Cf. *Ill Seen Ill Said,* p. 46, of the clock "ever regaining north," "ever attaining the last."

(a "Fizzle" of unknown date but unlikely to postdate *The Lost Ones**), especially in its description of

> an arena and a ditch. Between the two skirting the latter a track. . . . Room for millions. Wandering and still [to become *The Lost Ones*'s "searching" and "vanquished"]. Never seeing never hearing one another. Never touching. . . . Bed divided into lots . . . heat and dry air. (p. 199)

Every detail here finds expansion in *The Lost Ones:* the mention of dead leaves covering the track prefigures *The Lost Ones*'s rustle of dry skin "as of nettles or dry leaves." The latter text serves as genesis for the cyclical saga of inertia, separation from imaginative reality, and reduction of means. If *Ping* is in the most reduced form, then *The Lost Ones* is the most amply, almost generously written, the longest certainly, and it suggests that the voice relishes its descriptions of the vault, as though it were new ground as yet unexplored, about which there initially seems plenty to say. The "lots" into which the arena in "Closed Space" and *The Lost Ones* ends up divided seem anterior to the later concentration upon a single one of those lots, enclosed by walls and thus becoming a rotunda, in the other texts. Two more indications that *The Lost Ones* is intended as a genesis text are (a) the fact that the searchers, initially free, are then "vanquished," cease searching, and adopt the crouching position and motionless attitude familiar from *All Strange Away* and *Imagination Dead Imagine;* and (b) the fate of the searchers' eyes:

> And were it possible to follow over a long enough period of time eyes blue for preference as being the most perishable they would be seen to redden in an ever-widening glare and the pupils little by little to dilate *till the whole orb was devoured.* (p. 170, my italics)

This is precisely the state of the eye so terrifyingly uncovered in *All Strange Away* (see chapter 5, pp. 148–49). The "unappeasable turmoil," that metaphorical monster, is not even satisfied by "devouring the whole orb."

This image, together with the iteration of "the eye of flesh" throughout the cycle, illustrates that the human physical eye is

---

*In both manuscript form and as published in *Minuit,* "Closed Space" is designated "Fragment années 60." James Knowlson agrees that the manuscript paper is more likely to belong to the earlier sixties than to the later, when *The Lost Ones* was begun.

ruined by exclusive overuse in the service of a consciousness that ignores the physical eye's complement, the mind's eye. Blake says:

> the whole creation will appear infinite and holy, whereas it now appears finite and corrupt. . . . If the doors of perception were cleansed, every thing would appear to man as it is, infinite. For man has closed himself up, till he sees all things through narrow chinks in his cavern.[3]

The mind's eye is an icon for imagination; the "eye of flesh" delimits the fancy's fixities and definites. The pictures, forms, and colors in consciousness are seen by the mind's eye or imagination, whereas the *processes* of thought are, as it were, the mind's hands and feet.

Perhaps the above quotation from *The Lost Ones,* with its particular emphasis on the enormous amount of time needed to notice the change in the eyes, represents a speeded-up historical metaphor of the evolution of consciousness from before the scientific revolution to the present, from the imagination and seeing eye to the mechanistic "eye of flesh," not *seeing* but merely *registering,* like an insect's. This progress—or more accurately regression—is exactly the one which Blake denounces, locating the evils of the industrial revolution in the tabula rasa theory of education propounded by Locke and in the "universe-as-mechanism" popularized by Newtonian physics.[4] Beckett initiates an echo dialogue with Blake, replying in *Ill Seen Ill Said* to Blake's "if the doors of perception were *cleansed*" with the phrase "the *filthy* eye of flesh" (my italics in both cases).*

Blake avers that communications from the level of imagination need to enter a person through, not with,[5] the eye, through a clean mind's eye. No wonder then that an eye tainted by "fleshness," the eye of the Beckettian rotunda-character, can relate only to the dead, mechanical dealings of fancy. The scorched, dilated, bloodshot eye is the perfect symbol of overwrought, unduly predominant fancy. Notice that the blue color of the eye—its common factor with the blue sky, the heavens, the seat of Coleridge's primary imagination (to say nothing of "azure,"** the secondary imagina-

*Two other echo dialogues with Blake show Beckett's interest in this author: *Heaven and Hell*'s "The crow wished everything was black, the owl that everything was white" is echoed in *From an Abandoned Work:* "crows have done this . . . lovely creatures, white mostly." Also *Hell*'s seventieth and final proverb, "Enough! or Too Much," is echoed in *Enough*'s title and introduction: "Too much at a time is too much. . . . too much silence is too much."

**Cf. chap. 4, p. 107.

tion's "poetic fruitage"[6])—disappears in the extreme dilation typical of the fancy-ruled rotunda. Beckett had developed this symbol, perhaps unaware of how powerful a presence it would later assume, as early as *Murphy,* in describing Mr. Endon's eyes:

> the pupils prodigiously dilated, as though by permanent lack of light. The iris was reduced to a thin glaucous rim of spawn-like consistency. . . . All four lids were everted in an ectropion of great expressiveness, a mixture of cunning, depravity and rapt attention. (p. 140)

The Lost Ones shows the evolution of consciousness taking place graphically—it describes how the eye changes—whereas in *Imagination Dead Imagine* and *Ping* the change is assumed to be understood, and its horrific culmination is suddenly presented to us at the end of *All Strange Away.* Here *The Lost Ones* again serves as background. Other links are to be found between *The Lost Ones*'s "panting light" and *Imagination Dead Imagine*'s "convulsive light": both liken the oscillation of light to the mechanism of *disturbed* breathing; and in both texts the word *storm* describes the time measured out by these oscillations. If the physical is to the spiritual as fancy is to imagination, then it is obvious that the function of the physical body, exemplified here by breathing, will be as disturbed as the consciousness is by the death of imagination.

The most interesting part of *The Lost Ones* is its ending. This final paragraph contrasts the gaze of the *last searcher* in the eyes of the *first vanquished* (the redheaded woman, seen as the guide, "the north")* with that of the typical man and wife during the period when everyone was searching. This latter meeting of eyes is meaningless: "If they recognised each other, it does not appear. Whatever it is they are searching for it is not that." But the other exchanged glance, between the last searcher and the *first vanquished,* is a profound vision and, crucially, an *anagnorisis* or recognition (many have looked at the woman and not recognized her):

---

*Probably an allusion to Blake's Enitharmon, who, according to S. Foster Damon's *Blake Dictionary,* is "Spiritual Beauty, . . . the inspiration of the poet Los," who is "the expression in this world of Creative Imagination." The positions of both are said to be the North (pp. 124, 246), and the North symbolizes Imagination (p. 301). The penultimate paragraph of *The Lost Ones,* describing the redheaded woman, was published under the title *The North* in 1972 by the Enitharmon Press, London, with etchings by Arikha depicting the woman (see Appendix). See also T. J. O'Connor, *High Vision* (Cork: n.p., n.d.), sec. 2, pt. 2, "The Celestial North Pole." See also second footnote, p. 153.

> On his knees he parts the heavy hair and raises the unresisting head. Once devoured the face thus laid bare the eyes at a touch of the thumb open without demur. In those calm wastes he lets his wander till they are the first to close and the head relinquished falls back into its place. (p. 177)

After this the temperature ceases to fluctuate, the hellish light subsides, the "faint stridulence as of insects" is silenced. In other words, the *inferno* is past (or the *purgatorio,* if the redhead be seen as a Beatrice waiting in paradise). This can be interpreted: the last of the searchers is the only one to really see. Kneeling before the feminine incarnation of intuitive knowledge or imagination, he opens her eyes with a touch (the blind searchers had to drag up the lid, it was insisted) and dwells on the truth he sees revealed there, "lost" no longer. He drinks his fill at the fountain of inspiration; *his* eyes are the first to close—there is no lack in the goddess; if there were enough searchers to wander "in those calm wastes" instead of passing them by, her eyes would remain eternally open. Since the searcher has said yes to the search, since he has not given up but has persevered to its culmination in an intuitive vision of imaginative knowledge, his path separates from that of all who are still in the cylinder, who did not recognize the priestess when they raised her hair but simply walked away, and crouched down on their little space of floor to be rediscovered as occupants of the imagination-less world of *All Strange Away* and *Ping:* that world announced immediately that there was no way out of the chamber, whereas in *The Lost Ones* an exit still proposes itself to "amateurs of myth." Samuel Beckett, more than an amateur—though never ceasing to be a lover—of the Dantean myth, has made of *The Lost Ones* more of a *purgatorio* than an *inferno.* The ending suggests that the searchers are all given a choice, even though only one of them, it seems, makes the choice for heaven rather than hell. The "last searcher" is a kind of Dante; gazing into the eyes of Beatrice, a true daughter of inspiration, he is able, after the recognition of who she is, to go to paradise.

Considering all the Rotunda texts together, there is chronological continuity enough, in the various events and states described, to confirm that *The Lost Ones* is the mythological/narrative starting point of the cycle. From here onward the path divides. The destiny of the searchers who have given up is the subject of *All Strange Away, Imagination Dead Imagine* and *Ping,* followed by *Lessness* and *For to End Yet Again.* The destiny of the one searcher who did *not* choose hell is the province of the texts of the sixties and seventies that are not concerned with the rotunda: *From an Abandoned Work, Enough,* the *Still* texts, *Old Earth,* and finally *Company* and *Ill Seen Ill Said.* The dates of actual composition of the Rotunda texts are difficult to establish and in any case do not affect the narrative coherence of the cycle. Most important is that, read in a certain order, the six texts amount to a developing picture. The development is not subject to all the normal rules of time and space, since more than usual amounts of time and space are involved in the narrator's perception of the scenes: "Rediscovered after what absence in perfect voids it is no longer quite the same" and "no question now of ever finding again that white speck [the rotunda] lost in whiteness"; these phrases show how the vision encapsulated is the one and only intersection of an eternal line of being and an eternal line of perception. In *All Strange Away* the shape of the chamber changes from oblong to dome shaped; then back, after *Imagination Dead Imagine,* to oblong again in *Ping.* The development takes a dramatic new turn in *Lessness* and *For to End Yet Again.*

Lessness

Linguistic and formal analysis of *Lessness* abounds, so I will not repeat it here.* In this investigation the symbolic aspects of this work, or its iconography, are more important and interesting. Indeed the text's formal precision is itself a symbol, but only of the fancy's conjectural strides and exclusive concern with neatness and fixed units, as opposed to the mystery and resonance of the suggestions from imagination. In the words of *The Lost Ones,*

> Within the cylinder alone are certitudes to be found, without nothing but mystery. (p. 171)

Within the cyclinder, with the ample computer program of fancy in operation, certitude is of the greatest value, indeed the only value worth defining and searching for—a process which the laborious deductive reasoning of the narrator fittingly enacts. But outside, maybe, the imagination still lives, or in the "mystery" (Jakob Böhme's "Unground,"[7] perhaps) there is freedom for it to develop,

*Formal investigation of Shelley's *Prometheus Unbound* reveals the noun suffix *-ness* to be even more frequent in the poem than the adjectival suffix *-less,* which occurs no fewer than forty-two times.

without the strictures of certitude that "reduces the conceivable to the bounds of the picturable." We are reminded of the voice of Molloy: "to know you are beyond knowing anything, that is when peace enters in, to the soul of the incurious seeker."[8]

In *Lessness,* we are in fact *outside* the chamber of certitude. Its walls have collapsed to reveal the occupier in the midst of his ruins, on the earth, with the sky above. Earth and sky in *The Lost Ones* are the unreachable depth and zenith; in *Lessness* they are suddenly contacted by the prison's walls unexpectedly falling down. There is no color: imagination has not yet peopled it with "islands, waters, azure, verdure"; earth and sky are "as one," the "same grey" as sand and ash. The difference, for the occupier of what was once the rotunda, is that he can now see out of it, his "face to endlessness." Now his plight is a matter of the ignorance of freedom rather than the impotence of imprisonment. He seems to have emerged from the prison of *Ping:* in *Ping* the figure had all his limbs and moving parts "joined like sewn," but now he is indistinguishable from a half-cut carving of a person:

> Little body little block genitals overrun arse a single block grey crack overrun . . . grey face features overrun. (*Lessness,* p. 153–56)

Barren landscape and predominantly frigid syntax notwithstanding, there is a great release in *Lessness,* and not only in the literal sense of there being a breath of fresh air in the scenario. Indeed, the formal precision of the description of the actual landscape, effectively the same as *All Strange Away*'s "bleached dirt," sets off the extraordinary power of words which herald a return to the world, a world where the "blank planes sheer white" of the rotunda are "all gone from mind,* a world that is a potential expression or physical manifestation of the primary or universal imagination:

> On him will rain again as in the blessed days of blue the passing cloud.
>
> He will live again the space of a step it will be day and night again over him the endlessness.

In the dead matrix of "issueless" words, these sentences gleam like pieces of gold in gray rock. The matrix is the radically different, *Ping*-like telegraphic style reserved by Beckett for the structurings and machinations of fancy. The only musical sentence here

*The phrase "all gone from mind" was first used in *All Strange Away* (p. 123).

echoes in its small, grammatically coherent dimensions the perfection and completeness of cosmos, a world informed by imaginative intuition:

> Figment light never was but grey air timeless no sound. Blank planes touch close sheer white all gone from mind. Little body ash grey locked rigid heart beating face to endlessness. On him will rain again as in the blessed days of blue the passing cloud. Four square true refuge long last from walls over backwards no sound.

The contrast between the styles cannot be considered irrelevant: the text's message is contained in it. The fact that there was actually a random element in the composition[9] does not affect the diversity, or quality, of the original sentences used in the collage.

Rain is a nourishment which has been withheld from all the prisoners in all the various stifling vaults and chambers of the Rotunda texts, where a marked lack of moisture, together with unnatural heat, desiccated their skin and eyes. Notice how in *Lessness* all these references to a return to the world of earth, sky and rain, day and night, are in the future tense:

> He will stir in the sand there will be stir in the sky the air the sand.

The time for the union of man in the cylinder with the Imagination has not come yet, it is clear.* But there could hardly be a more intimate description of that union than this: when man stirs again and lives imaginatively, there will indeed be "stir in the sky the air the sand."

> It will be day and night over him the endlessness the air heart will beat again.

The lack of punctuation leaves open the possibility that another heart will beat again, besides the one that is already said to be beating in the "little body white upright": perhaps this is the air's heart, the heart or central organ of the atmosphere or cosmos, perhaps Coleridge's "living power," the "very power of growth and

---

*Cf. Heidegger's essay "Hölderlin and the Essence of Poetry": "It is the time of the gods that have fled and of the god that is coming. It is the time of need because it lies under a double Not: the no-more of the gods that have fled and the Not-Yet of the god that is coming" (*Existence and Being*, p. 289). Beckett criticism has mostly devoted itself to the Not of no-more in Beckett's works, seeming unaware of the not-yet that is obviously expressing itself.

production." The charge of pathetic fallacy could of course be brought against this argument and interpretation, but only with the dubious force which the concept always has: it assumes, without question or adequate grounds, a *one*-way relationship between man and the elements, what Barfield calls a sense of "outness congealed into absolute and idolatrous detachment" that ignores the possibility that the relationship may be interpenetrative or reciprocal.

Just as in *All Strange Away* and *The Lost Ones* a hint of the "universal human" crept into the narrator's exasperatedly humorous constructions of fancy, so in *Lessness*'s toneless gray cement there occur "tonal" outbursts, linguistic equivalents of color, which give the extraordinary sound the text has when read aloud. In a general matrix of absolute estrangement from being come the homely phrases "time out of mind," "fallen over backwards," "he will make it," "better days," "not a breath," "old love, new love," "face to the open sky," and, common in colloquial narrative discourse, "[There was] *this* wild laughter, *these* wild cries." The forbidding aspect of the general form obscures from us how simply made many of these texts are. The everyday phrases above are very close to the world, and indicate that *Lessness* is on the brink of a return to it, as does the introduction of dawn and dusk, rain, and the passing of the seasons. At present still declared "figments," these phenomena occupy the future realm prophesied in the cadenced sentence "On him will rain again as in the blessed days of blue the passing cloud." One is reminded of a semiprophetic hint in *All Strange Away* describing the faint longings and fears of the couple imprisoned in the rotunda:

> dread and longing sorrow all so weak and faint nothing more than faint tremors of a leaf indoors on earth in winter to survive until Spring. (p. 127)

In *Lessness,* the world is turning and spring is again possible. It is interesting that *Lessness,* one of a group of texts committed to testing the supposedly stale concept of imagination, ends up by making all the more striking an impression with the archetypes of Romantic poetry—blue sky, sun, rain, the seasons, "islands, waters, azure, verdure"—by the very force of contrast between them and the artificial, fancy-induced tribunal set up to sentence them. The trial has not confirmed the assumption that imagination is obsolete, and whether intentionally or not, it has refreshed and reaffirmed the traditional images.

For to End Yet Again

Though completed quite a long time after *Lessness, For to End Yet Again,* in many respects unyielding and difficult, recalls directly and reasserts (albeit in a less randomly collagelike manner) the state or imagination or nonimagination described there:

> grey sand as far as eye can see beneath grey cloudless sky same grey . . . as far as eye can see. (pp. 179–84)

This is a direct echo of *Lessness*'s "ash grey all sides earth sky as one on all sides endlessness." Similarly, *For to End*'s "mingling with the dust slowly sinking some almost fully sunk the ruins of the refuge" continues where *Lessness*'s collapsed "refuge" left off. More dust has accumulated ("after what absence in perfect voids miraculously rediscovered?")[10] and has begun to cover the remains. The same continuity attaches to the main character "the expelled," who still suffers from the curious immobilization of limbs and features which *Ping* so pointedly described as "joined like sewn" and *Lessness* as "features overrun." *For to End Yet Again* has it thus:

> The arms still cleave to the trunk and to each other the legs made for flight. . . . Little body last stage all stark erect still amidst his ruins all silent and marble still.

The recall of *Lessness*'s phrase "little body," the indication that this is the "last stage" of his destiny, and the strange title all reinforce the argument that the rotunda texts are effectively a cycle. The phrase "for to end yet again" is elliptical, with a hint of rebeginning as well as a sense of "the last stage of all": to *end again* is to begin anew the attempt to end. The word "marble" recalls *Lessness*'s description of the body as a "little block," as though it were petrified. The reader is more and more led to feel that the person is made of stone, and can hardly doubt it by the time in *For to End* he "falls unbending as a statue."

In that phrase, and in the text's scenario of desert and dust and ruins, there is an elaborate reference to Shelley's *Ozymandias:*

I met a traveller from an antique land
Who said: Two vast and trunkless legs of stone
Stand in the desert. . . . Near them on the *sand,*
Half-sunk, a shattered visage, whose frown
And wrinkled lip, and sneer of cold command,
Tell that its sculptor well *those passions* read,
Which yet survive, stamped on these lifeless things.
The hand that mocked them, and the heart that fed:
And on the pedestal these words appear:
My name is Ozymandias, King of Kings:
Look on my words, ye mighty, and despair!
Nothing beside remains. *Round the decay*
Of that colossal wreck, boundless and bare
The lone and level sands stretch far away.[11]

Compare a sample of phrases from *For to End Yet Again;* even the tone of ironic regret is reproduced:

> litter of laughable memory

> sand pale as dust ah but dust deep indeed to engulf the haughtiest monuments which too it once was here and there.

> Still amidst his ruins all silent and marble still.

> Mingled with the dust slowly sinking some almost fully sunk the ruins.

This landscape is described as "the last stage"; the "last change" of all, when the statue falls, has the same finality as Shelley's poem. It is no coincidence that Shelley, so at home in azure, verdure, islands and waters, should loom so large behind this "last" conclusion to a series of texts showing what happens, without imagination, to human beings in the world.*

This concluding Rotunda text, final though it seems, finally ends not with an assertion but with the only direct questions that occur anywhere in the entire cycle of texts:

> Sepulchral skull is this then its last state all set for always litter and dwarfs, ruins and little body grey cloudless sky glutted dust verge upon

*Beckett mentions Shelley in *The Unnamable:* "under the elms in se, murmuring Shelley" (p. 110), and quotes 'To the Moon' ("Art thou pale for weariness") in *Waiting for Godot,* p. 52. In Beckett's essay "Dante . . . Bruno. Vico . . Joyce" there is an echo of Shelley's *Defence of Poetry:* "Poetry is a prime condition of philosophy and civilisation" (*Disjecta,* p. 24). See also footnotes to pp. 115, 213, 215, 240.

> verge hell air not a breath? And dream of a way in a space with neither here nor there where all the footsteps ever fell can never fare nearer to anywhere nor from anywhere further away?

The second of those two questions refers to the dwarfs, who never arrive at the expelled figure but remain in uncertain orbit around him.* The reference of the dwarf metaphor is to relativism as it underlies thought in the present day, where absolute truth is outlawed, so that every affirmation is reduced to a gesture, a whim, or a "matter of taste," and neither a "here" nor a "there" exists: if you *always* fare either nearer or farther away, then you can never *be* anywhere, and nowhere is anywhere in particular. This is surely why the dwarfs—whose movement symbolizes some term which physical relativity determines is redundant, merely jostling for truth-status with innumerable other entities just as redundant—have such strange heads:

> atop the cyclopean dome rising sheer from jut of brow yearns white to the grey sky the bump of habitativity or love of home.

They yearn for truth, for home truths, perhaps, and for truth to be brought home to them. This amazing sentence partially explains the pointlessness which the three figures of the text are trapped in. Although in *Lessness* the occupant of the prison of consciousness was released and "expelled" into the world of night and day and "the passing deluge," *For to End Yet Again* shows that, in a persistently mechanistic or materialistic consciousness which denies the reality of the imagination, the laying aside of one constraint (the walls of the rotunda) merely gives way to a new one, the walls of the skull:

> no neck no face just the box

that is, essentially the same prison as ever. It is in assumptions about consciousness that the trouble lies. This is surely why the world of *For to End Yet Again* still seems barren and bleached, and as forsaken of its eagles[12] as the site of the rotunda is of any trace of "habitativity". The "hell air" is back again. In the prophetic words of *From an Abandoned Work,* written some ten years before *All Strange Away* and the associated works:

---

*Compare *The Unnamable:* "Molloy . . . wheels about me, like a planet about its sun" (p. 11). The "orbit of Malone" is also mentioned.

> *With so much life gone from knowledge* how know when all began, all the variants of the one, that one by one their venom staling, follow upon one another, all life long, till you succumb. (p. 135, my italics)

Life in knowledge is imagination. With that gone, all the variants of "the one"—all the imagination's manifestation in the physical world—must of necessity seem stale and arbitrary, like "mouldy old reliables." In a pitiful and lamentable attempt *not* to "succumb" to the prison walls of the skull, the dwarfs' minds, brains, try to reach for the heavens, stretching the bone up and outward like a balloon, as water on the brain does: on the "dome rising sheer from jut of brow yearns white to the grey sky the bump of habitativity."

A materialistic consciousness of the physical world or world of appearance, such as prevails in the age of Beckett, will seat the "imagination" in the skull of a human, forgetting that the organ contained by the skull usually performs far more perfunctory levels of thought than those of the imagination, in whose activity it only *assists*. This, I believe, is what is repeatedly being symbolized in the "Imagination Dead" or Rotunda texts, in which the infernal white-planed prisons are another image of entrapment in the "skull" of physical consciousness. (Compare chap. 4, pp. 120–25.) Other texts of the sixties and early to mid-seventies, those not concerned with the chamber and its occupants but written concurrently, tell a very different story. Significantly, they also prefigure the first expansion from smaller works to larger that Beckett has made since beginning work on the trilogy.

Part 4
Universal Visions (1977–1989)

7

Imagination Living (*From an Abandoned Work, Enough, Still, Sounds, Still 3, Old Earth*)

To the dispensations of the twilight dawn, to the first messengers of the redeeming world, the yet lisping utterers of light and life, a strength and power were given, because of the enemies, greater and of more immediate influence, than to the seers and proclaimers of a clearer day.

—Coleridge, "Notes on the Book of Common Prayer"

It looks as though the race of man needs a feeling of being accepted by the universe . . . if it is to live with mental health or perhaps survive at all in the world presented by modern science.

—William Empson

Form signifies the intelligible reality of a thing, and is quite independent of the thing's material existence. Form . . . is the synthesis of the qualities which constitute the essence of a thing.

—Titus Burckhardt, *Alchemy*

Of *Imagination Dead Imagine* Brian Finney writes: "The yearning poetic language betrays the hopelessly subjective bias underlying the sham knowledge. As doubt grows, Beckett places his use of scientific method . . . in ever more absurd contexts."[1] Although this can make sense when read loosely, it is not clear whether the subjective bias is attributed to the poetic language or to the "sham knowledge," though the illusion which he says is characteristic of poetic language in these texts would suggest that it is not the scientific mode which Finney thinks illusory. Yet I think Beckett's own finer equivocation suggests it is. Finney also says of the Rotunda texts in general that "illusion proves too attractive to be resisted," and implies that the subjects of the imagination, "time, beauty, love and memory" are just as sham as the pseudo-objective knowledge that they stand in contrast to. The conclusion to his essay does paradoxically raise some issues that really are essential to a discussion of Beckett's late prose pieces:

> . . . a gallery of unique and compelling images that reflect Beckett's lifelong search for that impossible shape that will capture in its own destruction life's ultimate shapelessness.

Such a view of Beckett's "lifelong search" is not afforded at all by the last three major prose works, which appeared in the eighties. As they become absorbed in the Beckett canon, certain conclusions Beckett critics may earlier have been drawn toward need to be, "if ever so slightly, altered."[2] Most significant is the change in perspective which *Company* and *Ill Seen Ill Said* offer on some of the sixties short texts: on those which, *not* being concerned with the rotunda and the "imagination-dead" state, pertain to the workings of the imagination when it is actually alive:

> Within the cylinder alone are certitudes to be found, without nothing but mystery. (*The Lost Ones,* p. 171)*

The Rotunda texts up to and including *For To End Yet Again* are dominated by the "vehemently rigorous" hunt for certitude; the remaining short texts—*Enough, From an Abandoned Work, Still, Sounds* and *Still 3, Old Earth,* and *One Evening*—are characterized by the "infinite suggestibility" of a vision of the mysteries *outside* the cylinder. Finney is right to say that when the "rigour and objectivity" lapse in the Rotunda texts, it is because the imaginative principle has forced, or rather stolen, an entrance; but to speak of what has entered as "illusory" and "hopelessly subjective" (what is the hope that subjectivity robs us of? one wonders) is to repeat the very aberration of taste and the philosophical sleight of hand which those texts are warning us against. *Company, Ill Seen Ill Said, Worstward Ho,* and some unpublished fragments that have appeared in 1987, along with their shorter sketches of the early seventies, refute that claim of illusoriness. They have made it obvious that the command to "endlessly omit" the "islands, waters, azure, verdure" has been carried out with a specific purpose in mind, which was the trial of an imagination that *How It Is* sus-

*All page references to the shorter texts discussed in this chapter are to the *Collected Shorter Prose, 1945–1980.*

pected of being purveyed by "cunning literary artificers," whose worn poetic platitudes still tried to "approximate to a universal language." Many critics take this to be a maxim to which Beckett, from the time of his first critical essays, fixed himself inflexibly: Enoch Brater's recent essay on *Worstward Ho* and *Ill Seen Ill Said* still equates the "figurative" with the "sloppily sentimental" and attributes the same to Beckett.[3] But these very works, along with *Company,* the *Still* texts, and *Old Earth,* show this one-sided reading of the trial of imagination to be far too simple. What Beckett's narrators find is that the attempt to rid language of outworn poeticisms, far from killing imagination, revives and brightens it. Brater speaks of "the ravages of figurative enticement," but the only "ravaging enticement" in the Rotunda texts and those that follow is the enticement of idle fancy, the *un*figurative counters of fixity and definition. In *All Strange Away* it is unarguably fancy which entices and ravages: but the figurative moments of imagination illuminate reality. There can be no doubt after *Ill Seen Ill Said* that Beckett has never forsaken the idea of a universal language but only doubted whether some poetic language—the "Wordsworthy"—can actually rise to speaking it properly.

* * *

In the four remaining short texts of the sixties and seventies, the Proustian time, love, beauty, and memory alluded to by Brian Finney predominate, and they set the scene for a deeper reflective contemplation than any Beckett has achieved before. The situations that encourage imagination and contemplation—nature and certain special times of day, for instance—are no longer excluded by imperatives to omit but accepted as what they are.

This strikes the reader in what the *environment* has to say: *From an Abandoned Work, Enough, Still,* and *Old Earth* all share a green world, alive with sun, wind, and rain. Man is open again to the "passing deluge" which *Lessness* prophesied; all these humanizing influences bring man from the margin of the world—"a white speck lost in whiteness"—into the center. "We lived on flowers." One feels that "islands, waters, azure, verdure"—all of them environmental phenomena—are no longer seen as redundant trappings or encrustations on the language of poetry so much as essences of it. This is a tremendous advance on the idea presented in the trilogy that nothing other than a thing's being *said* can conduce to its truth-status. *Imagination Dead Imagine,* at first averring "no difficulty there" in respect of continuing this trilogy principle, finally encounters, like its companion texts, the extremest of difficulties.

Of these texts, *From an Abandoned Work* is probably the least imbued with a sense that the phenomena of nature are of the essence of imagination, with its gray days and inhospitable landscape and its obvious affinity with *Molloy*—as regards the protagonist's attitude, his references to his mother, and his wandering through ferns and moorland—but its world is obviously very much alive nevertheless, with rain, "great ferns," "a family or tribe of stoats," and a white horse. Whereas in this work the world is a familiar one, in *Enough* it is fantastic and visionary with strange stemless flowers, expanses of water, steep hills, and a curiously stable climate, "as if the earth had come to rest in spring," with rain descending from a cloudless, windless sky, "eternally mild." Indeed, the strangeness is as marked in *Enough* as it is assiduously expelled in the process of doing away with all that is strange in the seminal Rotunda text. In the texts now under discussion, the *person* is more affected by grayness than the scene is: *Enough* and *From an Abandoned Work* have fertile landscapes but barren travelers.

In the three *Still* texts and in *Old Earth* (1973–74) the environment is much more intimate than in *Enough* and *From an Abandoned Work,* which relate to an earlier period in Beckett's oeuvre (1966 and 1954, respectively). The journey so crucial in those two texts is over by the time of *Still.* From this point onward the "scene" for nearly all of Beckett's prose will include a house, windows, a tree, a garden, or an open hillside. The "familiar" scene is no longer "one of grandeur and desolation"[4]—an attitude which began with *More Pricks*'s "Wicklow full of breasts with pimples" and ended in the desert waste of *For to End Yet Again*—but the familiarly familiar one of intimacy and short distances. If the circularity of the house tempts us to see it just as another rotunda, its lighted windows and wooden construction, along with the far more pervasive other differences between these texts and the Rotunda texts, should serve to dismiss the speculation. The intimacy is not of course always specifically social, since these texts all center around a person mostly alone, but it certainly calms the panic and nervous energy of the earlier works. An intimate environment like the log cabin cannot absorb impotent anger as "vast frescoes, dashed off with loathing[5] excellently can, and therefore such anger subsides, and other sensibilities take its place. In *Old Earth* the narrator is meditatively absorbed in the summer evening: cockchafer beetles are the immediate object of meditation. *Old Earth* shows especially clearly how an environment of the kind described in it and in the *Still* texts is essential to awakening the narrator to elevated, trancelike states and to his being "dreamt away," in the words of *Sounds.* The language of imagination is here, as it also was for Shelley and Coleridge, shown to feed directly from certain elements in the natural world, the world of appearances. From *Enough* onward, these are nearly always benign elements, especially so in the case of dawning and failing light, plants, rain, and birds. The "valley window" in *Still* and the tree on the hillside, common to the *Stills* and *Old Earth,* seem especially resonant, as do the *Stills*'s mysterious "nightbirds."* Although there is a search (not a journey) still going on in these texts, especially in the *Still* "trilogy," it no longer takes place in an inferno or desert.

It is a curious and significant fact that the *language* of imagination at this stage in Beckett's development, as it touches the environment, is not representational in the sense in which such language is said to be in some readings of Romantic poetry or the nineteenth-century novel. Having waged a war against threadbare poeticizing on the one hand and against representationalism on the other, Beckett is bound to have something new and interesting to say when he turns to the world of nature. Beckett's early works show how he scorned the habit qua habit of mentioning natural phenomena ("The pastures, in spite of the torrential rains, were exceedingly meagre and strewn with boulders"),[6] and his guardedness about this and about the "life in the light" in *How It Is* clearly had some influence in the extreme exercise, which I called the attrition of poetry, throughout the Rotunda cycle. But in *Imagination Dead Imagine* and *All Strange Away,* the narrator is notably powerless to prevent the color blue from appearing and unable to counter his language's insistence on softening occasionally to make a harmonious, not dissonant, music. This applies even in the middle of *Ping:* "Only just perhaps a nature a meaning one second almost never blue and white in the wind that much memory almost never."[7]

The power of imaginative reality is such that the narrator cannot simply rid his texts of it, as though scraping away dispensable material: the language of imagination has the hidden strength of weeds that push through roads and pavements. After such rigorous attempts to test the validity of this language, Beckett gives it free play in his most recent prose, covering the decade 1973–83. Beckett is aware that the truth of imaginative reality does lie not only in the experience of the phenomena referred to by language but also, for the artist particularly, in the iconography of language.

*A typically Joycean elision of usually hyphenated words. Compare Joyce's "sindark nave" ("Nightpiece," in *Pomes Penyeach*).

Certain words reproduce certain phenomenal worlds as spiritual substance, and are thus icons; others merely call up a photographic mental image. This is probably what Blake was trying to say in his criticism of Wordsworth's "Influence of Natural Objects": "Natural Objects always did and now do weaken, deaden and obliterate imagination in me. Wordsworth must know that what he writes valuable [*sic*] is not to be found in nature."[8] Blake's prophetic poems abound in icons of natural appearances; he obviously sensed in Wordsworth an objectizing of natural appearances that worked against the perception of spiritual substance. What Wordsworth "writes valuable" is, for Blake, not in images of objects but in the imaginative reality reflected in them, what the French Islamicist Henry Corbin has called the imaginal world, and world of intelligibles.[9] Beckett likewise sees that the verbal medium need not objectize and that poetic language can mark out new relations between the referential fixities contained in its own terms.

This special function, over and above the denotative power of words, is hinted at in *Enough* when the teller frustrates the photographic interpretation and invites the iconographic:

> I don't know what the weather is now. But in my life it was eternally mild. . . . I would not have noticed the windlessness if he had not spoken of it. Of the wind that was no more. Of the storms he had ridden out. (p. 143)

Since language is an attribute of consciousness, it is natural that the imaginative faculty should manifest as much involvement in language as it does in the contemplated. Beckett, paraphrasing Vico, says the same: "The first men had to create matter by the force of their imagination, and 'poet' means 'creator'. Poetry was the first operation of the human mind, and without it thought could not exist."[10]

The imagination seeks neither to locate itself only in grammatical relations nor to persuade the reader that it has no role in our perception of the world. Beckett's "nature-poetics," such as they are in the late prose texts, exemplify what Johnson calls "the force of poetry, that force which calls new powers into being, which embodies sentiment and animates matter."[11] Every time this perennial theme is reanimated, it gains in significance; for in proportion as it wears, it endures ever greater assaults of skepticism. There have been few more thoroughgoing skeptics of "the poetic" than Johnson and Beckett, and yet both persuade us finally of the vitality and reality of imagination.

Just as the environment, not exclusively the skull, signifies the true seat of the primary imagination, so humor and playful inflection are associated with the imagination's quickness or life. Of all Beckett's prose works, *From an Abandoned Work* must be the one in which there is the gayest abandon, glee almost, in the very act of speech. Whereas the "perfect" language of *Imagination Dead Imagine* attempted to pin the butterfly visions to a board of certitude, the "awful English" (of which *From an Abandoned Work* confesses it is composed) is profuse with life and affirmation, despite a darkening world. (It was written just prior to *How It Is*.) Characteristic of the language is its organization into breath-sized periods, many of them squeezing in at the last moment another piece of valid but extraneous detail, each defying at the same time as flaunting its superfluity; imperative in tone but far from imperative in substance:

> Birds with my piercing sight I have seen flying so high, so far, that they seemed at rest, then the next minute they were all about me, crows have done this.

> On the other hand I must have been quite one of the fastest runners the world has ever seen, over a short distance, five or ten yards, in a second I was there.

> Just under the surface I shall be, all together at first, then separate and drift, through all the earth and perhaps in the end through a cliff into the sea, something of me.

> All well then for a time, just the violence and then this white horse, when suddenly I flew into a most savage rage, really blinding. (pp. 129–37)

There is affability in this, as well as sophisticated, tendentious wit ("I might have been a professor, he had set his heart on it. A very fair scholar I was too, no thought but a great memory.") The narrator is in his element so that even when he suffers from narrative impotence, as a Beckett narrator will, he avoids turning it into a drama in the manner of *The Unnamable;* he merely says:

> . . .the rages were the worst, like a great wind suddenly rising in me, no, I can't describe.

As in the third extract above, there are occasional lapses in grammar, "all together at first, then separate and drift" into unclear relations, omitted pronouns and mixed tenses:

> other days quite quiet for me and have four or five.
>
> What happens now is I was set on and pursued by a family, or tribe . . . of stoats.
>
> Harsh things these great ferns, like starched, very woody, take the skin off your legs through your trousers . . .

What is funny in such examples is how the author so finely calculates the incompetence of the narrator.

There is a quieter humor in *Enough*, a text which has mostly been seen as hardly humorous at all:

> One day he halted and fumbling for his words explained to me that anatomy is a whole.
>
> His talk was seldom of geodesy. But we must have covered several times the equivalent of the terrestrial equator.*
>
> He loved to climb and therefore I too. He clamoured for the steepest slopes.
>
> We didn't keep tally of the days. If I arrive at ten years it is thanks to our pedometer.
>
> In order from time to time to enjoy the sky he resorted to a little round mirror. Having misted it with his breath and polished it on his calf, he looked in it for the constellations. I have it! he exclaimed referring to the Lyre or the Swan. (pp. 139–44)

It is surprising that such jokes should have been largely unremarked upon by commentators. The word "clamour" is singularly incongruous, considering the weak, garbled mental state of the old man, "fumbling for words." The practice of complete sentences without commas is responsible for the joke about geodesy. As a declaration, "His talk was seldom of geodesy" sounds disarmingly arbitrary, though the word is explained later in the paragraph about covering distance. The humor is in the division of two connected

*Did Beckett have this idea from *Rasselas* 13: "He that shall walk with vigour three hours a day will pass in seven years a space equal to the circumference of the globe"?

statements, for the full stop makes us think that nothing more will be said in explanation of "geodesy."* The exclamations of the old man remind us of Mercier's and Camier's laconic enthusiasm, and of Malone's cry "My things! My things!" Perhaps *Enough* has too often been cast by critics as somehow involved with *Imagination Dead Imagine* and *The Lost Ones* for its funny side to be worth mentioning,[12] but I think there is very little connection between the texts other than a close date of composition. And the inflections in *Enough* which carry a more "serious" note are differently serious from the tone of the Rotunda texts and often, as I have said, implicate the environment:

> Of the wind that was no more. Of the storms he had ridden out. Things that for him were no more and for me could not have been. The wind in the overground stems. The shade and shelter of the forests. (p. 144)

* * *

The infinitely subtle inflections of language in the *Still* texts reflect the quality—weak as the tremor of a leaf indoors—of the longings and dreads in *All Strange Away*'s chamber. The three *Still* texts may indeed be said to emit that tremor, but they also amplify its sound. On first inspection the language is hardly inflected at all, seeming almost as toneless as *Lessness,* relying on silent grammatical boundaries to communicate many omitted parts of speech and make attenuated links intelligible:

> never quite for nothing even stillest night when air too still for even the lightest leaf to sound no not to sound to carry too still for even the lightest leaf to carry the brief way here and not die the sound not die on the brief way the wave not die away.

These words from *Sounds,* the second of the *Still* texts,[13] remain remarkably stable and coherent, increasing concentration upon a single indicated meaning and yet drawing out the statement's musical substance into a thinner and thinner skein: a case, in the words of *Ill Seen Ill Said,* of "imagination spreading its sad wings." Imagination is neither dead here, nor dying, but rather flying with the slow wing-beat of *How It Is*'s albatross,** symbol of imagination.

---

*See Susan Brienza, *Samuel Beckett's New Worlds,* p. 77, for more examples.

**Cf. in this context Beckett's poem "Alba" and its "white planes of music" and the woman in *More Pricks Than Kicks* whom Belacqua names "*the* Alba." See also S. H. Nasr, "The Flight of Birds to Union," an essay on Attar's *Conference of the Birds,* in *Temenos* 4 (1983), p. 103. Nasr gives some impression of the metaphorical and metaphysical dimensions of the image of birds and flight.

In this passage the syntactical qualifications, "no not to sound to carry" and "the sound not die . . . the wave not die," actually produce the music, whereas earlier in the prose works they were often nothing more than parentheses, lies, or fatuous change ringing. This special characteristic is occasionally carried over into *For to End Yet Again*:

> place . . . where once used to gleam in the dark once used to glimmer a remain . . . by degrees there dawns and magic lingers a leaden dawn. (p. 179)

These subclausal attenuations are unusual by any standards and not a feature of Beckett's prose before *Still.*

What is more, the *Stills*' subtle, attenuated language serves to *indicate* something that is not stated. The *Stills* develop an inner language of indication in this sense. The first text describes a movement of the hand toward the head, then of the head toward the hand, and then, "because of what comes,"[14] resumption of the upright sitting posture. But this is not narrated merely for the sake of describing some physical movements, as it was in *All Strange Away,* but rather because the narrator (or narratee, for these texts do not explicitly identify the narrator with the person described as *The Unnamable* does) has had a sudden thought or intuitive impulse. Susan Brienza suggests that the text tries to "transpose the kinetic to the verbal"[15] but stops there, ignoring the indications of the kinetic, which it is the purpose of the verbal to suggest. Then in *Sounds,* the second text, a certain sound, unidentified, causes the figure in the chair to get up from it and go outside to a tree, probably the very tree that *Still* described as "that beech in whose shade once quite still till it goes" (p. 184). The tree is obviously the scene of a remembered event. Its exact description is not important, since it dissipates in a severed clause "in whose shade once . . .' What matters is that this memory carries itself through time much more strongly than the sound carries through the air; but that infinitesimal sound, at that particular point in time and in that certain place, is still needed in order to revive the memory. It is revived in such a way and with such force that it compels the narrator to "start up now snatching up the torch"—an astonishing break with the pervasive stillness—and to go up to the tree to see what there is to see and hear what there is to hear. He is even described as in "some moods" embracing the tree. In *Old Earth* there are parallel indications of this love for a potential source of inspiration: in that text another tree appears, of which the narrator says, "I reach up, grasp the bough, pull myself up and go in" (p. 201). After that "entrance" the distinction between physical reality and recollection becomes more and more faint, just as it became at the end of *From an Abandoned Work,* where "I just went on, my body doing its best without me."

In *Still 3,* the final text in this miniature Beckett trilogy, a long time has passed with the protagonist absent—"whence when back no knowing"—perhaps under the tree. Where he has been, and for how long, keeps him wondering for the first half of the text,

> till in imagination from the dead faces . . . try . . . for one in the end even though only once only for a second say back try saying back from there head in hand as shown . . . sudden white black all about no known expression eyes its at last not looking lids the ones no expression marble still so long then out.

The import of this momentary vision is again a puzzle, and since it is unspecified, it is probably less important than the fact of its occurring in the circumstances and with the stimuli described. Again, as subliminally in *Imagination Dead Imagine,* there is a sense that this moment is the only intersection of two lines, one an infinite line of being, the other a line of time, and that to trace something *back* from this momentary vision—"try saying back from there"—may bring illumination of that mysterious "what comes" in *Still.* It is clear that the narrator is searching for one among many persons or beings, and that a sound is needed to elicit memory of that one person or being and, most importantly, that the agent of perception here is in a world where there is

> no sound to listen for no more than ghosts make or motes in the sun

—in other words, where there are nonphysical modes of perception. This is the one convincing explanation for Beckett's concern at this period with manifestations of sound and color that survive only in the tones of a language endeavoring to divest them of all physicality. (Compare *Company*'s "a less faint made faint by farness not a true faint near at hand," "died on to dawn and never died," and "some soft thing softly stirring soon to stir no more.") This refusal to be "tied by interest to a corpse obedient matter"[16] is the essential characteristic of the language of indication that the *Stills* excel in. In an increasing sensitivity to what it is indicating, this language nevertheless shuns certitude, like a signpost with no writing on it but pointing definitely *some*where. Whether the recognition finally discovered at the end of *Still 3*—"eyes its at last lids the ones"—is as satisfying as that achieved at the end of *The Lost Ones* is difficult to say, but it is analogous to imagination, the valuing faculty which raises the profounder recollection above the many snapshot stills which fancy, Blake's "daughter of memory,"[17] has stored up.

In the *Still* texts and *Old Earth* it is clear that the time and place, the no-longer-barren environment as it is rendered in the language, coaxes even Beckettian man—so bowed down with physical consciousness that he cannot "raise his eyes to the sky"[18] but must use a mirror to see the constellations—into the world of visions, mysteries, and dreams, and into the powers of imagination, confident to face or willing to brave its "prevalent dangers."[19] But another difference between the Rotunda texts and the present ones, and a reason why the "inspiration" of memory is facilitated, is that the narrator is not identified with the person sitting in the chair or visiting the tree. The narrator no longer seems to be locked irrevocably in the place he once described (the rotunda) nor to be suffering the perplexity of what have become definite protagonists (not narrators) in the *Still* texts.

In this coaxing of existential man into the world of dreams, an Anglo-Irish equivalent of Bierbaum's "Traum durch die Dämmerung,"[20] there is involved yet another life-affirming element on top of those I have noted in the environment. This is a freer, more open expression of longings and emotions. I have already mentioned the impulse to embrace the tree in *Still*. Then there is the image in *Sounds:*

> quiet as when even the mother can't hear stooped over the crib but has to feel pulse or heart.

Beckett has not been much in favor of this kind of tenderness since the days of *Watt*, and even then it was rare (and inflected by a tongue in the cheek: compare the relationship between Watt and Mr. Knott).

Even more remarkable and truthful is the outburst in *Old Earth* addressed to the "old earth" itself:

> Not long now, how I gaze on you, and what refusal, how you refuse me, you so refused. (p. 201)

In this text, longings and dreads are by no means the faint tremors they were in *All Strange Away*. One wants to reverse the voice of

From an Abandoned Work and say, "Perfect English, this!" The repeated "refuse" is not just emotional iteration: the emphasis is each time shifted by changes in tense, word order, and verb-noun function; we sense only the force of repetition, not its tedium. Past and present are gathered up to multiply the size of the time span; an exclamation ("what refusal") mediates something of the very quality of refusal as well as how much of it there is; and to specify that it refused *him,* not everyone—and how!—drives the lament home. The loving, even though despondent, "how I gaze on you" rules out the risk of diatribe that attends such a cri de coeur; and it is not so much an accusation—an accusation would make this individual gesture seem small—as a gesture of "sad, helpless love" (to borrow the words of *From an Abandoned Work*). There is a dramatic power in this cry, however. It is anything but helpless. It does not fall into sentimentality even with the full sense of loss, "collapsion"[21] and failure which it bears and bears out. Crucially, this exclamation promotes a welter of sudden associations of "time, love, beauty and memory." The passion of "Ah to love at your last and see them at theirs" is consciously restrained with a question—"why ah[?] Uncalled for"—but the conscious attempt at restraint fails:

> No but now, simply stay still, standing before a window, the hand on the wall, the other clutching your shirt and see the sky, a long gaze, but no, gasps and spasms, a childhood sea, other skies, another body. (p. 201)

The grip of recollection is powerful and disorientating in this central prose statement of Beckett's later writing. Avoiding the ruthless banishment of sentiment along with sentimentality in *How It Is* and *Imagination Dead Imagine,* and with the imagination so disturbingly alive again, the artist faces the task of rendering and harmonizing these freed intimations and memories. This is what Beckett began to do about three years later as he started writing *Company.* Susan Brienza, quoting the speaker, sees *As the Story Was Told* as expressing the same need: "I did not know what the poor man was required to say, in order to be pardoned."[22] *Old Earth*'s painful crush of memories is a kind of punishment, rather like the torture in *As the Story Was Told.* It may be that the pardon required is for the sin of having neglected to contact the source and clarifier of these memories until it was almost too late.

8

The Imagination of Youth (*Company*)

Existing accounts of *Company,*[1] in particular Susan Brienza's section on it in *Samuel Beckett's New Worlds,* have paid most attention to the fact of its greater length, its style and autobiographical function, its alternations between the recalled scenes and the "devisings" of its narrative structure, and the situation of the speaker. The end of the book is seen, characteristically, as a "crescendo of despair."[2] But *Company*—from the point of view traced in the preceding chapters—is at once a smaller work than its length promises,* overall a lighter one than we would expect its inert, exhausted narrator to be capable of producing, and at moments a more serious one than it has yet been taken for.

All these points arise, in one way or another, from the most basic observation to be made about *Company*: there is a much more relaxed hand on the syntax than there has been for a very long time in Beckett's fiction, since *Malone Dies* and *From an Abandoned Work,* in fact. This provides opportunities that had been unavailable in the short, concentrated prose works. None of this is to suggest that the fine crafting and rigor of the sixties and early seventies has been abandoned; on the contrary, it surfaces readily at need:

> At each slow ebb hope slowly dawns that it is dying. (p. 22)
>
> As best to erode the drop must strike unwavering. (p. 47)
>
> All the way from calcaneum to bump of philogenitiveness. (p. 71)

But in *Company* the specific place of such language is marginal in

*Cf. John Pilling, "A Criticism of Indigence: *Ill Seen Ill Said*" in McCarthy, *Critical Essays on Samuel Beckett.* He sees *Company* as "more praised than studied" and, "weighed in the balance, found wanting" (pp. 137–38).

comparison to its role in a work like *For to End Yet Again*. *Company* is for the most part stylistically uncomplicated and unconcentrated, and can be read faster than any of the short texts of the decade before.

The looseness and speed of *Company*'s style is particularly evident in the hedgehog narrative and in the paragraph about the narrator's birth and his father's evasion of it (p. 15). The writing is so open as to introduce casual objects hardly mentioned in any of Beckett's prose after *Murphy*—real place names, for instance, or egg sandwiches, or the De Dion Bouton. Such objects keep reappearing, whereas they were expelled from the earlier texts or were introduced as extremely bizarre curiosities (e.g., Mercier's cream horn, or *Enough*'s pedometer, completely incongruous given the mythical scenario). *Company*'s familiarity with everyday objects is an aspect of the environmental intimacy newly characteristic in the *Still* texts and *Old Earth:* the influence is a humanizing one, but this perhaps also detracts from *Company*'s universality: the mention of "American billion" and the Longman Atlas localize things in a way Beckett has been unused to doing and to which, after *Company,* he does not return. This is an aspect of the work's comparative lightness, and also indicates its emphasis on location, which it shares with the Joyce of *Dubliners* and *Portrait of the Artist.*

But the ordinary or casual style of the passage describing the mother's labor and giving birth is not as harmless as it might appear: the claws, as it were, may be hidden, but emerge disconcertingly in

> The midwife was none other than a Dr Hadden or Haddon. (p. 16)

"None other" ordinarily prefaces a clearly recognized, unambiguous object, but hopes of recognition are dashed here by the indefinite article and the alternative spelling, both suggesting the midwife has *many* other possible identities, not "none other than" one. In the same passage there are other ironic touches, like "the first summit scaled" (p. 17), alluding glancingly to the passion for physical achievement prevalent in the family's social rank* or by the anticlimactic and consciously callous statement:

> he learned to his dismay from the maid at the back door that labour was still in swing. (p. 17)

*A preoccupation shown by Deirdre Bair to be attributable to Beckett's father (*Samuel Beckett,* pp. 6, 8).

Few of Beckett's clichés are more incisively adroit than "in swing." In the twinkling of an eye, it transfers the father's satisfaction at having avoided the scene of birth from his own guilty conscience to the mother's experience of giving birth. Similar in effect is the suddenly sedulous vocabulary of

> He at once hastened to the coachhouse some twenty yards distant where he housed his De Dion Bouton. (p. 17)

In the unusual positioning of "at once," so forwardly insistent, in the literary "hastened," the bureaucratic "some twenty yards distant" and "housed," a conscious formality reflects the loveless care expended on machines and suggests lack of regard for the mother, whose individual position is reduced to—and the father's attitude supposedly excused by—the phrase "pains and general unpleasantness." And yet, acutely though it alerts us to all this, the style is not set coldly or self-rightously against the father for beating such a hasty retreat. It is, rather, making fun of him for doing so: his fear is that of the squeamish boy, excellently disguised into emotionless formality. And his fascination with machines and climbing bring into play a Boys' Annual ethos.

The amplitude of style in *Company* allows for greater shifts of tone than have been possible since the trilogy, where, quite simply, there had been plenty of room for it. John Pilling has noted the greater range of emotions opened up by the disparate style of *All Strange Away,*[3] but that work achieves its range at the expense of homogeneity, whereas *Company* achieves both. Several of the autobiographical scenes in *Company* have this open, casual style, unafraid of specifying places and people, the tea parties of Dublin suburbia as Beckett experienced them in his youth. Even the second section of *Molloy,* which drew on largely the same social situation and the same landscape, was nevertheless severely refracted and filtered by the legalistic and at times almost surrealist tone of Moran.

Company's often looser syntax is constricted somewhat in the "other half-world," so to speak, of the text, when the "gropings of the mind" are proceeding in the skull of a man stretched out on his back in a darkened room. But the style is not rigorous in the manner of *The Lost Ones* or *Imagination Dead Imagine:* the skull-voice of more than half of *Company* is idly friendly, often wry, indulging in afterthoughts and the "nested clauses" that Brienza identifies.[4] One might suggest that the voice is almost too "downright human" to be speculating in this way about such an essentially inhuman, companionless state. Beckett is here again confronting us with the consequences of unmitigated fancy, the unmotivated cousin of imagination. On two occasions the voice asks directly

> What kind of imagination is this so reason-ridden? (p. 45)

> deploring a fancy so reason-ridden (p. 75)

and it administers an ironic put-down to the speculation that its story is narrated by an infinitely regressing series of selves and voices: amidst one such chain of speculation he interpolates

> Reserve for a duller moment

—as if this moment were not dull enough. Could another conceivably be duller? For forty-four of the fifty-nine paragraphs, the same basic permutative problem is being addressed (that of who the voices are and why they go on speaking meaninglessly) with an effect, to adapt a phrase from *All Strange Away,* of "some delight in that flashes of humour few and far now rive their sameness." But it is only a qualified delight: ultimately these speculative paragraphs are only to be swallowed along with the interspersed lyrical episodes.

It is notable that the open style does not succeed as well in the devisings of a mind in the dark as it does in the world of scenery, objects, people, and relationships, simply because there is nothing to hold, nothing upon which the language can hang properly. This is probably why Beckett's 1977 piece, *VERBATIM—The Voice,*[5] was abandoned, and its central theme (the provenance of a narrative voice) recast as *Company*'s double theme. We are returned to the issue discussed in chapter 1, the reassuring appearance of the outer world of objects to our besieged sense of knowledge and reality. This is why the "gropings of the mind" and its internal activities are of so "low an order" and are so "inert" and "ill-imagined." The voice, neither assisted by a perspective on objects that would liberate their essences nor encouraged in metaphysical affirmation, finds itself with only its mathematical, mechanical, and physical consciousness to empower it. Finally, its sole hope is merely to die, if it cannot find company. But it is clear by the end that none of the "devised" company has been satisfactory: nor do the locomotions, noises, and smells do more than arouse a faint amusement, what Joyce would have called a "mirthless" laugh.* True company cannot be devised or approximated by the fancy's "eye of flesh," an eye which can only register an object, not understand or relate meaningfully to it. The amount of space filled by ascertaining and repeating a proposition that is known to be untenable all along is what makes *Company* a smaller work than its length and scope promise.

Company is usually seen as divided into two modes, the "lyrical-memorizing" and the "rational-speculative." But in the lyrical passages there are in fact two distinct tones. One of them is earthbound, expansive, and casual, as in the paragraphs describing the fall through the fir tree or his birth or the "whiff of adulthood": in all these passages, the familiarity and simplicity of the subject almost justify our momentary sense that the book's large print is somehow appropriate in seeming to address learners rather than readers:

> Then climb the tree again. Your mother answers Mrs. Coote again, saying, he has been a very naughty boy. (p. 28)

But by the time the work is read through and we find a teasing remark like "From time to time with unexpected grace you lie" we begin to see that no reader of Beckett can ever be more than a learner. But there is another, different tone of recollection, which has a longer stylistic ancestry in that it seems to have developed from the sixties prose, and it evidently has more potential since it is developed to even more effect in *Ill Seen Ill Said*. The beach scene in *Company* is the finest example:

> A strand. Evening. Light dying. Soon none left to die. No. No such thing as no light. Died on to dawn and never died. You stand with your back to the wash. No sound but its. Ever fainter as it slowly ebbs. Till it slowly flows again. You lean on a long staff. Your hands rest on the knob and on them your head. Were your eyes to open, they would first

---

**Portrait of the Artist*, chapter 2, (in *The Essential James Joyce*, pp. 108 and 110), and *Ulysses* (pp. 47–49). *Watt* takes up the subject of mirthless laughter: "The bitter, hollow and . . . the mirthless . . . the mirthless laugh is the dianoetic laugh, down the snout—haw!—so. It is the laugh of laughs, the *risus purus*, the laugh laughing at the laugh, . . . at that which is unhappy" (p. 47). Compare Coleridge: "To resolve laughter into an expression of contempt is contrary to fact, and laughable enough. . . . It seems as if nature cut short a rapid thrill of pleasure on the nerves by a sudden convulsion of them, to prevent the sensation becoming painful" (*Table Talk*, p. 236).

> see far below in the last rays the skirt of your greatcoat and the uppers of your boots emerging from the sand. Then and it alone till it vanishes the shadow of the staff on the sand. Vanishes from your sight. Moonless starless night. Were your eyes to open dark would lighten. (p. 75)

This is interpretable as one of the autobiographical scenes, but the mystery of it—its sound and its lack of specifying objects—makes it generically different from the paragraphs in which Connolly's Stores and "wafer-thin bread and butter" feature so easily, and so appropriately to autobiography. This passage is more timeless, and it was obviously important enough to Beckett for him also to include it– from "Light dying" to "never died"—in his short play *A Piece of Monologue.*[6] In one sense it may be as abstract as the "narrative-present" passages describing the crawling and devising, but it is connected in sound, reference, and style with something much larger than the everyday world, its objects, and "the common light of day." In fact it is connected not to what *Watt* called "things in the normal sense" but to "the emptinesses between them."[7] This is why it is more mysterious than the ratiocinative passages.

The difference between this second lyrical tone and the first is evident in two ways: in the case of the strand scene, light defines and qualifies reality, rather than reality's objects defining and qualifying light, as they do in the references to blue sky, gorse, and red sheep's placentas elsewhere in the autobiographical part of the book. "Were your eyes to open they would first see far below in the last rays the skirt of your greatcoat." The words "far below" contribute to the larger-than-life atmosphere; the figure has suddenly grown to superhuman size. The very phrase "in the last rays" becomes one of the linchpins of *Ill Seen Ill Said,* and indeed the whole passage closely foreshadows the style and imaginative center of that work. Light is not introduced in order to allow the identification by color and form of everyday objects: it is introduced here to modify the terms upon which, in the cold light of day, we see them related. The second sense in which the nonmateriality of the scene is made clear is contained in the words "were your eyes to open, dark would lighten." These bear two meanings, whereas the earlier description of the eye—"the globe . . . hooded. Bared. Hooded again. Bared again."—bore only one, that of the physical "eye of flesh" or "eye of prey" ubiquitous in the prose since *How It Is.* The phrase "Were your eyes to open dark would lighten" has the overt meaning that dark seems less dark when you open your eye in it, combined with an implied sense that some imaginative intuition is about to occur (cf. the phrase "Lighten our darkness"), an intuition arising directly from contemplation of the staff's shadow and the sound of the tide, and the advent of night. A "moonless starless night" could not be imagined darker. Yet "were your eyes to open, dark would lighten"—that is, "if the doors of perception were cleansed,"[8] if our inner eyes were opened to the intimation—then the dark surrounding the supine narrative consciousness, and the darkness which encloses everyone who shares his debility, would disperse. The sentence just mentioned is not equivalent, incidentally, to the remark on page 25, "Had the eyes been open, they would have marked a change," for at that point it is still assumed that the light in the chamber of the narrative consciousness still has the same hellish, sourceless oscillation as it has in *The Lost Ones*. The presence of such light suggests that the voice which the slight change of light accompanies is a voice from hell, the voice of rational certitude without imagination, whose sound *Ill Seen Ill Said* calls "the howls of laughter of the damned."[9]

This latter interpretation of the voice originates in the fact that in the narrative present (as opposed to the cameos of memory) there are two distinct kinds of light: on the one hand the "faintly luminous," gray, "shadowy light" in the narrator's "little void," without source and clearly related to the rotunda's light; and on the other, the light of the sun and moon, in short, of the living and known universe. It is decisively significant that this *natural* light appears to *Company*'s man on his back in the dark on only one occasion. When it does, the blind ratiocination and the laborious scrutiny of fancy on the watch face, along with the "invented," unnatural hell light, are instantly dispelled:

> . . . the very distance itself between hand and shadow varies as the degree of slant. But however great or small this distance it invariably waxes and wanes from nothing to a maximum 15 seconds later and to nothing again 15 seconds later again respectively. More might have been observed on the subject of this second hand and its shadow in their seemingly endless rotation round and round the dial and other variables and constants brought to light and errors if any corrected in what had seemed so far. But unable to continue you bow your head back to where it was and with closed eyes return to the woes of your kind. Dawn finds you still in this position. The low sun shines on you through the eastern window and flings all along the floor your shadow and that of the lamp left lit above you. (pp. 82–84)

Even the "low sun" is strong enough to eclipse the artificial light of the lamp, "left lit" but serving now only to cast a shadow. Not only the narrator's fatigue but also the dawn of natural light are needed to put an end to the lucubrations of the "reason-ridden" fancy. This is the same light that creates the staff's shadow in the beach scene. The final sentences of the quoted passage contain in their sound and tenor the release and unexpected climax of the watch-face speculation. A return to sentences of normal length, the mention of "sun" and "window," and the amplitude of "flings all along the floor your shadow" all are symptoms of the transformation of a paragraph which until that point is rigidly in the tone of a reporting document, the guise of empty reason. Does it seem arbitrary to equate the natural light of the universe with the highest forms of imagination and to argue that the artificial light belongs to a lower order? The evidence provided by the Rotunda texts (already discussed in part 3), and by the reappearance of natural light in all the succeeding texts not concerned with the death of imagination, is overwhelming. More still is furnished by *Ill Seen Ill Said.*

Just as the assumption that *Company* is simply divided into recollective and scrutinizing modes—the one past, the other present—can be faulted because there are two different modes of recollection, so the supposition that the recollections are separate from the scrutinies can also be found to be incorrect. On at least three specific occasions in the book, the lyric past and the analytic present occur fused in the same passage. In this fusion, more than a compound—virtually a new element—seems to result; it is neither of the past nor of the present, neither nostalgic nor rational. In the following passage the themes of light, youth, and the power of recollection all interact with the concerns of the analytic voice:

> The light there was then. On your back in the dark the light there was then. Sunless cloudless brightness. You slip away at break of day and climb to your hiding-place on the hillside. A nook in the gorse. East beyond the sea the faint shape of a high mountain. . . . The first time you told them and were derided. So now you hoard it in your heart with the rest. Back home at nightfall supperless to bed. You lie in the dark and are back in that light. Straining out from your nest in the gorse with your eyes across the water till they ache. You close them while you count a hundred. Then open and strain again. Again and again. Till in the end it is there. Palest blue against the pale sky. You lie in the dark and are back in that light. Fall asleep in that sunless cloudless light. Sleep till morning light. (pp. 33–34)

In a remarkable throwback to the same position in youth that the narrator has now in age—lying in the dark—Beckett shows how drastically the imaginative faculties have atrophied in the interim. The first appearance of the phrase "on your back in the dark" in this paragraph signifies the two possibilities: on your back in the dark "then" and on your back in the dark "now." The image of the child contemplating a mountain for a whole day, and not growing tired of it, is familiar from Wordsworth's poetry. The mountain is beyond and higher than all the circumstances of the conditioned human plane. It is also beyond the derision of the narrator's family who are so tellingly immolated in Beckett's ironic twist of Keats's "supperless to bed."[10] But the irony is double: at once sardonic in its invocation of Keats's virgins (who are so breathless with anticipation of love-deams that they dare not eat) and decisively inviting to our sense that the delight of the dream, here in *Company* as well as there in the castle of Keats's poem, is going to outweigh the physical hunger. Once out of his family's way, the child has it within his power to summon back the light he had seen, and in it the mountain, "palest blue against the pale sky." In the sentence "You lie in the dark and are back in that light"—the axis of *Company*'s two strands—we are brushed with a glancing sense of relief that in the word "back" placed next to the phrase "in the dark," only a punning echo remains of that naggingly repetitious refrain "on your back in the dark."* *Back*'s first and only change of grammatical status in *Company* also signals subtly a change of perception: this vision of the mountain, and the solace which it brings to the child's sleep, is one of the best evocations of paradisial experience in all Beckett's work. "Fall asleep in that cloudless light. Sleep till morning light" is far from the "cacodemons" of *All Strange Away.*

It is as though Beckett has finally found an acceptable approach to the "islands, waters, azure, verdure" of imagination and has retrieved *Old Earth*'s "childhood sea" and "other skies."[11] It is no coincidence, firstly, that a child should be the only one to display a power and level of imagination that are so desperately lacking in the murmurings of *Company*'s old fabler; and secondly, that natural light should be the stimulus for it, a light beginning "at break of day" (the same time that the "low sun" dispelled the watch-face rigmarole) and pausing "at nightfall" only to be re-created during the night and to disappear in the "morning light." The deliberate echo of the narrator's supine position, and the disparity between the young and old self's power of imagination, shows unarguably

*Cf. *More Pricks Than Kicks:* "nothing for it but to lie on his back in the dark" (p. 174).

to what a minimal level consciousness sinks when fancy is uppermost in it over a period of years. Fancy is the mode of consciousness associated with the "calm eye of reason" (*Lessness*), rationalism, and, ultimately, the "eye of flesh" confined to "devouring" such physical objects as it can register. This is why the light which the eye sees in the rotunda is so deliberately described as *without source:* light, life, and knowledge from their source and fountain are not admitted solely by physical perception. All that the rotunda's light gives evidence of is objects. The natural light is the light of the higher or primary imagination,* and in Beckett it is summoned to the world of the texts by an *inner* activity of the kind that the boy narrator makes in the dark, remembering the light. It cannot merely be invented or "fancied up"; it requires repeated effort: "then open and strain again. Again and again." Rationalistic certitudes, such as are "within the cylinder alone to be found," never connect with the sun. For a "reason-ridden" consciousness, the solar light of the sky is indeed nothing more than a "myth."[12]

Company's recourse to childhood imagination is further illustrated by a paragraph immediately following the fall through the fir tree; this paragraph is another instance of the merging of the two modes.

> What with what feeling remains does he feel about now as compared to then? When with what judgement remained he judged his condition final. As well inquire what he felt then about then as compared to before. When he still tarried in the remains of light. As then there was no then so there is none now. (p. 29)

Three time periods are implicit: "now," "then," and "before then." "Now" is a period of minimum judgment, minimum feeling, minimum reason even, although reason is what the narrator is trying to live on. "Then" is the period of childhood, a period more fully illuminated because he "moved or tarried" in more light than he does now. A "before then" is also posited, which is either still earlier childhood or prechildhood. The occurrence of "tarried" is interesting, because in Romantic poetry it sooner has associations of lingering in a delectable place than of loitering or dawdling in any place.** Its slight archaism serves a special purpose, as unusual

---

*See chap. 5, pp. 142–45.

**Cf. Wordsworth, *Prelude* 14, line 352: "Roamed, tarrying at will in many a pleasant spot."

vocabulary always does in Beckett's prose. Again, light is significant: in the descending periods "now," "then," and "before then," the most mysterious and yet the most insightful period was the one in which he "tarried" in the "remains" of light. The words recall *For to End Yet Again*'s "where used to glimmer a remain." But that period is also the most unreachable, because even in childhood one is not conscious of it: "As then there was no then, so there is none now." Only "before then" could there have been anything more than "remains of light." The whole passage echoes Wordsworth, albeit with a radical shift of tone:

> Heaven lies about us in our infancy!
> Shades of the prison-house begin to close
>   Upon the growing boy
> But he beholds the light and whence it flows
>   He sees it in his joy;
> The Youth, who daily farther from the east*
>   Must travel, still is Nature's priest
>   And by the vision splendid
>   Is on his way attended;
> At length the man perceives it die away
> And fade into the light of common day.[13]

The third occasion on which the speculative reason of the "narrative present" gets directly involved with the lyricism of the memory passages, or where the "head" and the "heart" interpenetrate, is just before the "aspen-idyll" scene, in which the narrator's voice asks where the other voice he can hear is coming from:

> From ranging far and wide as if in quest the voice comes to rest and constant faintness. To rest where? Imagine warily.
>
> Above the upturned face. Falling tangent to the crown. So that in the faint light it sheds were there a mouth to be seen he would not see it. Roll as he might his eyes. Height from the ground?
>
> Arm's length. Force? Low. A mother stooping over her cradle from behind. She moves aside to let the father look. In his turn he murmurs to the newborn. Flat tone unchanged. No trace of love. (pp. 65–66)

The voice dwelt on at the beginning of *Company,* coming to the narrator out of the dark with a peculiarly "flat tone" (p. 26), here merges—imperceptibly to the narrator, but perceptibly enough to

*The mention of the east in *How It Is* (see chap. 4, p. 124) is possibly related to this poem.

the reader—with the voices of his parents above his cradle, part of the childhood memories. This is one of the most interesting links between remembered past and desiccated narrative present. The flat tone of voice is *un*consciously remembered by the narrator, for fully conscious memory of the cradle is difficult if not impossible (even though Beckett himself claimed to remember life even earlier than that, in the womb, but *how* conscious such memories are is left unclear); but the connection between the flat tone of the voice and the loveless murmur of the parents steals in on the narrator when his thought is directed to something quite different, that is, to the probable distance of the unidentified voice from him once it has ceased to move in the dark. The link between this voice and the parents' voice is established in terms of recognition, whereas earlier in the work the "flat tone" was an unrecognized, though experienced, effect. As Beckett put it, describing a very similar situation in *À la recherche du temps perdu:*

> A subconscious and disinterested act of perception has reduced the object . . . to its immaterial or spiritually digestible equivalent, and the record of this pure act of cognition has not merely been associated with this sound . . . but centralised about it. (*Proust,* p. 73)

The parents have a tendency to steal into *Company*'s narrative present at other points, too. In the "bloom of adulthood" passage, for example, the pregnant abdomen of the woman "dissolves" for a moment to the memory of "your father's straining against the unbuttoned waistband," and, in fact, the whole of the lovers' scene is played out in the same wooden summerhouse that was the scene of exchanged chuckles of friendship between father and son years earlier. Actually, about a third of the "bloom of adulthood" episode is taken up with this memory of the brighter blossom of childhood.

So, apart from the occasional flicker of humor ("A rat long dead. What an addition to company that would be"), the "reason-ridden" speculations of the narrator have nothing to do with life in any way except on the occasions already discussed where memory joins, supplies, or explains what it is that has been lacking or lost in the endless ratiocination. One further characteristic that saves *Company*'s edifices of fancy from the delusory truth-status which they still tried to weather in *Imagination Dead Imagine* is the rather wry, faithless, and *un*scientific tone in which they are built up and delivered, together with typical doubts as to the utility of all the reasoning, given the decrepitude of the faculties themselves: "With what reason remains he reasons and reasons ill."

Accompanying the doubts there is a fear, still incipient but nevertheless new to Beckett's prose, that fancy might have a grim, rancorous, and destructive power, and that experiments in speculation, once set up and in motion, might be impossible to arrest or dismantle:

> Mental activity of a low order. Rare flickers of reasoning to no avail. Hope and despair and suchlike barely felt. *How current situation arrived at unclear.*
>
> Which of the two darks is better company. Which of all imaginable positions has the most to offer in the way of company. And similarly for the other matters not yet imagined. *Such as if such decisions irreversible.*
>
> Which of motion or of rest the more entertaining in the long run? And in the same breath too soon to say and *why after all not say without further ado what can later be unsaid and what if it could not? What then?* (pp. 35–62, my italics)

This fear, which is expressed in varying moods in *Company,* perhaps relates to the unexpressed sense of emergency at the end of *The Unnamable,* where we encounter an urgency—and yet a reluctance—to "speak of me," since all the figments and stories previous to (and in) *The Unnamable* were evasions and lies. The lack of discrimination between the lie and the truth—"I simply believe I can say nothing that is not true"—began as an amusement (and an escape from "corpse-obedient matter") and ended in *The Unnamable*'s tragic self-division. But none of the earlier long works was as clear about the reason for this emergency as *Company,* following the sixties texts, is. Whereas in *The Unnamable* truth made a contrary claim against lies and caused anguish, in *Company* imagination makes a contrary claim against fancy and insists on knitting together the lower faculties of consciousness with the higher, thereby uniting the two divided worlds of Beckett's man.

The physical and associated sides of consciousness cannot by themselves sustain the narrator without an atrophy of imagination taking place. Nor can the imagination or imaginative immanence be made visible in the world of conditioned relativity, unless human imagination unites it with manifest objects and uses rational consciousness as an adjunct or mediator (See chap. 5, pp. 141–45). In the light of *Company*'s proliferation of images, and the comparison I have made with Wordsworth's and Coleridge's understanding of inspiration, a comment Owen Barfield made in his book on Romanticism makes especial sense in a reading of Beckett:

> There is a concrete thinking (experience alone can prove it) which is independent of the senses, and there is an abstract, logistic thinking, which is entirely dependent on them. But between these two there is an intermediate stage at which consciousness takes the form of pictures or images. . . . Imagination is the marriage of spirit and sense. Therefore the Consciousness Soul, which is the ego cut right off from sense by its abstract thoughts, will have, in its passage back to its home in the spirit, to pass through the intermediate stage of imaginative consciousness.[14]

Company advances still further than the Rotunda texts in illustrating this point. It gives a greater proportion of time to imaginative inspiration (recollection) and its formation into images such as the strand scene, as opposed to the tedious logistics of "imagination on the decline."[15] So although the truest light in *Company*—the "remains of light" in which youth tarries—is still no more than a glimmer, the circumstances that favor it are bodied forth with a breadth and concentration unthinkable in *Imagination Dead Imagine* or *For to End Yet Again.*

9

Cleansing the Doors of Perception (*Ill Seen Ill Said*)

Ill Seen Ill Said (published in English in 1982) is the climax of Beckett's late period. It is as extended as *Company,* but profounder; it has the same tragic overtones as *Worstward Ho,* but is richer. It is the axis of more traditions, methods, cultures, and preoccupations than any other work of Beckett's (except perhaps the trilogy as regards range), and it is probably the most difficult to understand of all.

Susan Brienza, like many before her on the preceding texts, has given quite illuminating and interesting commentary on what James Hansford[1] and others refer to as narrative or imaginative strategies, and has shown how *Ill Seen Ill Said* follows *Company* in its vision of the world, consciousness, and fiction. But unlike the position taken by Nicholas Zurbrugg in his recent essay,[2] her conclusion is that, once again, Beckett has produced a book "obdurately about writing."[3] David Read remarks on the "absence at the core of being" and "the perennial conflict of being."[4] But if, after *Company,* any Beckett work should make us wonder if these diagnoses are not becoming stock interpretations of post-Modernism, *Ill Seen Ill Said* should be the one to do it. Adept narrative strategist though Beckett remains—this work is no exception in showing his mastery of that skill—the impact of *Ill Seen Ill Said* has far less to do with narrative strategy than that of *Watt* or the trilogy. Indeed, the great majority of the qualities of narrative consciousness identified by Brienza in *Ill Seen Ill Said* are also profusely present in *Molloy,* many of them (the review of declarations, the search for modifiers, etc.) discussed in chapter 3.

Beckett's antepenultimate prose work is not concerned with renewing or recapitulating these matters, which in all cases are incidental not essential, factors. If *Ill Seen Ill Said* does have a central theme, it is the changes in the universe revealed by the sinking sun and the rising dawn, and the night lying between, and their reflection in human consciousness:

> Something far more deeply interfused
> Whose dwelling is *the light of setting suns*
> And the round ocean and the living air,
> And the blue sky, and the mind of man:
> A motion and a spirit that impels
> All thinking things, all objects of all thought . . .[5]

> It is down there in deep sleep that Beckett lives and where all of us live, but few in our time have been so expert in visiting that region, in staying there and bringing back a living report. It isn't just a matter of visiting—one needs a specially made, specially trimmed vocabulary to bring back true reports. One must understand the rhythms of the realm. One must bring back words and images, its particular music too.[6]

These two poets' remarks are of great pertinence to Beckett's late works. *Ill Seen Ill Said*'s essential factors are the threshold times of human existence, the half-death of sleep and its initiator, dusk; and the resurrection educed by the dawn.

Twilight: An *Urphänomen*

If this is what *Ill Seen Ill Said* is really about—and the insistence on these twilight times of day is obvious even on a first reading—then the evidence of preparation for it in Beckett's oeuvre pre-1982 is immense, quite as much as in the case of narrative strategy or ontological abstraction. From the end of *Murphy* (1938) onward, hardly any memorable scene or perception occurs outside the hours of dusk or dawn. Watt is virtually only alive at night, or in the evening (see particularly the first pages of chap. 4 of *Watt*). Molloy's reflections on the universe, on the "planet rolling eager into winter" and on "the sound the earth makes as it rides the deeps and wildernesses" all take place at dusk—"the dying day when I always felt most alive"[7]—in gardens under the open sky. Moran returns home at evening to his own garden, to his perished bees, and to a recognition of the truth of his situation. It is at dusk and in the night on the hillside next to the sea that Malone remembers the sound of the stonecutters' hammers. In *How It Is*, Klopstock's shadow grows gigantic in the westering sun. In the short works of the sixties concerned with the death of imagination, dawn and dusk become icons of the living universe, entering the "void" where, strictly speaking, no being should enter. In the sixties and seventies prose pieces leading up to *Company,* the evening is vibrantly present, with an effect so potent that it controls both universe and consciousness in *Old Earth* and the *Still* texts, and falls hardly short of being the balm of inspiration. The necessity and effect of the changing light of morning and evening and its link with heightened human perception were pointed out in *Company* (the beach and watch-face episodes, and the childhood memories of light). It is this power of daybreak and nightfall, of the change lived through by the universe and the "mind of man" as light and shadows brighten and darken, that is, if anything is, Beckett's favorite theme: certainly more than the themes of the skull and isolated man. Morning, evening, and night are literally the crucial times for Beckett's fiction. They are crucial because pervasive, and crucial also by virtue of the fact that, as *Company* tells us, "Christ at the *ninth* hour cried and died" (p. 77) and rose again in the early dawn. (This is not to say that Beckett's work simply subserves a Christian interpretation but rather to indicate that the Christ event, however it happened, is hardly ever ignored in Western art.)

From *How It Is* onward, Beckett's fiction has been more and more concerned with light and, as noted several times earlier, with the distinction between normal light (of which dawn and dusk are examples) and artificial, "sourceless" light. This preoccupation can now more clearly be seen as a preparation for *Ill Seen Ill Said,* particularly in the contrast between the two groups of sixties texts, one stream maintaining the "convulsive," "panting," "oscillating" light of hell, the other immersed in an "endless equinox," in "the afterglow," in the comparatively slow, serene change from day into night and night into day, and in the "flights at nightfall" of the cockchafer, or whatever being it is that flies in that form in *Old Earth. How It Is* also has an interesting hint of what is to come, in its metafictional harping on *azure* and in its distant allusion (via the *OED*'s quotation from Carlyle) to Klopstock, whose shadow is said to be so long in the "huge sun" (see chap. 4, pp. 112–14). Whereas, in one sense or another, these texts (and all Beckett's earlier fiction, notably the novellas) depended upon these crucial times, *Ill Seen Ill Said* revolves, and revolves around, the subject itself.

The realities of dawn and dusk, "poetic" though they may seem, have never been merely adventitious in Beckett's work. Yet *Ill Seen Ill Said* makes us feel that the earlier settings were only groping their way toward this one, and were therefore emergent rather than complete—even in *Lessness,* where dawn and dusk are in the same breath called "figment" and "dispeller of figments." *Ill Seen Ill Said* illustrates, too, how great the contrast is between the fast, tortured breathing, to which the rotunda's hell-light is likened, and the deep slow breathing of the cosmic atmospheres symbolized by the changes of natural light in the world. For in *Ill Seen Ill Said,* whilst there is still fear, frustration, isolation, and impotence on the human scale, the world evoked is one of "silence merging into music infinitely far and as unbroken as silence," "ceaseless celestial winds in unison," and "endless evening"; in other words, of the calm, majesty, and wisdom similarly evoked by the mountain which the boy in *Company* glimpses in the distance. The universe of *Ill Seen Ill Said* is sufficient to itself and complete, and is evoked with a power that is uncanny in view of the minimalist style the narrator adopts, and given the difficulty he finds in narrating the "story." How far these prenocturnal and postnocturnal phenomena are essentially connected with that hobbyhorse of post-modernist theory, the process of writing, is difficult to establish; but the preeminence of the light/no light question and its twilit scene seems to me obvious and never to have been mentioned in discussions of the late prose (even the best of them, like Zurbrugg's essay "A Sense of an Ending"). This is surprising given the amount of attention this subject has received in studies of Beckett's drama.[8]

In *Ill Seen Ill Said,* language is becoming related to something much farther away from, and larger than, "the act of writing itself." For that act is in a sense almost perversely tied to the "locality" of the particular creator: "what matters in the later prose," says Brienza, "is not the world but the mind creating a world; not the substance but the dynamics of its creation: style."[9] This assertion is typical of the current thinking on Beckett, and to an extent it frees readers of some unnecessary presuppositions. But such a "style" is worth anything only when it brings forth a world, or, in Heidegger's terms, when

> we are able to characterise creation as follows: to create is to let something emerge as a thing that has been brought forth. The work's becoming a work is a way in which truth becomes and happens. It all rests in the essences of truth. . . . Truth is the unconcealedness of beings. . . . Precisely where the artist and the process and the circumstances of the genesis of the work remain *unknown,* the thrust, the "that it is" of createdness, emerges most purely from the work.[10]

In *Ill Seen Ill Said,* it is not the *genesis* and *process* of writing but the "being" that is to be "unconcealed" which needs, if it also defies, comment.

The issues raised and the explorations invited by the sunset and night—the "created centre" of *Ill Seen Ill Said*—do not, however, contain any solution or answer to the question *why* these times of day should be so heavily concentrated upon, and why that center should be there:

deepening gloom . . .

in the light of the moon . . .

It is evening. Yet again.

Silver shimmers some evenings when the skies are clear . . .

At break or close of day . . .

Suddenly it is evening. Or dawn.

The buttonhook glimmers in the last rays.

Quick enlarge and devour before night falls.

It will always be evening. When not night.

She casts toward the moon to come her long black shadow.

Black night henceforward. And at dawn an empty place.

This great silence evening and night.

Shroud of radiant haze. Where to melt into Paradise.

She lit aslant by the last rays . . .

Winter evening in the pastures . . .

Death again of deathless day.

They cast to the east-north-east their long black shadows.

Dazzling haze. Light in its might at last.

> The westering sun . . . the eastering earth.
>
> Day no sooner risen fallen.

The fact that such phrases as these span the entire fabric of this text suggests, however, that *Why?* might be the wrong question. Goethe's outlook as a scientist as well as an artist ran counter to the generally accepted inductive reasoning of why and wherefore:

> Look for nothing behind phenomena: they themselves are what is to be learned.[11]

According to the Goethean view, when the observer comes upon "primal phenomena" (*Urphänomene*) he endeavors, as Owen Barfield wrote, "rather to sink himself in contemplation *in* that phenomenon than to form further thoughts *about* it. The blue of the sky, says Goethe, *is* the theory. To go further and weave a web of abstract ideas remote from anything we can perceive with our senses in order to 'explain' this blue—that is to darken counsel."[12] It is meaningless to try to penetrate behind these apodictic *Urphänomene,* the true "laws of nature." But if the observer is conscious *in* them, as Beckett is in the twilight in *Ill Seen Ill Said,* the contemplation will nevertheless yield counsel. Not all verbal moves toward the truth take the form of explanations; and it is in this fact more than any other that the essential relationship between truth, language, and imagination becomes apparent. The essential attribute of a contemplation of twilight as an *Urphänomen* is that vision is involved: it cannot merely be a matter of words or reasoning. In vision we have the paradigm of sensory perception unified with imaginative or spiritual interpretation of phenomena.*

Change

The first observation to make about dawn and twilight is that they are two of the most powerful expressions of change that there are

*Heidegger (in "The End of Philosophy and the Task of Thinking") sees lighting, unconcealment, or opening (*Lichtung, aletheia*) as both a "primal phenomenon" in the Goethean sense and a necessary condition for truth to be perceived. "Light can stream into the clearing, into its openness, and let brightness play with darkness in it. But light never first creates openness. Rather, light presupposes openness. However, the clearing, the open region, is not only free for brightness and darkness but also for resonance and echo, for sound and the diminishing of in the world. Dusk is a period in which change floods into human consciousness. *From An Abandoned Work* illustrates the characteristic Beckett day:

> The sky would soon darken and the rain fall and go on falling, all day, till evening. . . . Then blue and sun again a second, then night. (p. 129)

The rain is continuous (it goes on falling), as is the sky's darkness. But the blue and sun occur only in the time of transition: "blue and sun again a second, then night." *Enough* hints mysteriously that reality is a journey, a change, measured out by the periods of dawn and dusk:

> Night. As long as day in this endless equinox. It falls and we go on. Before dawn we are gone. (p. 144)

Where to? Everyday reality seems to dissolve here; they go on when night falls, but where do they *stay,* in order that "before a dawn" they may be "gone" again? Something similar obtains in *Still,* whose opening sentence

> Bright at last close of dark day the sun shines out at last and goes down.

indicates a period of change in which the journey of memory is undertaken by the old man in the chair in *Sounds* and *Still 3*. But *where* the old man goes, or *how long* he has been away are not known and are referred to only by questions: "whence when back no knowing," and so forth. In these texts what *is* clear is that impending night gives birth to otherwise impossible intuitive knowledge. In *Ill Seen Ill Said,* the pervasive dusk is once again the only situation in which the mix of memory, fact, and reflection can form a compound experience.

Recognition

> *Stars how much further from me fill my night.*
> *Strange that she too should be inaccessible,*
> *Who shares my sun. He curtains her from sight,*
> *And but in darkness is she visible.*
>
> —William Empson, "To An Old Lady"

---

sound. The clearing is the open region for everything that becomes present and absent. . . . *Aletheia,* unconcealment thought as opening, first grants the possibility of truth. For truth itself, just as Being and thinking, can be what it is only in the element of the opening (*Basic Writings,* pp. 387–89).

The "story" of *Ill Seen Ill Said* posits a rememberer, that is, the narrator, and an old woman remembered but continually evading memory. The upsurge of frustration is similar to that of the searcher in *Still 3,* who is looking through hundreds of half-remembered faces for *the* face. But just as *Why* the dusk? is the wrong question, so *capture* of the memory is the wrong aim. The memory can be vouchsafed only in the period of change, and in the incertitudes of twilight. In both *Ill Seen Ill Said* and *Still 3,* a relationship between "rememberer" and "remembered" is understood, and in *Ill Seen Ill Said* it feels as if the "old dying woman" still elicits a sense of guilt in the rememberer for not getting his leavetaking right or complete, or not distancing himself enough from a limitingly personal involvement in it: "How say farewell? . . . How need? How need in the end?" (p. 16) No other figures are discernible in the story, despite the man Brienza suggests is "threatening to become another character," who is actually the same man as the observer/rememberer, the guilt-ridden son or lover of the woman. I am not extrapolating this detail in order to situate the book in "biographical" or "interpersonal" terms, although these matters are more germane than it has been the habit of "second-generation" Beckett criticism to acknowledge. The autobiographical possibility is qualified by another possibility—that Beckett may be remembering the dead grandmother he mentions twice in *Proust,* "this mad old woman, drowsing over her book, overburdened with years" (p. 28):

> Now a year after her burial, thanks to the mysterious action of involuntary memory, he learns that she is dead. But he has not merely extracted from this gesture the lost reality of his grandmother: he has recovered the lost reality of himself, the reality of his lost self. (p. 41)

This prefigures the narrator's state in *Ill Seen Ill Said* remarkably.

If there is a value to Beckett's memories—autobiographical or literary—here, it is that while not excluding readings which would cast recollection as merely subjective, *Ill Seen Ill Said*'s memories encourage an insight into the form of all recollection. This form is not a formula, nor a "question answered," nor yet a Platonic "Form," but a form or way of life, which in its turn answers many interesting questions other than "what is recollection itself?" Just as the Goethean scientific principle ignored conventional deductive reasoning until it had gained full awareness of *what* a phenomenon is, and thus stood a better chance of one day lighting on an explanation, so the recollecting imagination in *Ill Seen Ill Said* gains in effect from evoking the appearance and vanishing of the old woman in the twilight rather than probing into what the pervasive twilight and the vision of the woman mean.

The search for recognition in *Ill Seen Ill Said* also depends on the changing light to succeed, just as it was shown to do in the *Still* trilogy. The recognition itself is similar to *Company*'s:

> Quick the eyes . . . Suddenly they are there . . . thinly misted with washen blue. No trace of humour. None any more. Unseeing. As if dazzled by what seen behind the lids. The other [eye] plumbs its dark. Then opens in its turn. Dazed in its turn. (*Ill Seen Ill Said,* p. 39)

> The violet lips do not return your smile. . . . You go back into your mind. She too did you but know has closed her eyes. (*Company,* p. 58)

In both cases it is a matter of "recognition lost" with no sure hope of a "recognition regained" to counter it.

In the exchange of looks between Murphy and Mr. Endon, the same need for recognition was expressed: "The relation between Murphy and Mr Endon could not have been better summed up than by the former's sorrow at seeing himself in the latter's immunity from seeing anything but himself."[13] Lack of recognition is as good as—or as bad as—lack of relationship, since Murphy sees his own incipient problem, an inability to relate to the world, in Mr. Endon's advanced state of derangement. Beckett puts it axiomatically: "The last Mr Murphy saw of Mr Endon was Mr Murphy unseen by Mr Endon. This was also the last Murphy saw of Murphy." The irony is that Mr. Endon's eyes were the last mirror in which Murphy saw himself, both literally and metaphorically, before his death. It could be said that Murphy, having seen someone so much like him and so much older than him in a state which we recognize to be the same as the prisoners' in the rotunda, simply opted out of the continuing effort to survive. For, a mere seven lines after he speaks those diagnostic words "Mr Murphy is a speck in Mr Endon's unseen" and exchanges that glance, he is prophetically said to be feeling "incandescent." A few pages later the adjective is proved grossly and literally true, far from the euphoric figure of speech it seemed at first. Beckettian man cannot sustain the consequences of "recognition lost" at this stage; he gives up on life and burns to death, perhaps is even condemned by the authorial consciousness to the death of heretics. But at the end of *Ill Seen Ill Said,* the longed-for "grace to breathe that void" is the grace of acceptance of a "dark age," in which, perhaps, the mission of consciousness is to heal the wound caused by the division of man from the universe. In this sense, the "grace" is to accept one's destiny of self-consciousness and carry through the effort of reintegration that "this age" (p. 11) demands of man. The Rotunda texts were a first step: they faced, rather than escaped, the hell of a consciousness like Mr. Endon's. The *Still* texts and *Ill Seen Ill Said* try to use the dispensation of "grace": to use consciousness in such a way as to transform it.

The Eye of Flesh

Another characteristic of the *Urphänomen* of twilight is that it offers rest to the tired physical eye, so that the imagination can free itself of the material world to which it is tied during the day. One of the advantages of dusk is that it does not consign the "eye" (and hence the human being) to reliance on the mind alone, since things are still visible; but neither does it tie the "eye of flesh" to the flesh itself, to external objects. *Ill Seen Ill Said* makes much of "the eye having no need of light to see," that is, the mind's eye. The eyes of people continually subjected to *glaring* light (in *The Lost Ones* and the related texts) dry up, dilate, redden, and desperately need rest, such as would be offered by the milder influence of dusk's natural light. The Rotunda's light, it will be remembered, was sufficient to render visible anything visible as an *object,* but it had no source and no perceptible rays: "its omnipresence as though every square centimetre were agleam of the some twelve million of total surface."[14] For the "eye of flesh," an eye divorced from its imaginative function, it is a strain to keep seeing these lurid objects, walls, tunnels, and unrecognized other people. But it is characteristic of natural twilight falling on objects that it does not emphasise their objecthood so much as their existence as a term in a relationship of phenomena ranging from the material to the immaterial, all interacting. Objects lose their separateness—"outness"[15]—in twilight, where "idolatrous detachment" is less of a danger.

This avoidance of separation between the material and immaterial is exactly what *Company*'s strand scene achieved, whose relation to *Ill Seen Ill Said*'s narrative and theme is obviously strong. Shadows in the "dying light" are as much a part of the reality as the staff in the sand upon whose *shadow*—the union of object, light, and darkness—the reader is asked to concentrate. The objects only "unconceal their being" in the light of the universe lighting them up. If Heidegger is right to say that "at bottom, the ordinary is not ordinary; it is extra-ordinary"[16] then the light of common day is the least fit of all lights to give us an idea of the object's extraordinariness. The mysterious dusk light is what shows the object to be "at bottom, extraordinary." What lights the staff and boots in the sand, and the entire scenario of *Ill Seen Ill Said,* is the changing light:

> Blue and sun *again a second,* then night.

Thus, rest for the physical eye encourages the activity of the inner eye. Without cooperation from the imaginative eye, the narrator of *Ill Seen Ill Said* becomes a "widowed eye" in both senses of the word: bereft of a human partner and bereft of its "second sight." The "widowed eye" terminates the "marriage of spirit and sense" that Barfield, after Coleridge, calls the imagination.[17]

Night, the permanent habitation of the onlooker and the woman, releases still more perceptions in the narrator as to the nature and danger of the physical eye, the "eye of flesh" so often present earlier in Beckett's prose. This eye first became sinister in *All Strange Away,* where it was "jammed open, glaring, unseeing," and it remained so in *Imagination Dead Imagine, Ping,* and *The Lost Ones.* In *The Lost Ones* it is revealed that none of the population in the cylinder recognizes anything essentially human; the commentator/narrator could just as well be regulating and reporting on the social life of ants. In *Company,* mental activity has almost ceased for the man on his back in the dark, "whose eye of flesh" is "hooded, bared, hooded again. Bared again." All these references suggest the limited vision of animals or insects; and a human consciousness which is physically dominated actually makes its eyes equivalent to photoelectric cells in the end. This is the lamentable condition symbolized by the failed recognitions in *Company* and *Ill Seen Ill Said,* referred to on p. 204. In the latter there is a very poignant double entendre in the words "no trace of humour" used of the woman's eyes: the absence of an aqueous humor indicates the woman's long-departed physical wholeness, and the absence of "humour" indicates at the same time the death of sentiment. Each eye, dazed by the fact that in the other person's eye it sees and is seen by a mere globe of flesh ("Unspeakable globe. Unbearable"), closes to the outside world and in so doing closes on the inspiring possibility of either uniting object and light or establishing the lost relationship between the two protagonists. It is in this sense—of having described the plight of modern man's consciousness—that Beckett is a modern tragedian, much more so than in the commonly accepted "absurd" sense. The symbol of the engulfed pupil is almost as pervasive as that of the dusk. But the connection between them becomes clear when the eye *ceases* its perfunctory registering at dusk and at dawn. At such a moment the universe offers momentary repose to a consciousness in thrall to its own history (that of Western thought) and, incidentally, to its own choice in accepting the possibly dubious authority of a materialist *Zeitgeist* regarding the provenance of knowledge and the nature of reality.

Ill Seen Ill Said's narrator finally dares to take up a challenging attitude to the kind of eye that has suffered—and done—so much damage:

> Close it for good this filthy eye of flesh. (p. 30)

Borrowing a phrase from the blinding of Gloucester in *King Lear*, Beckett further calls it "the vile jelly." According to empiricist thought, the agent of perception has always been taken to be the physical eye (as it is illustrated in Beckett's *Film*), not the imagination or mind's eye, as Coleridge, Blake, and Shelley took it to be.

The Motion of the Planets

The motion of the planets is at its most apparent at twilight. The earth turns and the stars and moon appear. This is a hint that at such a time the cosmos undergoes something approximating what the human undergoes in breathing. Thus the condition of the old woman, whom the observer contemplates, is absorbed into a contemplation of the universe: if she no longer breathes, the changing light breathes for this "old, so dying woman" her diffused being. Compare what happens to Lucy in Wordsworth's "A Slumber Did My Spirit Seal":

> No motion has she now, no force;
> She neither hears nor sees.
> Roll'd round in earth's diurnal course
> With rocks, and stones, and trees.[18]

There are elements in *Ill Seen Ill Said* correlating to virtually every detail in this stanza: motionlessness, frailty, the unseeing eye, the "diurnal course" of the earth (a reprise of *Molloy*'s "planet rolling eager into winter"[19]) and lastly the "zone of stones" (p. 13). The dead woman, "not of this world," is a kind of oblique Lucy figure: her appearing coincides with the moonlight, ushered in by the visible rendering of "earth's diurnal course" at nightfall, the "sun low in the southwest sinking" according to *Still,* the "eastering earth" in *Ill Seen Ill Said*'s remarkable phrase, which again stresses the related motions of the planets.

It cannot be a mere coincidence—if it is, then it is a meaningful one—that at precisely the times when the motion of the universe is most clear to our eyes, Beckett always sees a "sudden gleam": "sun again a second, then night." Uncannily similar words float up in contexts where no evening scene is being depicted but where the faint stirrings of imagination in a gray world are taking place. They occur first in *The Unnamable:* "gleams . . . measurements, gleams, as at dawn, then dying, as at evening, or flaring up, they do that too" (p. 129); then again in *All Strange Away:* "But sudden gleam that whatever words given" (p. 122); "Sudden gleam" in that context means "sudden thought," the equivalent of "it occurs to me that . . ." *Enough* furnishes another peculiarly apt gloss upon *Ill Seen Ill Said*'s world:

> I belonged to an entirely different generation. It didn't last. *Now that I'm entering night I have kinds of gleams in my skull. Stony ground but not entirely.* (p. 140, my italics)

This suggests that *Ill Seen Ill Said*'s "zone of stones," however influenced it may have been by memories of the Dublin mountains where Beckett's oft-cited stonecutters worked, is principally of allegorical significance. "Entering night" is the crucial time referred to continuously throughout *Ill Seen Ill Said* (as previously also in the *Still* texts). In *For to End Yet Again*

> The skull makes to *glimmer* again in lieu of going out. There is the end all at once or by degrees there dawns and magic lingers a leaden dawn. (p. 179, my italics)

That this icon of change, the dawn, should linger at all—compare it with the refrain "last change of all"—is indeed a "magic"; and the aperçu which follows this glimmering dawn is thanks to a slight extension of the normally swift passage from night into day. The period's very brevity is what roused the dead still protagonist of *Sounds* to "snatch up the torch" while the going, so to speak, was good. All these details suggest that the "sudden gleams" associated with nightfall in *From an Abandoned Work, Still,* and *Ill Seen Ill Said,* and associated with consciousness in *Enough* and *For to End Yet Again,* postulate a restored link between man and the universe. In this way the gleams of sunset or sunrise in the characteristic Beckett day are equivalent to inspiration as understood by the Romantics. *Tintern Abbey* speaks pointedly of "an eye made quiet," "the light of setting suns," and "the mind of man," connecting the universal appearances, sky and sea, with consciousness, "all thinking things, all objects of all thought." *Ill Seen Ill Said* is a modern parallel.

Knowledge

The last aspect of Beckett's vision of dawn and dusk which I wish to consider takes us from Romanticism to Modernism and concerns knowledge. Twilight is the time farthest removed from certitude, and the physical eye's perception is then at its most unreliable. In *Ill Seen Ill Said* this is represented by a groping, opportunistic struggle to "seize her," whenever the woman happens to become visible in the gloom. Certitude, however, is a false friend in the world of Beckett's late prose, which concerns itself with a journey in search of *reality,* not merely certitude. Certitude is the correlative of fancy; the real, the correlative of imagination. The fancy's ravenous desire to ascertain, or to acquire certitude from nothing, had disastrous consequences for the consciousness of the rotunda; and as the prose of *Enough,* the *Still* texts, and *Old Earth* testifies, the "mystery of the without" which *The Lost Ones* warned of is much more inspiring and less confining than the certitude which is "within the cylinder alone to be found." Certitude proves to be no more genuine an article of knowledge than the idle speculator's drawing up of coordinates in a barren chamber. All this makes it quite plain that the late prose texts discussed in this chapter do no eschew the world, as the grammatologists* and Brienza's "New Styles" claim they do. On the contrary, these

*The hardened Derridian cannot seek to persuade, because he knows he is outside intelligent comprehension: "The inscription of the trace succeeds only in being effaced," Hansford quotes Derrida as "reminding us" (*Skullscapes,* p. 14). A theory of knowledge can as well eschew the world as bury its head in the sand. That said, I find it hard not to share Christopher Norris's commendation of "Derrida's refusal to subjugate style to the kind of repressive regimen which treats figurative language as a blemish on the surface of logical thought" ("The Margins of Meaning," *Cambridge Quarterly* 9, no. 3 [1980]: 283).

works attempt the difficult task of referring to, or indicating, the world in a nonconfining manner. The negation in the *Still* texts and in *Ill Seen Ill Said* is not the negation characteristic of nihilism, but rather that of Romanticism. Keats's "negative capability," rather like Beckett's dusk, is an inspiring abeyance of certitude, an abeyance of that "irritable reaching after fact and reason" evident to us in Beckett's less inspired, obsessively rationalistic longueurs. It is interesting that Keats's poetry, according in the same way as *Ill Seen Ill Said* does to the principle of negative capability, should be so crepuscular.

Ill Seen Ill Said is notable for the fact that the terror of the rotunda is past: the narrator's and woman's faces are, to quote *Lessness,* "to endlessness," and therefore capable of reading the iconographic phenomena and movements of the cosmos. In *Company* the narrative consciousness was overtly feeble, occupying the low level of the practically unthinking brain and virtually unseeing eye, in other words very much still in the trap of the skull/box/rotunda, and only roused from its torpor to record memories, but not integrated enough to move toward *knowledge* won from contemplation as well as from reasoning; a knowledge which, if Murphy had had it, would have saved him from the 'incandescence' to which in the event he was condemned. But in *Ill Seen Ill Said* the narrative consciousness is wide awake and alert, like the narrator of *Sounds,* for the slightest chance to receive the intuitive message he is convinced is about to appear somehow or somewhere, and is also in a position to understand it as knowledge. Fancy does not bog the speaker down in the pages of change-ringing that intrude even into *Company;* and he is not fancy's slave, although acutely aware that, as a human consciousness, he is always inclined to fancy at every turn, to "that dislike of vacancy and that love of sloth, which are inherent in the human mind"[20] but which are not, as the writer of those words would be quick to add, insuperable. The idly speculative impulse is kept at bay in *Ill Seen Ill Said* by the tempering voice "Gently gently. On. Careful." The legitimate activity of deduction is still acknowledged, but it is no longer the only accepted agent of knowledge. Coleridge never stated his theory of knowledge more clearly, nor provided a better gloss to the evocations of consciousness in Beckett, than here:

> Thus the act of thinking provides two sides for contemplation,—that of external causality, in which the train of thought may be considered as the result of outward impressions, of accidental combinations, of fancy, or the associations of memory,—and on the other hand, that of

internal causality, of the energy of the will on the mind itself. Thought, therefore, might thus be regarded as passive or active; the same faculties may in a popular sense be expressed as perception or observation, fancy or imagination, memory or recollection.[21]

The New Vision

Of the *Urphänomen* which we have contemplated from various points of view, *Ill Seen Ill Said* itself suggests, on page 49, "the explanation at last": that what is seen with the eyes open and what is seen with the eyes closed are two different things. Beckett thus assumes another sight is possible—so that things can be "re-examined rid of light"—the possibility being to look *through* the eye instead of *with* it. The eye of flesh, open and staring, looks *with* itself, but sees, identifies, and understands nothing. But the eye's master, the soul, understands by virtue of having seen through the eye:

> The eyes then agaze for the viewless* planet are now closed. On other viewlessness. (p. 50)

After "closed" an ellipsis is implied: "*and reopened* on other viewlessness"; that is, a viewlessness "re-examined rid of light," Beckett then adds, "of which more, if ever, anon.," by which he means, if ever I have need to write again on the subject of imagination and perception. The question of distinguishing the physically seen—one "inspection"—from the spiritually seen—another "inspection"—is addressed clearly for the first time in Beckett's prose:

> Re-examined rid of light, the mouth changes. . . . Between the two inspections the mouth unchanged. Utterly. Good. But in what way no longer the same? What there now that was not there? What there no more that was? (p. 50)

Beckett shifts attention from the object to the mode of perception. Compare Blake: "If perceptive organs vary, objects of perception seem to vary. If the perceptive organs close, their objects seem to close also."[22] In the passages from *Ill Seen Ill Said* quoted above,

*Cf. Keats's "Ode to a Nightingale": "For I will fly to thee . . . / On the viewless wings of poesy" (*Poetical Works*, p. 259).

the sunset light is singled out as deceptive: "True that light distorts. Particularly sunset." The sunset light belongs to the crucial time, again, where perceiver and perceived cannot occupy fixed ontological positions. This is a liberation for consciousness, and this liberation is not gained at the expense of knowledge so much as to favor a rediscovery of knowledge.

Imagination, as *Ill Seen Ill Said* illustrates, allows a fluid, interpenetrative ontological system. Mere linguistic constructs, on the other hand, produce fixed ontologies or the excess bulk of fancy's ratiocinative inscriptions, and promote the feeling in narrator and reader that they are ultimately lies. Blake summed it up:

> We are led to Believe a Lie
> When we see with not through the eye
> Which was Born in a Night to perish in a Night.[23]

It is likely that, in a manner unthought of by many Beckett critics approaching the late prose now,[24] the preeminence of half-light *does* have an affinity with the process of creation. But it is light, the burgeoning and fading light, and not the creator, less still the mere deviser, that brings the work into its existence.

10

A Pox on Void
(*Worstward Ho*)

. . . nothingness
in words enclose?

These words are from the poem beginning "Who may tell the tale of the old man?" which was used once by Beckett as a tailpiece to his second novel, and once again as a tailpiece to his *Collected Poems, 1930–1980,* when the celebration of Beckett's birthday gave added point to the poem's opening question. *Worstward Ho,* the tailpiece to his "late trilogy" (now published in one volume, *Nohow On*) is yet another tale from the old man (and *of* him, for *Company*'s tramping figure reappears) and also an answer to the question with which *Watt*'s poem ends: whether nothingness can be a content or not. Attempting to give an answer, *Worstward Ho* also continues the exploration of another question: whether imaginative works can afford to ignore the potentiality of knowledge inherent in imagination. Are the contraries fact/fiction and reality/figment reliable? Both *Worstward Ho* and the cultic modernist trends* which it addresses are a surprising instance of "calculation outrunning conception," "till nothing is but what is not."** If existence, and hence knowledge, is no longer defined either by content or by meaning but only by form, then there are a number of problems that an imaginative work which is aware of them will feel itself obliged to state.

Of all Beckett's later prose works, *Worstward Ho* is the most manifestly aware of its presence within a "literary climate," with

---

*Peter Murphy's *Reconstructing Beckett* and Lance St. John Butler's *Samuel Beckett and the Meaning of Being* are the only extended antiformalist readings of Beckett's prose to date.

**Shelley, "A Defence of Poetry," *Essays and Letters,* p. 33; Shakespeare, *Macbeth,* I iii (ll. 141–42).

its plays on the sign-signifier-signified conception in the search for sound analogues, as in:

> boundless/beyondless,*
> never to nought be brought

and:

> Throw up for good. Go for good, where neither for good. Good and all. (p. 8)

Think of the multiplicity of signifieds that are "thrown up" in our minds by the last example. Do we throw up our hands in despair, or does the narrator throw up—give up—the task of "going on"? Or do narrator and reader simply vomit in disgust? And, in a text in which good *is* good insofar as "failing better" is better than nothing, does "Go for good" mean "exit for eternity" or "pursue the good"? "Where neither for good"? So both—"throwing up" and "going"—are not for good, only temporary. Or neither "throwing up" nor "going" conduces to the good. The sense of good as opposed to evil in those three sentences is more or less outlawed by the "good and all" that so decisively concludes them. "All" sounds all too easily as "ill," however: one senses that with such multivalent words as "good," "go" and "all," and with so little in the way of context to bind them, any of their senses would "do as ill" as any other.

Although these ploys are reminiscent of the tactical games played by a Derrida or a "concrete poet," they also exemplify what Susan Brienza calls "baby-talk," the "inane words" which *Company* suggested were not so much the way to carry on as an author but, instead, the way to bow out:[1]

> With every inane word a little nearer to the last. (p. 88)

In *Company* last maybe: but since *Company*'s words were not the last, *Worstward Ho* translates "last" to "least" ("With leastening words say least") and suggests that a number of its formulations are "wanting in inanity" (p. 20). Thus, while showing a lively awareness of the post-Structuralist distinctions between words and what they stand for—if indeed they stand for anything according to those

---

*Cf. note to page 158.

distinctions—Beckett finds a new vein of humor, a definitively inane way of saying things:

> So leastward on. So long as dim* still. Dim undimmed. Or dimmed to dimmer still. To dimmost dim. Utmost dim. Leastmost in utmost dim. Unworsenable worst. (p. 33)

Combining superlatives in ever-tightening circles, and reversing their direction (by alternating "utmost" with "leastmost"), Beckett's sentences act out an infinite regression of the means of representation. This paring down, a ruthless attempt to strip the literature of Romanticism to the bone of its very truth,** has been an exercise characteristic of Modernism: post-Structuralist literary theory can be said to be an analogy in the realm of literary criticism. *Worstward Ho*'s metafictional element, commenting (like *How It Is*) on its own conduct, locates the later work firmly in both the Modernist "tradition" and the post-Structural theoretical debate.

One of *Worstward Ho*'s most characteristic contributions to the debate, however, is that in the repetitions that seek to enact a paring down, there is a hint of deliberate silliness. Each verbal element—the positive/negative cancellations "better worse," "least most," "unnullable least"—carries with it something like enjoyment of the meaningless sound of words and of their constituent vowels and consonants, as though an abacus user were forgetting the reason for his calculation and taking positive (if somewhat idle) pleasure in the slide of bead and the click of wood against wood. As meaning recedes, implicit criticism of the method grows. The weight of the long monosyllable "worst" drops heavily and finally on the profusion of shorter vowels scattered so conspicuously through the previous phrases, and thus gives the text back the tonality it has consciously tried to lose. So this apparently most opaque of Beckett's fictions turns out to have a distinct character. The inanity is, on a metafictional level, polemical, questioning the modes and means of this text and its literary milieu. The rather childlike way in which "unworsenable worst" tries to wrap up the argument gives way elsewhere to other inanities: for instance, the faintly obnoxious play on certain particular sounds for their own

*Cf. Shelley, *Prometheus Unbound* 3.4.204: "Pinnacled dim in the intense inane," *Dim* occurs nine times in the poem, *ooze* twice, *void* and *embers* once.

**What Livio Dobrez calls "the Beckett irreducible" (*The Existential and Its Exits,* chap. 1).

sake or for idle amusement, as in the disconcerting choice of "ooze"* for "progress":

> ooze gone. Till ooze again and on. Somehow ooze on. . . . No trace on soft when from it ooze again. In it ooze again. Ooze alone for seen as seen with ooze. Dimmed. No ooze for seen undimmed. For when nohow on. No ooze for when ooze gone. (p. 40)

Studied inanity is the only excuse for such an unembarrassed insistence upon merely physical softness, especially as "ooze" is the verb applying to the "thoughts" which the "soft" brain produces. The "drops" of *Ill Seen Ill Said*'s "strangury"[2] are revitalised here—if revitalized is the word—and turned into a metaphor for the telling of a "story": "ooze on." Having reduced the mind to the brain and having exposed the brain's "soft" as "ooze," Beckett has brought the reader's consciousness to an extreme point. If this insistence were not an implicit judgment of the process it has chosen to adopt, the result would be tasteless. As it is, Beckett's gesture is complexly distasteful, more a matter of emphasising how necessary distaste is to the recognition of taste than of evoking a distasteful subject groundlessly, for its own sake.

Then there is the inanity manifest in the work's disregard for grammatical links. In a prose which takes ellipsis as far as it will go—

> Said is missaid. Whenever said said said missaid.

—there are inevitably moments when it is taken beyond comprehensibility:

> Back unsay better worse by no stretch more.
>
> Not till for good nohow on poor worst missaid. (p. 36–37)

Yet most of *Worstward Ho*'s grammatical obscurities, as in these examples, are sins of omission rather than commission, and are therefore implicitly a critique of the reductive process. It is notable that the most confusion is usually caused by the paring of such paired concepts as come/go, back/on, say/unsay, utmost/leastmost; and where the omissions can be accounted for, we find that the

---

*Cf. *Murphy*, p. 25, "You suffer a dreary ooze of your being into doing," and *Proust*, p. 91, when Beckett adverts to Keats's "Autumn" oozings, and speaks of the "red ooze" of pomegranates in "Il Fuoco."

obvious point is being labored: there is not really very much difference between the supposed contraries. The insolence and inanity derive from the obviousness of this conclusion. It is usually the lack of content that equalizes the contraries and takes their force away; *Worstward Ho,* in playing the process out, enforces its implicit argument that form cannot exist without content:

> Longing the so-said mind lost to longing.
>
> Vain longing that vain longing go.
>
> Back is on. (pp. 36–37)

That the poles be stated is, of course, as necessary to their cancellation as their cancellation is to a sense of fitness, which even here Beckett does not forsake: this is one facet of Aristotle's doctrine of the mean,[3] which presupposes the (statable) existence of two extremes. But the voice of *Worstward Ho,* realizing fully how boring it is to pursue such an exercise, limits it to forty-six pages, keeps the tone light and "inane" for the execution—in both senses—of the word-pa(i)rings; and the narrator also still finds, much like his mud-bespattered forebear in *How It Is,* that other foreign beings and "contents" keep entering in on his oozing trip, spoiling the inane game. The narrator tries to play it, but the author frustrates the effort.

What does enter in is quite sinister. The games played in *Worstward Ho* remind us of the lies in the early fiction and the trilogy:

> Say bones. No bones but say bones . . . No ground but say ground. (p. 8)

These words are a concentrate of many themes characteristic of Beckett that have been traced throughout the previous chapters. There is the assumption that merely to say something is to render something real: there are no bones, we are told, but to say them creates them. This is a more conscious application of the principle illustrated in the description of Mr. Knott's garden: "Of vegetables there was no sign." But the text "says" vegetables in the same way as *Worstward Ho* "says" "bones" and "ground," although we are reliably informed in the same breath that there is no ground, and no bones. This is a prime example of the dangerously splintered axis of epistemology that Beckett can create and, by so doing, draw our attention to first principles without laboring the exposition of them. There is no verb *to be,* and this takes away any confidence in an *existence* centred on grammar: that only *exists* which *is.*

Here, however, the ellipsis of "no bones but say bones" serves another purpose than mere compression. The pun on "no bones" hints at another truth-value: to "make no bones" about something means, in effect, to tell the unadorned truth and make no fuss; to seek the truth is, likewise, to remove a "bone" of contention. It is true to say that after saying "no bones" on page 8 of *Worstward Ho,* the narrator goes on to make more and more bones, whereas, if he had kept his word, he would have said nothing more. The words "no ground" are equally cannily chosen: there are indeed no grounds for going on, but to "say" that there are forces you to go on "living the lie," as it were. In this way he also goes on both "making bones" and "saying bones"; because if we analyze the sentence "No *x* but say *x*" strictly, we assume that the truth is on the left-hand side of the equation, whereas the right must necessarily be subsidiary, the said. The silent "there are" prefixing the left side has more force than the said "said" on the right. To make bones is to obstruct the course of the truth; therefore it is natural that, if there *are* no bones in the scene imagined by the narrator, then any *said* bones will amount also to bones of contention, bones that should not be made. That there is *no* "ground" in *Worstward Ho* is clear enough; the figures tramp a groundless abyss at the same time the narrator makes a groundless statement. It is equivalent to saying "There *is* nothing, but *say* something," which must inevitably remind us of *Watt*'s words: "The only way you can speak of nothing is to speak of it as though it were something" (See Introduction, p. 24). Only content will make form real: just as an overemphasized bond between language and the world creates the deadening habit relationship described in the first chapter, so an attempt to divorce language from reference to the world turns that language into lies, as happened in the trilogy. Merely *saying* content will not bring it into being. Meaning has to be contacted, absorbed, imagined, thought about, and then finally it is known. Then, in being said, it will not *merely* be said. The same applies to human relationships as opposed to relationships with objects: a human being is a thing but not only a thing; therefore human relationships, which Beckett's characters are markedly poor in establishing, demand the flexibility to relate to an object and to more than an object at the same time.

Bones become more sinisterly multivalent in *Worstward Ho* than ever before in Beckett's prose, with all their connotations so sharply pointed up: bones of death; bones of contention; bones that are "gnawed" by the nameless fear that expresses itself throughout *Worstward Ho* in the form of present participles ("preying," "gnawing," "longing"); the bone of the skull or the islanded consciousness; and, lastly, the bone associated with truth, the bone which is, in the common phrase,* stripped of all the flesh of hypocrisy by "truthful" people.

Since, however, nameless fear is the one by definition not spoken of, so it is most likely to be the closest to the truth in a text in which the said is *not what is* ("No ground but say ground"). It is also significant that the attributes of personality and passion—"longing," "preying," "gnawing"—do not vanish during the inane cancelling of pairs of words: language seems not to be patient of this trick when a certain content, that nameless gnawing at the doubtful bones, is uppermost:

> Longing the so-said mind lost to longing. . . . Vain longing that longing go. (p. 36)

There is no such problem in the theoretical "Back is on," which defuses itself quite easily.

But the inanity of cancellation would be unmitigated if it were not so knowing, and so aware of the nameless obstacle to the game:

> The say? The said? Same thing. Same nothing. Same all but nothing. (p. 37)

This "all but nothing" is actually a considerable something, something positively "unnullable." This was not nearly so evident in the trilogy, where the narrator could get away with "I simply believe I can say nothing that is not true," nor even in *Enough,* where the speaker could say, "I set the scene of my disgrace just short of a crest. On the contrary it was a flat calm" and still assume that the mere function of producing or saying those elements of language would disclaim responsibility for the presence or absence of truth-value. *Worstward Ho* is much more honest. Although much of the book is based on the "no ground but say ground" principle, there are still certain things in it that cannot be simply unsaid, "said away," or burbled out of existence altogether by way of sophistries.

---

*E.g., Bob Dylan's song "Most of the Time" contains the lines: "I can deal with a situation / Right down to the bone" (*Oh Mercy,* 1989, CBS 465800).

There is an ungainsayable unease in what preys and gnaws most relentlessly, the

> Stare undimmed that words had dimmed. (p. 39)

This stare horrifies the narrator. It is once again the stare of imagination dead, which in this text is the only content that is fully imagined rather than merely said into or out of the linguistic fabric.

Worstward Ho is saying the same things as the Rotunda texts, *Company,* and *Ill Seen Ill Said* say about imagination, but in the awkward, inane temper of the work there is no chance for a contemplative discussion of "imagination alive" as there is in some of that group of texts, as shown in chapter 6. A fragile hold on that extraordinary cliché "a ring of truth" is all that is left:

> How almost true [words] sometimes almost ring. (p. 20)

> Held holding hands. That almost ring. (p. 32)

The ring of truth? And, because of the hands, the ring of humanity in a text almost devoid of it? The echo is faint, and only half the phrase is supplied, so that the other half depends entirely on our knowing the rest of the cliché; the sound is an almost ring, "a sound no more than ghosts make, or motes in the sun," as *Sounds* puts it. But the ringing is a metaphor; it is essentially of the imagination, in Johnson's words "embodying sentiment and reanimating matter."[4] And the faintness of the ring is usually a mere *tinkle;* the biblical cymbal tinkles in its meaninglessness or triviality. An *unfaint* ring, on the other hand, has connotations of purity, loudness, amplitude, and, like imagination, its sound includes rather than dissipates the hearers that gather in its field. So that even in the deserted field of Beckett's prose, the ring of truth and imagination remains; an almost ring, but by no means a tinkle.

One is reminded of the "ring" in *Imagination Dead Imagine:*

> a plain rotunda, all white in the whiteness, go back in, rap, solid throughout, a ring as in the imagination the ring of bone. (*CSP,* p. 145)

Here the sense of "ring of truth" is not so much invited as fended off by the supply of an alternative, albeit a pregnant one in view of *Worstward Ho*'s bones; whereas "that almost ring" encourages the reader's proverbial completion, "of truth." But the implication of *Imagination Dead Imagine* is that unless it were *in* the imagination, bone would not ring but only rap. And rap is also the name given to the hollow talk of an empty mind.* As imagination lends to "that almost ring" its only ring of truth, so it also turns a solid "rap" into a ring, into a sound of greater amplitude and inclusiveness. And if to pare something to the bone is to reveal its most naked truth, then the ring of bone is doubly significant, especially in view of *Worstward Ho*'s harping on bones. But the significance has only come about owing to a retrospective dialogue between the later work and the earlier.

The speaker's nameless fear is of the monstrous physical eye that hovers over a ruined imagination and claims (with its "soft" partner, the brain) to be "the seat and germ of all." The almost hidden play on "germ" here is especially interesting, suggesting both the origin of forms and the disease of those very forms. There is enough evidence in Beckett's work from *Murphy* onward to suggest that the sundering of man and the environment by a materialistic conception of consciousness is an evil: the correlation of this with disease is not unexpected, given the "ooze" and "soft" which are characteristic of decayed, once-living matter. The contexts admittedly differ, but I find it impossible not to recall *Company*'s words "the mush. The stench"[5] when I read of *Worstward Ho*'s oozing "soft." In *Ill Seen Ill Said,* the skull is the jakes,** the "so-said" container of the soul, reinforcing the taint of decay and excrement apparent in *Worstward Ho*'s description of the brain and of thought. "Ooze" was notably used in Beckett's first close reading: "Shakespeare uses fat, greasy words to express corruption: 'Duller shouldst thou be than the fat weed that rots itself to death on Lethe wharf.' We hear the ooze squelching all through Dickens' description of the Thames in *Great Expectations.*"[6] The ill-at-ease murmur which preys on and gnaws at the narrator's consciousness causes the physical eye and hell to be mentioned again as mutual agents:

> One dim black hole mid-foreskull. Into the hell of all. Out from the hell of all.

The single, cyclopean eye (recalling the dwarfs' "cyclopean" skulls in *For to End Yet Again*) theorizes the eye in a manner which has only been hinted at in Beckett's previous prose: as early as *Mur-*

*Cf. *Collins Dictionary of the English Language,* edited by P. Hanks (London: Collins, 1979); S.V.: "rap: to talk, esp. volubly; . . . the least amount."

**The name of an assuredly decayed consciousness can be read as Ja[k]es Moran.

phy, it was Mr. Endon's *eyes,* not eye, that interested the hero, and terrified him. Beckett thereafter mentions the eye in the singular abstract, but makes it clear enough that even the protagonists in the Rotunda texts and after have two eyes (cf. "fit ventholes of the soul . . .," *Ill Seen Ill Said,* p. 58). But in *Worstward Ho* the skull becomes container for a single eye, its singleness suggesting at once its readiness for clinical dissection and its lack of perspective: only through two eyes can one perceive distance and thus relate properly to the objects of the world.

One thing that the mostly audacious "inane" narrator will not dare to do is to say "brain" for the "soft" from which and in which its thoughts ooze. Whereas "sight" and "eye" have such richly variant metaphorical uses, brain can only be brain, and at its most figurative the word is never unmisgivingly complimentary—to be brainy or a brainbox is to be no more than restrictedly intelligent. The "soft" or brain, being the seat of fancy or of ratiocinative consciousness, can have no imaginative overtones. It stands to reason—to a higher reason* than the brain's—that the word used to denote a limited intelligence or mere intelligence can have no metaphorical power. It is for this reason that the narrator so pointedly refuses to utter it, preferring to shift "soft" from adjectival to noun status. Brienza says of *Worstward Ho* that in "exploring being, language and imagination" it favors insight into the "very workings of the human brain."[7] One wonders why, after being so ghoulishly exposed by Beckett to the brain's oozing lethargy, we should particularly value any insight into it, and even more why it should be assumed that the perfunctory synapses which are termed its "workings" should be given the name of imagination. Such a mechanistic explanation of perception and imagination is nothing less than the "unworsenable worst" for Beckett's narrator, who describes it unmistakably and with evident revulsion.

> Next the so-said seat and germ of all. Those hands! That head! That near true ring! Away. Full face from now. No hands. No face. Skull and stare alone. Scene and seer of all. (p. 23)
>
> Preying since last worse the stare. (p. 38)
>
> Black hole agape on all. Inletting all. Outletting all. (p. 45)
>
> Dim black. In through skull to soft. Out from soft through skull. (p. 43)

---

*Cf. Coleridge's description of reason in "An Essay on Faith" in *Aids To Reflection,* quoted in part in the footnote to p. 147.

Behind this instinctively negative evocation of mechanistic perception—that brusque alternation of the softest and the hardest consonants in the last example is calculated to disconcert us—there are other indications of a humanly active agency and therefore of a live imagination.* These essentially human impulses constitute a vision or story or, if a story never quite gets into the telling, a dramatic/poetic icon: a man, a woman and a child, sometimes together, sometimes apart, but, prima facie, related. Their motion and attitude recall the couple in *Enough,* the dwarfs in *For to End Yet Again* and, most of all, the family in *Company* and its scenes in which the narrator tramps the hills with his "father's shade"[8]:

> Backs turned, both bowed, with equal plod they go. The child hand raised to reach the holding hand. Hold the old holding hand. Hold and be held. Plod on and never recede. Slowly with never a pause plod on and never recede . . . joined by held holding hands plod on as one. One shade. Another shade. (*Worstward Ho,* p. 13)

The moody "inanity" principle often tries to "unsay" these images of humanity but does not succeed. This example shows the attempt visibly failing:

> Nothing but ooze how nothing and yet. One bowed back yet an old man's. The other yet a child's. A small child's. . . . Nothing and yet a woman. Old and yet old. On unseen knees. Stooped as loving memory some old gravestones stoop. In that old graveyard. Names gone and when to when. Stoop mute over the graves of none. (p. 45)

There is something consciously wayward, indeed inane, about the use of "yet" in the first six sentences, where the archaic use diminishes progressively, reaching its customary grammatical function only to be followed by a flagrant abuse of custom again in "old and yet old." But along with the father and child of *Company,* the woman and the world of *Ill Seen Ill Said* reappear, despite the ooze and the inertia, occasioning one of Beckett's most remarkable multifaceted sentences: "Stooped as loving memory some old gravestones stoop." The gravestones themselves seem to love memory and stoop to the beings lying below them, at the same time as stooping *in* loving memory, as the phrase goes. (Recall *Still*'s "some moods" for "*in* some moods".) Also vividly conveyed

*Not, as Enoch Brater would have it, the "ravages of figurative enticement" (*Beckett's Later Fiction and Drama,* p. 171).

is the sense that the woman has actually stooped *in the manner of* an old gravestone, and that, kneeling, she is probably also kneeling in loving memory of the dead person whose name has worn off the stone (cf. *Ill Seen Ill Said,* p. 11). On top of this, both those notions are themselves the author's "loving memory" of the old woman. The cliché is bound into a multiple axis: it is this that makes such elements in *Worstward Ho* less a matter of "ooze" than of what Beckett was in 1986 to call "faint stirrings still,"[9] and hence more vitally stirring to the mind.

This fearful portrait of the ruined imagination (the "skull and soft") coupled with the essentially human "subtext" we have just seen, together suggest that the fashionable language games and post-Structuralist theoretical standpoints which this work flirts with (and to some extent performs) are the least important of its contents. *Worstward Ho* illustrates much more closely the conflict between truth and relativity. The cancellations and equations are an apotheosis of linguistic relativity: the barest tools of comparative judgment are displayed, more/less, here/there, good/ill, on/back, somehow/nohow, better/worse/worst, little/less/least (though "little," in this text, is often too much: it appears very seldom). But their mere existence amounts to nothing unless there is a content for them to fashion; and hardly any of the content that Beckett does want to express is expressed in anything like self-cancelling terms. The eye, the brain, and the three human beings will not respond to the vanishing trick: that is the great problem for the narrator's ambition to prove the viability of language games. The drawback to what Beckett might have called "the post-Structuralist solution" had he been writing criticism today, is that, ultimately, lack of content worries away any existing interest in form (legitimate as far as it goes), and prevents the reciprocity of both.* The sense of purpose in *Worstward Ho* derives from an attempt to cope with an emergency. This emergency is presented to the authorial imagination by the "preying," "staring" eye of flesh first witnessed in *All Strange Away*—the mental state of "no content" transformed into an all-too-disturbing content—and by the soft, jellylike receptacle, the seat of perception according to the natural sciences from which relativity, as it is now understood, derives.

Apart from when they function as icons for the eye and for the family, words are seen by *Worstward Ho* as inevitably tools of

---

*Cf. "Dante . . . Bruno. Vico . . Joyce": "The form that is an arbitrary and independent phenomenon can fulfil no higher function than that of stimulus for a

relativity, as is illustrated in a shrewd passage which recalls *The Unnamable*'s sense of words sinning against silence:

> Blanks for when words gone. When nohow on. Then all seen as only then. Undimmed. All undimmed that words dim. All so seen *unsaid.* (p. 45, my italics)

But, unlike the linguistic roundabouts of *Watt* and the trilogy that I discussed in the first two chapters, the language of *Worstward Ho* does rise to dealing with what, according to the above quotation, is only to be seen dimly or not at all when language "clenches," that is, clinches and at the same time relativizes it. When words seek to "undimmen" that sight, the result is the horrific stare of dead imagination or hell. Words do cope with it after all, but it is anything but a game. Blake would have agreed:

> The whole creation . . . now appears finite and corrupt. If the doors of perception were cleansed, everything would appear to man as it is, infinite.[10]

The "soft" of *Worstward Ho*'s eye of flesh, filthy and finite indeed, is the very contrary of cleansed, and nothing if not corrupt.

---

tertiary or quartary conditioned reflex of dribbling comprehension" (*Disjecta*, p. 13).

11

Disembodying Western Tradition (*Stirrings Still*)

We die with the dying:
See, they depart, and we go with them.
We are born with the dead:
See, they return and bring us with them.
—T. S. Eliot, "Little Gidding"

Although *Stirrings Still* is not a finalized text—it was once titled "Fragments: For Barney Rosset"—it is the last statement of any length that Beckett had to make to the world.* It recalls his earlier works and unlocks the meaning of earlier images, motifs and themes; it also says something which to my knowledge Beckett never came closer to saying than here, that is, that there are states of consciousness in which the relative conditions of existence, the everyday world, the limits of time, space, and language, are transcended. Whether this state, which *Stirrings Still* is wholly concerned with, is a trance state; or an out-of-body experience such as those recorded by people seriously wounded or undergoing an operation; or a state experienced after death or before birth is not explicitly stated. But what is clear is that a consciousness and an individuality which has known life as a human in the quotidian world is now so far from it that it is unsure whether it wishes to return there. This individuality is the third-person subject, the "he," of the text. The narrative voice is not strictly identified with the voice of this third-person subject, but it seems likely that the two might be associated, since the narrator does not intrude with doubts about the veracity of what he is describing, as often happened in Beckett's earlier texts. As far as the reader can tell, the

*Now collected in *As the Story Was Told: Uncollected and Late Prose, 1981–1989*. All page references to *Stirrings Still* in this chapter are to this edition.

narrator's "he" could as well be "I": a transparency is assumed. So unlike some of Beckett's earlier work, *Stirrings Still* is concerned with the predicament of a narrated self and its relation to life, not with the predicament of narration per se. All the tonal qualities evident in this text—deliberation, occasional colloquialisms, patience, the attempt to be "regardless," or unswayed by desire (p. 127)—are attributable to a narrator in sympathy with if not wholly identified with the narratee, whose problem obviously needs to be approached with these qualities.

So *Stirrings Still* speaks of a level of consciousness beyond the physical. But also it describes the acute problem of one who for whatever reason—trance or death—finds himself in this state. And it is the treatment of this problem which gives the text its impetus, its tone, almost its "story" and denouement. It also seems, on a more figurative level, that Beckett is comparing the old age and loneliness of a person to the dying out of a civilization and mentality, and comparing the void of an isolated consciousness to the space waiting to be filled by a new civilization.

To briefly state the texts' main landmarks and what is recalled and reclaimed in *Stirrings Still* from Beckett's earlier work: the first section (of three) describes an old man confined in a space, perhaps a room, with a skylight (recalling *Endgame, All Strange Away,* and *Company*) and imagining himself moving elsewhere by a mysterious process in which he forgets how he has moved and how long it took him (recalling *Still, Sounds,* and *Still 3*). A clock strikes the hours; the voices of people crying out (possibly being beaten) are heard; but both these sounds are very faint (recalling *Company, Ill Seen Ill Said, As the Story Was Told,* and *Catastrophe*).

It becomes clear that the change of place is an illusion, that when the protagonist moves he ends up in the same place again: "another place in the place where he sat at his table" (p. 115), as he did at the start. The protagonist, as in *Company,* is seen to be walking "the back roads." Manuscript 2935/1 describes people coming and reading to the narrator (recalling the trilogy and *Horn Came Always*). Manuscript 2935/2 mentions Watt, Mr. Knott, and Mr. Hackett. The phrase "he saw himself rise and go" in the first sentence of the published text recalls a sentence written more than fifty years before, in Beckett's short story "Ding Dong" in *More Pricks Than Kicks:* "The mere act of rising and going, irrespective of whence and whither, did him good."

The second section of the published text consists of reflections by the narrator on "seeking help," seeking "a way out" from the seemingly endless return to life in the everyday world, symbolized by the clock and the cries. Help is sought first in memories of love and of suffering, then in the thought that memory is unreliable, then in the power of sight, then in the power of hearing, and finally in meditation (thought separated from the other senses). None of these is found to be of any use to allay "time, grief, self and second self his own." In this section the thought of watching Venus rising floats up from *Ill Seen Ill Said,* and the phrase "the remains of reason" from *Company.*

The third and last part speaks of a time when the narrator will find himself not back in confinement, as so many times before, but "stayed": the section begins, "So on till stayed" (rather than "so on till back again") and he hears "from deep within oh how and here a word he could not catch it were to end where never till then," to cease to be, to cease at a place or at a stage which he has never reached before and therefore never known before. The climax of the text's metaphysical journey is here. The protagonist has been wishing to end at "a place where never till then"; and suddenly realizes that he has been there all the time:

> was he not . . . already there where never till then? For how could even such a one as he having once found himself in such a place not shudder to find himself in it again which he had not done nor having shuddered seek help in vain in the thought so-called that having got out of it then he could somehow get out of it again which he had not done either. There then all this time where never till then (p. 127)

The final question—whether to return again to everyday life, to strive for a world higher than the intermediate state he is in, or simply to stop altogether—hangs on the nature of the "missing word he could not catch," which, being an adjective, would serve to describe the state "where never till then," which he realizes, logically, he has always been in. Why the adjective cannot be caught is actually the solution to the whole puzzle, and this will be described at the end of this chapter.

These are the principal external features of the text as printed. Chapters 5 to 10 of the present book discuss how the oddly specific locations and scenarios in Beckett's work from *All Strange Away* (1963) through to *Worstword Ho* (1983) are in fact the indices of a spiritual landscape, and how the loss of the power of imagination is shown by Beckett to cause hell on earth, the despotism of reason over imagination, what Blake calls "the delusion of Ulro and a ratio of the perishing vegetable memory," and what René Guénon called the "reign of quantity."[1] When, on the other hand, contact is reestablished with the powers of imagination, it becomes possible once again to understand one's relationship to existence. In *Stirrings Still* and the five associated prose fragments,[2] a new dimension is added to this symbolic landscape already described by Beckett in *Imagination Dead Imagine, Lessness, For to End Yet Again,* and *Ill Seen Ill Said.*

The Guardian, publishing *Stirrings Still* for the first time in 1989,[3] introduced it as "a meditation on loneliness and old age," which is certainly part of what it is, given the emphasis on past deeds (p. 118) and memories (pp. 116–17, 122) and solitude. But it has an extraordinarily explicit spiritual content, which might have seemed odd to emphasize were it not for the factors in the printed text and the manuscripts which bear it out so strongly.

To anyone familiar with Buddhism or esoteric Christianity,[4] the first paragraph of *Stirrings Still* gives the rest away. It should be quoted in full:

> One night as he sat at his table he saw himself rise and go. One night or day. For when his own light went out he was not left in the dark. Light of a kind came then from the one high window. Under it the stool on which till he could or would no more be used to mount to see the sky. Why he did not crane out to see what lay beneath was perhaps because the window was not made to open or because he could or would not open it. Perhaps he knew only too well what lay beneath and did not wish to see it again. So he would simply stand there high above the earth and see through the clouded pane the cloudless sky. Its faint unchanging light unlike any light he could remember from the days and nights when day followed hard on night and night on day. This outer light then when his own went out became his only light till it in its turn went out and left him in the dark. Till it in its turn went out. (p. 114)

The exoteric explanation is simply that the paragraph describes an old man in a room, his wits deserting him along with his memory. The esoteric explanation—that it describes the narrator's speculations about individual existence on planes beyond the familiar world—does not deny the former explanation but adds to it, and arises from the following facts.

First, the protagonist's consciousness is divided into two and he perceives himself as another: "He saw himself rise and go," just as the speaker does in Beckett's 1937 poem "Arènes de Lutèce":

J'ai un frisson, c'est moi que je me rejoins,
Je me retourne, je suis étonné
De trouver là son triste visage.[5]

Second, the scene is not the familiar world. An actual room is not mentioned, only the term "confinement" (p. 121). The light is not the light of the physical sky: it is "unlike any light he could remember from the days and nights when day followed hard on night and night on day" and implies further that the perceiver has passed into a different type of existence, a step beyond the life Beckett's adjective suggests: the "hard" life of the conditioned, relative world. The "sky" he sees here is the sky of the sphere he has entered during the period between one incarnation and the next: a state of extracorporeal existence.

Third, following from this, the time scheme is definitely not the world's: the protagonist imagines himself dead or beyond the body's confinement, and his perceptions are therefore a preview of this state. (The references to confinement suggest that the "room" to which he always finds himself returning is in fact the body, the "confining" receptacle, as it were, of the individual in the world. In the sixties and seventies Beckett used the skull as a variation on the image of confinement in the body, with special reference to self-consciousness.) This is clear from the absence of the normal "diurnal course" and from the words "when his own light went out he was not left in the dark."

So from this second confinement in a spiritual "interworld," the bodiless individuality of the narrator can survey "what lay beneath" (the earth) and what is above (the sky of the next sphere) and ask himself whether he wants to incarnate again, as the Buddhist or esotericist says he usually must, or whether he is to throw himself into a new sphere of existence altogether and leave the earth behind. This interpretation is supported by the sentence "Perhaps he knew only too well what lay beneath and did not wish to see it again." And this is also why he later wishes for the "one true end to time and grief and self," which are precisely the mystic's three indices for life in the relative world: causality, suffering, and egoism. This question lies behind the sudden introduction of warning in the last part of *Stirrings Still:* was the protagonist to "press on" or "stir no more"

> as the case might be that is as that missing word might be which if to warn such as sad or bad for example then of course in spite of all the one, and if the reverse then of course the other that is stir no more. (p. 128)

Perhaps the clearest of all the clues to the real suggestion of this text is the fact that any conventional view of the location and of what the narrator is doing there is radically compromised by the extraordinary sentence:

> So he would simply stand there high above the earth and see through the clouded pane the cloudless sky.

in which the spiritual language bids fair to break the surface of the material one and leaves us in little doubt as to what is being meant. No ordinary room is that "high above the earth." Also implied here, in the words "clouded pane," is the fact that in all mystical disciplines, preoccupation with one level of existence makes one blind to the next level above. Mirrors and windows in Sufi terms, for example, do not stand only for the place of manifestation—"Man is the mirror of God"—but also require polishing in order to minimize the blinding with which one level of existence always endangers the next. Beckett also speaks here of his seeker as "blind":

> In a strange place blindly in the dark of night or day seeking the way out. A way out. (pp. 116–7)

The second paragraph of part 1 reveals even more about the contemplation of the journey from the physical world to the incorporeal state, possibly from incarnation to incarnation. Plato claims that Lethe is the *forgetting* which all reincarnating individuals have to go through in order to bear coming back at all.[6] Thus the "light of a kind" (the light of the narrator's present spiritual state) is said to become "his only light" when his own (that of his previous condition) has gone out:

> This other light then when his own went out became his only light, till it in its turn went out and left him in the dark.

That last dark mentioned is the obscurity of Lethe, to precede and prepare for the incarnating individual's having to see "what he did not wish to see again," that is, the world.

It is significant that, in the second paragraph, at precisely the spot where the exoteric content fails to convince, the esoteric one breaks in. There is no material explanation why the narrator cannot tell how he moves from place to place, nor why his feet are "unseen"; nor why he can not tell how long it has taken to move, nor why in the end he finds he has not moved at all. The explanation is the travel from the state of incarnation to an extrasensory state or another incarnation, which involves a partial "amnesia" and might involve a change of place. Thus the narrator sees himself

> start to go. On unseen feet start to go. So slow that only change of place to show he went. As when he disappeared only to reappear later at another place. Then disappeared again only to reappear later at another place. So again and again disappeared again only to reappear again later at another place again. (p. 115)

The change of place, though mentioned several times in this part of the text, is shown to be illusory from the point of view of the transcendent perception reached by the protagonist's consciousness "high above the earth." Later again in the paragraph quoted above there are mentioned the "hope" and "fear"—the types of *desire* which, according to the Buddhist or Hindu, bind the human to the wheel of repeated incarnations.

> Head on hands half hoping when he disappeared again that he would not reappear again and half fearing that he would not.

"Hoping" because he wishes to escape suffering; "fearing" because he loves life too much to forsake it without a struggle. Beckett coupled hope and fear in just this way in chapter 4 of *Watt:* "It was as he feared, earlier than he hoped."[7] It may seem an odd claim that a Beckett character should love life. But the protagonist's only surviving wish late in the paragraph, that "the strokes would cease and the cries for good" and that he "was sorry that they did not," suggests that compassion springs from a source that could not actually be loveless.

The esoteric content I have described is of course implicit; Beckett, as always, hesitates to commit himself to one form of statement or ideology, and thus he makes what he writes accessible to all readers at whatever level is appropriate. Stating the subtext is necessary partly because it offers us new light on a writer who has often been misrepresented by commentaries which use his work to support a materialistic ideology, but mainly because of the evidence provided by the second of the five *Stirrings Still* manuscripts held in the Reading Beckett archive. In this fragment the narrator refers to the faint sounds of voices reading to him from out of an obscure darkness or invisibility. As an example of what they say, he chooses the sentence "Mr Knott turned the corner and saw his seat," which would suggest to a seasoned reader of Beckett that the voices coming out of the dark are, as he explained in *Proust*[8] of the narrator's hearing his grandmother's voice in a telephone, the voices "of his lost self," or past self. We need hardly speculate further when Beckett then writes:

> Whenever the lame hexameter occurred however mangled and he happened to be heeding at the time it seemed to him he had heard it somewhere before, and most likely in the course of some previous incarnation to judge by his experience of the current now coming to a close. As much might be said of other fragments and shall if time permits. . . . Be said of how spoken and misspoken and of how eerily familiar.[9]

As much, albeit in less explicit form, *was* said in the published version of the text, in the allusions I have already pointed to. Although this fragment was not in the event published, the faintness and uncertain provenance of sounds and the mysterious way in which the narrator perceives himself as moving from place to place, all referred to in the published version, probably have their origin in this second manuscript fragment.[10] They certainly bear a close relation to it. The manuscript exists in several drafts, some written and some typed. In the above-quoted paragraph, Beckett experiments with using the terms "previous existence" and "previous life" before arriving at the term "previous incarnation." This supports the case that Beckett was not merely thinking of a purely literary self-incarnation.

The question might be raised as to why Beckett more or less hid the esoteric discourse in the published version, having gone deeper into it in manuscript. A possible answer is that to publish a direct reference might have seemed absurd in view of the strong prejudice against reincarnation held by twentieth-century Western thought, certainly by Beckett's generation. But a coded reference, in the manner of the published version's opening paragraph, does not expose Beckett to attack, yet still makes itself apparent to those readers "with eyes to see and ears to hear."

The same, precisely, goes for the references to Buddhism, which while not being direct, are wholly congruent with the universal perspective common to mystical thinking in Buddhism, Hinduism, Taoism, Sufism, Rosicrucianism, and the like. *Stirrings Still* reiterates the view of existence taken by these traditions. The cycle of life in this world is indicated by the clock (linear time); the cries and strokes (greed, cruelty, suffering); the head on the hands, and walking, and "confinement" (space-time conditions, relativity); and most important of all, the "self so-called," which precisely encodes the illusion of identity which the ego builds for itself and which all mystical schools seek to dissolve. And in a like manner the indices of the spiritual world are given, in the "light unlike any he could remember"; in the reference to "the one true end to time and grief and self"; and in the last section of the work, which speculates on the existence of a place beyond the round of incarnation in the world, in Beckett's formidably lapidary phrase, a place "where never till then," where one has never been until one arrives at it, where, logically, a previous incarnation could not have happened. And significantly, Beckett sees this place as a place without qualities, beyond adjectives, a place without conditions, therefore absolute and of the other world, not relative and of this one:

> from deep within oh how and here a word he could not catch it were to end where never till then
>
> from deep within oh how and here that missing word again it were to end where never till then (p. 126)

Why "a missing word" "he could not catch"? Arguably because the Unconditioned has no words: a word would *locate* the place the narrator longs for, locate the unlocated, "eff the ineffable," as Beckett once put it.[11]

Longing for this place, and longing, if end one must, to end there, is the only legitimate desire for the old narrator, contemplating his death and the sojourn in a spiritual interworld soon to come upon him. Desire for anything else only leads one back into incarnation again. Thus the second section of *Stirrings Still* is a litany on the vanity of human wishes and the futility of "seeking help" from the memories, wishes, and rationalizations of life in the world, what Beckett calls, in very Johnsonian idiom, "vainly delving" (p. 124). Sense perception, too, that cornerstone of the positivist and materialist philosopher, the "table" being "clung to" in the first part of *Stirrings Still,* is dismissed: being "all eyes" or "all ears" or "looking closer" only "makes matters worse," availing nothing. The one true solution, as Beckett hinted long ago in *Proust,* is "not in the satisfaction, but in the ablation, of desire."[12] As he put it in *How It Is:*

> an oriental my dream he has renounced I too will renounce I will have no more desires[13]

and as he puts it in *Stirrings Still:*

> Unknowing and what is more no wish to know nor indeed any wish of any kind nor therefore any sorrow save that he would have wished the strokes to cease and the cries for good and was sorry that they did not. (p. 125)

Here again appear two veiled references—one to *The Cloud of Unknowing,* one of the key mystical texts, the other to the one pure emotion allowed to the Buddhist: compassion. At the beginning of Beckett's writing career, in his story "Dante and the Lobster," in *More Pricks Than Kicks* (1934), compassion was the only emotion to escape the knives of his irony and depreciation: Belacqua, having been enjoined to reread Dante's "movements of compassion in Hell," is transfixed, as is the reader of the story, by the final event in it—the dropping of a live lobster into boiling water. The pervasive emphasis on compassion in all Beckett's subsequent work, often to the virtual exclusion of the other emotions, invites the conclusion that Beckett was influenced by Buddhism, almost certainly via Schopenhauer.[14] In *How It Is* "an oriental" sitting "under a bo" tree is mentioned in two passages, and is almost certainly to be associated with Gautama Buddha.

Perhaps the most memorable thing to emerge from a study of the *Stirrings Still* papers and the published text is the unprecedented way in which Beckett finds it possible to reconcile the post-Structuralist and the mystic in his portrayal of the self. The work of Gaston Bachelard is probably the only precedent for such a reconcilement. At first glance, the post-Structural theory of identity, with its principles of "the construction/constructedness of self" and its rejection of metaphysical planes, would seem to be the adversary of the Buddhist or esoteric view. But as far as the self is concerned, the mystic takes the same view as the post-Structural theorist: the self as perceived is "false personality," a deceptive construction on which we would do well not to rely. This has always been Beckett's message, but in *Stirrings Still* it has a much more obviously metaphysical context than it had in many earlier works.

Yeats attempted to forecast some of the trends which might affect the future of literature and culture in an essay called "The Autumn of the Body,"[15] written eight years before Beckett's birth. Contrasting the "old" and "new" Romanticism, Yeats mentions the protagonists typical of the new Romanticism as "persons from whom has fallen all even of personal characteristic except a thirst for that hour when all things shall pass away like a cloud." These words, which Yeats himself seems to borrow from prophetic tradition, are apt to describe the kind of consciousness evident in the narrator of *Stirrings Still.* Yeats later avers, repeating four times a word which Beckett is to use often in his late work and very often in *Stirrings Still,*

> I see . . . in the arts of every country those faint lights and faint colours and faint outlines and faint energies which many call "the decadence" and which I, because I believe that the arts lie dreaming of things to come, prefer to call the autumn of the body. (p. 40)

Yeats, of course, meant the nineteenth-century decadence. But the twentieth century has seen another possibly comparable decadence, that of Romanticism and Modernism into post-Modern cynicism and nihilism. The faintness, weariness, and sense of loss of bodily vitality which Yeats pointed to are all characteristic of Beckett's portrait of our own fin de siècle; and Yeats's further comments are again relevant to what Beckett saw as perhaps the "one true end to time and grief and self so-called": "such silence since the cries were heard that perhaps even they would not be heard again." Both these evocative sentences refer not only to the close of a stage in a person's life but also to the end of the world we know; and both of them suggest it is possibly the only way for us to go. Yeats put it like this:

> Man has wooed and won the world, and has fallen weary, and not, I think, for a time, but with *a weariness that will not end until the last autumn, when the stars shall be blown away* like withered leaves. He grew weary when he said, "These things that I touch and see and hear are alone real", for he saw them without illusion at last, and found them but air and dust and moisture. And now he must be philosophical about everything, even about the arts, for he can only return the way he came, and so escape from weariness, by philosophy.[16]

And for the protagonist of *Stirrings Still,* even philosophy is not enough to allay the weariness of "vainly delving": he has been a thinker, as is made obvious by the phrase "even such a one as he" in the final section (p. 127); and it is his thinking which has blinded him to the "true end," to the truth of the matter, which is that he has been, all along, in the place "where never till then," the place of union with the Unconditioned source of all existence. *Re-cognizing* one's essential union with the source is a quite different matter from a supposed *discovery of* a source. And philosophy is not an exclusive means to that re-cognition: the final lines of *Stirrings Still* dismiss it as chaos, a "hubbub of the mind."

So man's mastery of the physical world in the scientific revolution, a mastery reflecting itself in positivism and materialism, is equivalent to the assertion of egoistic personality, to the pursuit of desire, to the strokes and cries, at least in the eyes of Yeats and of Beckett's narrator in *Stirrings Still.* The latter is disenchanted with material reality, sick of the world as we know it, to the point of not even wishing to reincarnate on earth, should such a choice exist. No one could deny that he is like Yeats's man, weary, with a weariness that will not end until this world ends, until we realize we are in a place "where never till then." The individual weariness, as we have seen, is echoed in the general weariness of a culture which Yeats alludes to. Speaking of "cultures in their terminal phase," George Steiner also refers, in *In Bluebeard's Castle,* to a "phenomenology of ennui" and "longing for dissolution" as a "possible constant in the history of social and intellectual forms once they have passed a certain threshold of complication."[17]

As the ego crumbles for the post-Structuralist mind, so does it also for the initiate:

> One never says "I" but one can say "me". But if the student has reached the point of real knowledge, has come into the realisation of Reality, he will not even say "me", because in his gnosis he will know there is no-one to say it and there is no-one to say it to. This is the state of complete annihilation of the self, annihilation meaning not a loss of the Self, but an absolute dissolution of identity in favour of the identity of Ipseity.[18]

Beckett's last paragraph of *Stirrings Still* is an attempt to indicate such a gnosis as Bulent Rauf draws attention to here. It is indeed "an end to time and grief and self so-called" when one finds "there is no-one to say it (I, me) and no-one to say it to," and this is precisely why Beckett's "voice from deep within" does not say "I" or "me" in relation to its longing, but simply "oh" and then lacks an adjective to qualify what it would be like to "end where never till then." Adjectives are too near to identities, and the only identity involved in gnosis is the identity of the Unqualified: the "one true end."

Conclusion

Our "understanding," our science and idealism have produced in people the same strange frenzy of self-repulsion as if they saw their own skulls each time they looked in the mirror. A man is a thing of scientific cause-and-effect and biological process, draped in an ideal, is he? No wonder he sees the skeleton grinning through the flesh.

—D. H. Lawrence, *Fantasia of the Unconscious*

Eine Wortstürmerei, im Namen der Schönheit [Storm(ing) of words in the name of beauty]

—Beckett to Axel Kaun, *Disjecta*

Beckett's fiction has the effect first of symbolizing, then of disarming, the world picture inherited by modern culture and science from Rationalism. This effect invites in the reader a change of consciousness which Heidegger calls a "surrender of previous thinking to the determination of the matter for thinking."[1]

In the move from empirical knowledge toward imaginative knowledge during the course of Beckett's prose we find that, as the move progresses, the artistic means of treating problems of knowledge become closer and closer to the agencies of knowledge itself.

This fact accounts for the extraordinary inclusiveness of Beckett's art. Problems of knowledge, if faced as directly as possible, involve not only a search for solutions to abstract problems but also a search for the truth about the knower, the human being who takes the trouble to ask all the questions in the first place. Beckett's prose narrator is led, inevitably, from the empirical problems of subject/object relations and some of their consequences (*Murphy, Watt,* the novellas and the trilogy) into an investigation of individual destiny (*How It Is*). This investigation compulsively involves a simultaneous address to the matter of imaginative activity. Beckett seems to be saying that it is only with the faculty by which man can truly imagine that he can also find who he potentially is and become that person. And side by side with the ability to perceive the truth about himself, the knower has to develop the strength of will—not to be confused with willful strength—to remain faithful to that higher aspect of the self which makes a life into a biography instead of a mere aggregation of events. Beckett's later prose demonstrates, rather as Blake's prophecies did two centuries ago, some of the reasons why spiritual activity or imaginative perception is necessary to human development, individually and collectively. It has been intimated earlier, but now becomes clear, that an impoverished theory of knowledge—narrowly empirical, fancy without imagination—makes imagination impossible; or, if it does not kill imagination altogether, still it cripples the human's potential to live and act according to what imagination teaches him about why he is here.

This move from empirical knowledge to imaginative knowledge is not only to be understood as a progress, but also as a completion or continuation of an evolution of consciousness in which Rationalism and its legacy may be merely an aberrant interval. The Arabic scholar Titus Burckhardt takes issue with much the same world picture that Blake insisted was misrepresenting a reality that has been known for centuries:

> A science based on quantitative analysis, which "thinks through actions or acts through concepts" (rather than seeing and experiencing integrally and directly), must of necessity be blind to the infinitely fruitful and many-sided essences of things. For such a science, what the ancients call the "form" of a thing (i.e., its qualitative content), plays virtually no role. This is the reason why science and art, which in the pre-rationalistic age were more or less synonymous, are now completely divorced from one another, and also why beauty, for modern science, offers not the smallest avenue towards knowledge.[2]

Wordsworth, rather like Goethe, looked to a future which might see a possible healing of the divorce without the loss of beauty:

> If the labours of science should ever create any material revolution, direct or indirect, in our condition, and in the impressions which we habitually receive, the poet will sleep then no more than at present, but he will be ready to follow the steps of the man of science, not only in those general indirect effects, but he will be at his side, carrying sensation into the midst of the objects of science itself . . . the poet will lend his divine spirit to aid the transfiguration, and will welcome the being thus produced.[3]

For Shelley, even that divorce itself could be no more than an illusion. He establishes the reciprocity of

> reason and imagination. . . . the former may be considered as mind contemplating the relations borne by one thought to another, however produced, and the latter, as mind acting upon those thoughts so as to colour them, as from elements, other thoughts, each containing within itself the principle of its own integrity. . . . Reason is the enumeration of qualities already known; imagination is the perception of the value of those quantities, both separately and as a whole. Reason respects the differences, imagination the similitudes of things. Reason is to imagination as the instrument to the agent, as the body to the spirit, as the shadow to the substance.[4]

Imagination, relegated by the scientific age to secondary status, is precisely the faculty which can perceive "the fruitful and many-sided essences of things"; the imagination which Coleridge called "the living power and prime agent of all human perception . . . essentially *vital*" and D. H. Lawrence "the living principle."

Beckett—notwithstanding or perhaps reacting against his close contact with empirical rationalism—always agreed: "The only reality," he said in *Proust* (1931), "is provided by the hieroglyphics traced by inspired perception. The conclusions of the intelligence are merely of arbitrary value, potentially valid" (p. 84). Beauty, if it is present in inspired perception, is certainly an avenue toward knowledge for Beckett. It has become an artistic possibility in his later works, whereas in *Proust* it was still a theory, and lacked a distinction between higher and lower self. And such a vindication of inspired perception has come only after the most thorough and courageous exhaustion of the materialistic world picture that any author this century has performed.

Jonathan Culler and others have seen poetic language and other forms of consciously composed language as exploring and subverting certain "grammars" of discourse. Beckett, as we have seen in the first two chapters, is very good at subverting those grammars whose status is dubious because they derive from dead conventions and authoritarian ideologies. But the conviction of the Marxist schools that good art is subversive* is a confining frame of reference within which to read Beckett. This is not to deny the humanly necessary subversive functions of art, but to add that there are some "grammars" which, far from perpetuating a deceptive or destructive status quo, are the very faculties by which a more inclusive meaning for reality can be contacted and experienced. If these grammars, the "hieroglyphics of inspired percep-

*A good example in recent Beckett commentary is Kateryna Arthur's "Texts for Company," in Acheson and Arthur, *Beckett's Later Fiction and Drama,* p. 136.

tion," were really subverted (as Enoch Brater claims they are)[5] by a work such as *Worstward Ho,* the hellish one-eyed stare would destroy its witness completely, and its fancy's obsessive game would prevent the reader from taking that destruction seriously, or, at worst, might prevent him even from seeing it. The sting in the tail of that mocking and acutely rhetorical work is that if the grammar of imagination is subverted by the mechanisms of fancy or materialism, the fountain of inspiration will dry up, or be swamped in mud and ooze, and become perceptible only by the pain of its absence. It is highly significant that Beckett's last writings are wholly concerned with the "grammar" of imagination. Like the *Still* trilogy, *Old Earth, Company, Ill Seen Ill Said,* and the "uncancellable" elements in *Worstward Ho, Stirrings Still* also pledges itself to Romanticism. But, far from representing and endorsing what Dobrez calls "a modern Romanticism pledged to defeat,[6] they issue a challenge to it.

If Nicholas Zurburgg is right to say that the Modernist period of 1885–1935 was prevailingly optimistic,[7] Beckett's occupation of the Modernist stage of culture has not been blindly optimistic, any more than his domination of the post-Modern "scene" has been the dour affair the critics have supposed. "Make it new," said Pound, justifying with a hint of brashness Zurbrugg's view of the Modernists. Beckett has said very little to the post-Modernist audience, but the ever less that he has said suggests more and more the brevity of hieroglyphics, and also a sense of inspired perception of reality such as Blake envisioned. That Beckett, on the heels of Pound, should twice use "hieroglyphics"[8] in connection with imaginative writing suggests that the ancient source is as important to him as the new. In rediscovering an inspired perception, he has overcome the debilitating narrowness of Rationalism whilst keeping its virtues of clarity, always evident in his style. A naturally philosophic writer such as Beckett was at home in the self-reflexive literary world of this century: he can write a good novel and in it ask what it is for and who is writing it. But he did not have the smallness of many rational introspectives. He rather asks with Heidegger: "Is the manifest character of what *is* exhausted by what is demonstrable? Doesn't the insistence on what is demonstrable block the way to what is?"[9]

Appendix: Beckett's Blake Riddle

The publication in 1972 of a limited edition of a portion of *The Lost Ones* under the title *The North,* with etchings by Avigdor Arikha, is probably the most extraordinary example of Beckett's recondite tributes to William Blake; consequently also a strong piece of evidence for Beckett's interest in a higher knowledge related to imagination as understood by the Romantics and outlined in this book.

The first clue is that this extract from *The Lost Ones,* the paragraphs centering on the redheaded woman described as "the North," was published by the Enitharmon Press. Following up this name in S. Foster Damon's *A Blake Dictionary* (to which Beckett could have had access by 1966, when *The Lost Ones* was in progress) we find references like these:

> Los . . . His position in the North . . . his emanation is Enitharmon. Los is Poetry, the expression in this world of the creative imagination. (p. 246)

> ENITHARMON is Spiritual Beauty, the twin, consort and inspiration of the poet Los . . . her emblem is the moon, her oustanding emotion is pity. [She is one of the] Emanations of the Zoas, . . . Their position is the North, for they were originally one as the Zoa Urthona. . . . By herself, Enitharmon is "the eternal Female", . . . the Great Mother. She is the moon of love to Los's sun. (p. 124)

She appears as "vanquished" in Beckett's text because she is cut off from the light of the sun (in Blake, Los; in Beckett, imagination), thus also cut off from creativity, in a prison cylinder of "fixities and definites."

If this were not sufficient evidence, the Enitharmon Press's logo (fig. 1) and Beckett's title *The North* reflect one another unambiguously, almost as if the Press were devised for the occasion, not the occasion for the Press. The presentation of the text—in a small circulation on handmade paper, with Arikha's drawings of a female

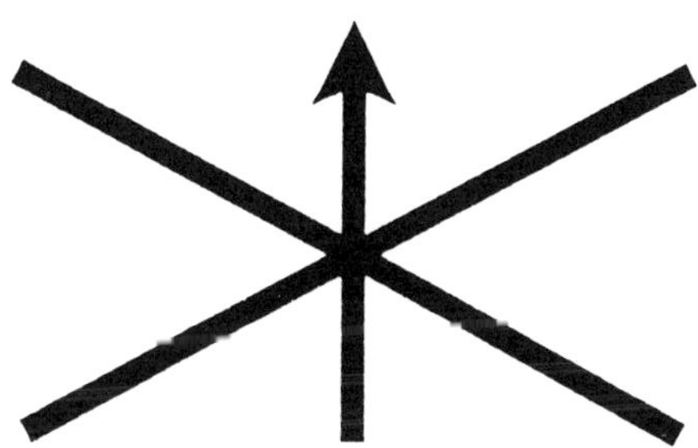

Figure 1.

figure we can only take to be Enitharmon—resembles so closely Blake's own method of presenting his poems and prophecies that the link between them comes to seem less and less fortuitous and more and more intentional.

And if we return to the *Blake Dictionary* and look under NORTH we find

> The NORTH symbolizes the Imagination. As the North is the place of spiritual warfare, war on earth is the result of the perverted imagination. When Enitharmon suppresses sex, it is reduced to the erotic dream in the North, where it is transmuted into war. (p. 301)

The *Dictionary* illustrates this aspect of Blake's vision—the suppression of sex—with virtually the same symbol as the Press's logo (see Fig. 2). Beckett readers may wish to compare the eventuality described by this diagram, and in Blake's poem "Europe," with the perverted imagination of sexuality in *All Strange Away* (*CSP*, pp. 119–120): the erotic dream, rather than the reality?

On the subject of "suppressed" sex energy and its connection with war, P. D. Ouspensky records from a conversation with Gurdjieff that

> The energy of the sex center in the work of the thinking, emotional and moving centers can be recognised by . . . a vehemence which the nature of the affair concerned does not call for . . . The emotional center preaches Christianity, abstinence, asceticism, or the fear and horror of sin, hell, the torment of sinners, eternal fire, all this with the energy of the sex center . . . Or on the other hand it works up revolu-

THE REPRESSION OF SEX UNDER ENITHARMON

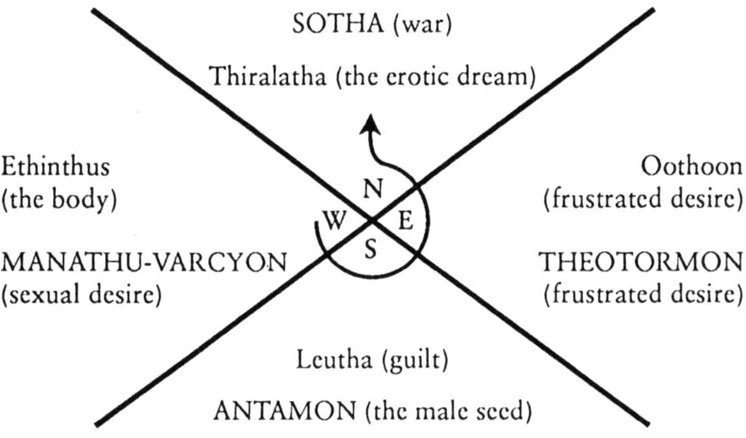

The movement is counterclockwise. Males are indicated by capital letters. When the sexual impulse is reduced to a mere dream (Thiralatha), the male (SOTHA) takes precedence again and explodes into war. (Eur. 13:9 - 14:28)

Figure 2.

> tions, robs, burns, kills, again with the same energy . . . This is an example of 'the abuse of sex'.[1]

This bears sustained comparison with Foster Damon's Blake diagram reproduced above, even to Damon's identification of Enitharmon's "suppression" with the "error of official Christianity . . . a false religion of chastity and vengeance."[2]

The conclusion of *The Lost Ones* is the last part of this esoteric riddle. One of the searchers dares to look into the eyes of the North woman, and it is at that point that the inferno of the dead or denied imagination gives place to inspiration and intuition. This event is foreshadowed by the well-known anecdote of Blake's and Catherine's engagement: *Blake:* Do you pity me? *Catherine:* Yes, indeed I do. *Blake:* Then I love you.[3] The *Dictionary* identifies Enitharmon not only as the embodiment of pity, but also as a being modelled on Blake's wife.

Notes

All books and articles referred to here are detailed fully in the bibliography.

Introduction. What Is Man? The Search for Reality

1. "The Voice," RUL MS. 2910, p. 4.
2. *U,* p. 87.
3. *CSP,* p. 135.
4. See *Company,* p. 15; *CSP,* pp. 195, 197.
5. See my essay, "Three Novels and Four *Nouvelles:* Giving Up the Ghost Be Born at Last," in John Pilling, ed., *The Cambridge Beckett Companion* (1994), chap. 3.
6. Guirdham, *Man: Divine or Social,* chapters 3 and 8.
7. *CSP,* p. 36.
8. *CSP,* pp. 195, 197.
9. See Jung, *The Spirit in Man, Art and Literature,* chap. 4, and passim.
10. See McMillan, *transition, 1927–1938: The History of a Literary Era,* chap. 4.
11. Beckett, English translation of a French quatrain entitled "Là"; and "Samuel Beckett on the Word: From a Conversation with Suheil Bushrui," *Temenos* 11 (1990): pp. 85–87.
12. Alvarez, *Beckett.*
13. *Watt,* p. 239.
14. Guirdham, *Man: Divine or Social,* p. 17.
15. Greenwood, "Literature and Philosophy," *Essays in Criticism* 20 (1978): p. 11.
16. Coleridge, *Miscellanies, Aesthetic and Literary,* p. 162.
17. Hartman, *The Unremarkable Wordsworth,* p. xxviii.
18. Wittgenstein, *Culture and Value,* p. 24.
19. Heidegger, "The End of Philosophy and the Task of Thinking," in *Basic Writings,* p. 391.
20. See Thomas Mann, *Der Zauberberg,* chap. 5, "Forschungen."
21. *Proust and Three Dialogues,* p. 103.
22. *Watt,* p. 74.

Chapter 1. Trusty Things? (*More Pricks Than Kicks, Murphy, Nouvelles*)

1. *First Love, CSP,* p. 13.
2. William Hazlitt, "Merry England," in *Sketches and Essays,* p. 44.
3. *Company,* p. 7.

4. *Watt,* p. 137.
5. *Proust,* p. 24 and passim.
6. *The End,* in *CSP,* p. 66.
7. *Proust,* p. 63.
8. *Murphy,* p. 57.
9. *Watt,* p. 115.
10. *Proust,* p. 23.
11. Ricks, *The Force of Poetry,* p. 369.
12. Keats, *Poetical Works,* p. 208.
13. Interview in *Rolling Stone,* January 1978.
14. *First Love,* in *CSP,* p. 6.
15. See Connor, *Samuel Beckett,* p. 49.
16. Barfield, *Romanticism Comes of Age,* p. 74.

Chapter 2. Laughing at the Referent (*Watt, Mercier and Camier*)

1. Wittgenstein, *Culture and Value,* p. 26.
2. *Watt,* p. 19.
3. *The End,* in *CSP,* p. 54.
4. *Watt,* p. 149.
5. Joyce, *Ulysses* 2:779–81.
6. *Mercier and Camier,* p. 19.
7. Quoted in Heller, *The Ironic German,* p. 214.
8. Barfield, *Romanticism Comes of Age,* p. 74.

Chapter 3. Lies in the Trilogy (*Molloy, Malone Dies, The Unnamable*)

1. Coleridge, *Biographia Literaria,* chap. XIV, p. 161.
2. Plato, *Republic,* chap. 3 and 10.
3. *M,* p. 10.
4. *U,* p. 20.
5. *Proust,* p. 76.
6. *U,* p. 85.
7. Ibid., p. 15.
8. See J. L. Austin, *How to Do Things with Words,* pp. 91, 98–132, 144–51; Eagleton, *Literary Theory: An Introduction,* chap. 3.
9. Bair, *Samuel Beckett,* pp. 135–36.
10. *Watt,* p. 92.
11. Guirdham, *Man: Divine or Social,* p. 144.
12. *M,* p. 89; *The End,* in *CSP,* p. 50.
13. *M,* p. 86.
14. *U,* p. 16.
15. *The End,* in *CSP,* p. 54.
16. Bair, *Samuel Beckett,* p. 327.
17. *Watt,* pp. 29, 224.
18. *MD,* p. 22.
19. Ibid., p. 94.

20. Quoted in Bok, *Lying,* p. 22.
21. See ibid., chap. 6, "Justification."
22. *M,* p. 36.
23. Weil, *Waiting for God,* p. 172.
24. *M,* p. 33.
25. Barfield, *Romanticism Comes of Age,* pp. 213–15.
26. Ibid, p. 73.
27. Ibid, p. 72, italics mine.
28. William Blake, preface to *Milton,* in *Complete Writings,* p. 481.

Chapter 4. The You That Is Not You (*How It Is*)

1. F. S. Hoffman, "The Elusive Ego," in Friedman, *Samuel Beckett Now,* pp. 55, 58.
2. *MD,* p. 46.
3. Kenner, *Samuel Beckett,* p. 189.
4. E.g., Alvarez, *Beckett,* p. 189.
5. *How It Is,* pp. 28, 29, 82.
6. Ibid., p. 25.
7. *U,* pp. 19, 113.
8. Bair, *Samuel Beckett,* pp. 512–15, 526.
9. *How It Is,* pp. 42, 112.
10. Barfield, *Poetic Diction,* p. 72.
11. *M,* pp. 51–52.
12. *MD,* p. 39 (my italics).
13. Mercier, *Beckett/Beckett,* p. 64.
14. Frederik N. Smith, "A Land of Sanctuary: Allusions to the Pastoral in Beckett's Fiction," in, *Beckett Translating/Translating Beckett,* p. 128.
15. Baldwin, *Samuel Beckett's Real Silence,* p. 154.
16. *How It Is,* p. 68 (my italics).
17. Barfield, *Romanticism Comes of Age,* pp. 70–71.
18. Samuel Beckett, "Dante . . . Bruno. Vico . . . Joyce" in *Our Exagmination Round his Factification for Incamination of Work in Progress,* p. 18.
19. Smith, "Land of Sanctuary," p. 135.
20. Baldwin, *Samuel Beckett's Real Silence,* p. 159.
21. Fletcher, *The Novels of Samuel Beckett,* p. 175.
22. Wordsworth, *The Prelude* 12.1.286.
23. Wordsworth and Coleridge, *Lyrical Ballads,* p. xxviii, quoted in Friedman, Rossman, and Sherzer, *Beckett Translating/Translating Beckett,* p. 124.
24. *The End,* in *CSP,* p. 69; *Cascando,* in *Collected Shorter Plays,* p. 141.
25. Jakob Böhme, *Six Theosophic Points and Other Writings,* p. 139.
26. Barnard, *Samuel Beckett: A New Approach,* pp. 70, 78.
27. Coleridge, "On the Principles of Sound Criticism," *Miscellanies, Aesthetic and Literary,* p. 34.
28. Novalis, *Hymnen an die Nacht,* p. 148 (my translation).
29. John Pilling, "*How It Is*" in Knowlson and Pilling, *Frescoes of the Skull* p. 70.
30. Novalis, *Hymnen an die Nacht,* p. 148 (my translation).
31. *The Calmative,* in *CSP,* p. 42.
32. Santomasso, *Origins and Aims of German Expressionist Architecture,* p. 263.

33. In Raine, *William Blake,* pp. 55, 81.
34. Barfield, *Romanticism Comes of Age,* p. 120–21.
35. Ibid, p. 129.
36. Wordsworth, preface to *Lyrical Ballads* (edition of 1802); reprinted in *Penguin Critical Anthologies: Wordsworth,* p. 50.

Chapter 5. Fancy and Imagination in the Rotunda (*All Strange Away*)

1. Shelley, *Essays and Letters,* p. 72.
2. Cohn, *Back to Beckett,* p. 256.
3. Lake, *No Symbols Where None Intended,* p. 119.
4. Barbara Hardy, "The Dubious Consolations in Beckett's Fiction: art, Love and nature", in Worth, *Beckett the Shape Changer,* p. 112.
5. Brian Finney, "*Assumption* to *Lessness:* Beckett's Shorter Fiction," in Worth, *Beckett the Shape Changer,* p. 81.
6. Pilling, "The Significance of *Still,*" p. 143.
7. Samuel Johnson, *Rasselas,* chap. 44.
8. See Al Ghazzali, *Mysteries of the Human Soul,* pp. 54–55.
9. William Hazlitt, "On Poetry in General," in *Lectures on the English Poets*, p. 1.
10. Barfield, *What Coleridge Thought,* pp. 711, 82.
11. Murphy, "The Nature of Art and Love in *Enough,*" p. 102.
12. Barfield, *What Coleridge Thought,* p. 83; and Coleridge, *Biographia Literaria,* chap. 1.
13. *Proust,* p. 33.
14. Coleridge, *Table Talk,* p. 232.
15. Barfield, *What Coleridge Thought,* p. 87 (my italics).
16. Beckett, "Dante . . . Bruno. Vico . . Joyce," *Disjecta,* p. 19.
17. *Disjecta,* p. 30.
18. Barfield, *What Coleridge Thought,* p. 89.

Chapter 6. Exits for Amateurs of Myth (*Imagination Dead Imagine, The Lost Ones, Lessness, For to End Yet Again*)

1. Heidegger, "The Origin of the Work of Art," in *Basic Writings,* pp. 176–83.
2. Cohn, *Back to Beckett,* p. 250.
3. Blake, *The Marriage of Heaven and Hell,* in *Complete Writings,* p. 154.
4. See Capra, *The Tao of Physics,* chaps. 1–4.
5. Blake, "Auguries of Innocence," in *Complete Writings,* p. 433.
6. Barfield, *What Coleridge Thought,* p. 83.
7. See Nicolas Berdyaev, "Unground and Freedom," introduction to Böhme, *Six Theosophic Points and Other Writings,* p. xix.
8. *M,* p. 68.
9. Cohn, *Back to Beckett,* p. 265.
10. *Imagination Dead Imagine,* in *CSP,* p. 146.

11. Shelley, *Complete Poetical Works* 2:320, my italics.
12. *For to End Yet Again,* in *CSP,* p. 181.

Chapter 7. Imagination Living (*From an Abandoned Work, Enough, Still, Sounds, Still 3, Old Earth*)

1. "*Assumption* to *Lessness:* Beckett's Shorter Fiction," in Worth, *Beckett the Shape Changer,* pp. 76–77.
2. Eliot, "Tradition and the Individual Talent," in *The Sacred Wood,* p. 48.
3. Enoch Brater, "Voyelles, Cromlechs and the Special (W)rites of *Worstward Ho*" in Acheson and Arthur, *Beckett's Later Fiction and Drama,* p. 160.
4. *The End,* in *CSP,* p. 61.
5. *M,* p. 67.
6. Ibid., p. 144.
7. *CSP,* p. 150.
8. William Blake, "Annotations to Wordsworth's Poems," *Complete Writings,* p. 783.
9. See Corbin, "Mundus Imaginalis, or the Imaginary and the Imaginal," pp. 1–19.
10. *Disjecta,* p. 24.
11. *The Rambler* 26, no. 168 (October 1751).
12. E.g., Finney, "*Assumption* to *Lessness:* Beckett's Shorter Fiction" in Worth, *Beckett the Shape Changer,* p. 78.
13. Beckett, *Sounds* and *Still 3* in *Essays in Criticism* 28, no. 2 (1978): p. 156; *Still* in *CSP,* p. 183.
14. *CSP,* p. 183.
15. Brienza, *Samuel Beckett's New Worlds,* p. 201.
16. *Murphy,* p. 108.
17. Blake, preface to *Milton,* in *Complete Writings,* p. 480.
18. *MD,* p. 20.
19. Johnson, *Rasselas,* chap. 44.
20. Otto Julius Bierbaum, "Traum durch die Dämmerung," Translation and original text (set by R. Strauss, op. 29, no. 1) to be found in Prawer, *The Penguin Book of Lieder,* p. 153.
21. *Ill Seen Ill Said,* p. 55.
22. Brienza, *Samuel Beckett's New Worlds,* pp. 201–2.

Chapter 8. The Imagination of Youth (*Company*)

1. E.g., David Read, "Beckett's Search for the Unseeable and Unmakeable: *Company* and *Ill Seen Ill Said*" and Frederik Smith, "Three on Beckett: An Essay Review," in the Beckett Issue of *Modern Fiction Studies* 29 (ed. S. E. Gontarski); Kateryna Arthur, "Texts For *Company*", Brian Finney, "*Still* to *Worstward Ho*: Beckett's Prose Fiction since *The Lost Ones*" and *S. E. Gontarski, "Company* For Company: Androgyny and Theatricality in Samuel Beckett's Prose" in Acheson and Arthur, *Beckett's Later Fiction and Drama*; and H. Porter Abbott, "Beckett and Autobiography", Linda Ben Zvi, "Phonetic Structure in Beckett: from Mag to Gnaw", and Brian Fitch, "The Relationship Between *Compagnie*

and *Company:* One Work, Two Texts, Two Fictive Universes," in Friedman, Rossman, and Sherzer, *Beckett Translating/Translating Beckett.*

2. Brienza, *Samuel Beckett's New Worlds,* p. 228.
3. John Pilling, "Ends and Odds in Prose," in Knowlson and Pilling, *Frescoes of the Skull,* p. 144.
4. Brienza, *Samuel Beckett's New Worlds,* p. 226.
5. RUL MS. 2910.
6. *Collected Shorter Plays of Samuel Beckett,* p. 267.
7. *Watt,* p. 81.
8. Blake, *The Marriage of Heaven and Hell,* in *Complete Writings,* p. 154.
9. *Ill Seen Ill Said,* p. 54.
10. Keats, "The Eve of St Agnes", *The Complete Poems,* p. 313.
11. *Old Earth,* in *CSP,* p. 201.
12. *The Lost Ones,* in *CSP,* p. 164.
13. *Ode on Intimations of Immortality,* in *Poems of Wordsworth,* p. 195.
14. Barfield, *Romanticism Comes of Age,* p. 79.
15. *How It Is,* p. 112.

Chapter 9. Cleansing the Doors of Perception (*Ill Seen Ill Said*)

1. James Hansford, *Skullscapes: Imaginative Strategies in the Late Prose of Samuel Beckett.*
2. Nicholas Zurbrugg, "*Ill Seen and Ill Said* and the Sense of an Ending" in Acheson and Arthur (eds), *Beckett's Later Fiction and Drama,* p. 152.
3. Brienza, *Samuel Beckett's New Worlds,* p. 239.
4. Read, "Beckett's Search for the Unseeable and Unmakeable," p. 111.
5. Wordsworth, "Tintern Abbey," in *Poems of Wordsworth,* p. 243.
6. Robert Lax, quoted in Zurbrugg, "*Ill Seen Ill Said* and the Sense of an Ending", p. 152.
7. *M,* p. 49.
8. E.g., Knowlson, *Light and Darkness in the Theatre of Samuel Beckett.*
9. Brienza, *Samuel Beckett's New Worlds,* p. 238.
10. Heidegger, "The Origin of the Work of Art," in *Basic Writings,* pp. 143–88.
11. Goethe, *Maximen und Reflexionen,* no. 488 (my translation), in *Goethes Werke* 12:432.
12. Barfield, *Romanticism Comes of Age,* p. 36.
13. *Murphy,* p. 140.
14. *The Lost Ones,* in *CSP,* p. 159.
15. Barfield, *What Coleridge Thought,* chap. 2.
16. Heidegger, *Basic Writings,* p. 176.
17. Barfield, *Romanticism Comes of Age,* p. 79.
18. In *Poems of Wordsworth,* p. 145.
19. *M,* p. 52.
20. S. T. Coleridge, Lectures 1813, "On the Use of Fiction," *Miscellanies, Aesthetic and Literary,* p. 162.
21. Ibid.
22. Blake, *Jerusalem,* in *Complete Writings,* p. 661.
23. Blake, "Auguries of Innocence," in *Complete Writings,* p. 433.
24. See: Kateryna Arthur, "Texts for *Company*"; Brian Finney, "*Still* to

Worstward Ho: Beckett's Prose Fiction Since *The Lost Ones"; S. E. Gontarski, "*Company* for Company: Androgyny and Theatricality in Samuel Beckett's Prose" in Acheson and Arthur (eds.), *Beckett's Later Fiction and Drama;* Susan Brienza, *Samuel Beckett's New Worlds;* H. Porter Abbott, "Beckett and Autobiography", Linda Ben-Zvi, "Phonetic Structure in Beckett: From Mag to Gnaw"; Brian Fitch, "The Relationship Between *Compagnie* and *Company:* One Work, Two Texts, Two Fictive Universes"; Angela Moorjani, "The *Magna Mater* Myth in Beckett's Fiction: Subtext and Subversion", in Friedman, Rossman and Sherzer (eds.), *Beckett Translating/Translating Beckett;* John Pilling, "*Ill Seen Ill Said:* A Criticism of Indigence", in P. A. McCarthy (ed.), *Critical Essays on Samuel Beckett;* David Read, "Beckett's Search for the Unseeable and Unmakeable: *Company* and *Ill Seen Ill Said*" in *Modern Fiction Studies* 29 (1983).

Chapter 10. A Pox on Void (*Worstward Ho*)

1. Brienza, *Samuel Beckett's New Worlds,* pp. 254, 255.
2. *Ill Seen Ill Said,* p. 52.
3. Aristotle, *Nicomachean Ethics,* p. 100. See also par. 6 of Barnet's note to his 1900 edition, pp. 69–70.
4. Samuel Johnson, *The Rambler,* no. 168 (26 October 1751).
5. *Company,* p. 41.
6. "Dante . . . Bruno. Vico . . Joyce", p. 15.
7. Brienza, *Samuel Beckett's New Worlds,* p. 262.
8. E.g., *Company,* p. 19.
9. RUL MSS 2935–38.
10. Blake, *Complete Writings,* p. 154.

Chapter 11. Disembodying Western Tradition (*Stirrings Still*)

1. Blake, *Milton* 28.1.45; Réné Guénon, *The Reign of Quantity.*
2. RUL MSS 2935/1–2935/5.
3. *Guardian,* Friday 3 March 1989, p. 25.
4. See, for example, Baldwin, *Samuel Beckett's Real Silence;* Büttner, *Samuel Beckett's Novel "Watt";* Foster, *Beckett and Zen.*
5. *Collected Poems, 1930–1978,* p. 52.
6. Plato, *Republic,* book 10, passim.
7. *Watt,* p. 228.
8. *Proust,* p. 41.
9. RUL MS. 2935/2.
10. Only one of the manuscripts, no. 2935/2, p. 2, is dated: "June 87."
11. *Watt,* p. 61.
12. *Proust,* p. 18.
13. *How It Is,* p. 62.
14. See Pilling, *Samuel Beckett,* p. 133.
15. Yeats, *Selected Criticism,* pp. 38–42.
16. Ibid. (my italics).

17. Steiner, *In Bluebeard's Castle: Or, Some Notes towards the Redefinition of Culture,* p. 26.
18. Bulent Rauf, *Addresses,* p. 46.

Conclusion

1. Heidegger, "The End of Philosophy and the Task of Thinking," in *Basic Writings,* p. 392.
2. Burckhardt, *Alchemy,* p. 61.
3. Wordsworth, preface to *Lyrical Ballads,* (1802), in *Penguin Critical Anthologies: Wordsworth,* p. 51.
4. Shelley, *A Defence of Poetry,* in *Essays and Letters,* pp. 1–2.
5. Brater, "Voyelles, Cromlechs and the Special (W)rites of *Worstward Ho*" p. 160.
6. Dobrez, *The Existential and Its Exits,* p. 128.
7. Zurbrugg, "*Ill Seen Ill Said* and the Sense of an Ending," p. 145.
8. "Dante . . . Bruno. Vico . . Joyce", *Our Exagmination Round His Factification for Incamination of Work in Progress,* pp. 11, 15; *Proust,* p. 84.
9. Heidegger, in "The End of Philosophy and the Task of Thinking," in *Basic Writings,* p. 391.

Appendix: Beckett's Blake Riddle

1. P. D. Ouspensky, *In Search of the Miraculous: Fragments of an Unknown Teaching* (London: Routledge and Kegan Paul, 1950), p. 258.
2. S. Foster Damon, *A Blake Dictionary,* p. 125.
3. Mona Wilson, *The Life of William Blake* (London: Rupert Hart-Davis, 1948), p. 16.

Bibliography

Works by Samuel Beckett

As the Story Was Told. RUL MSS 1396/4/12–14, 3–8 August 1973.

As the Story Was Told: Uncollected and Late Prose, 1981–1989. London: John Calder, 1990.

Collected Poems, 1930–1978. London: John Calder, 1986.

Collected Shorter Plays of Samuel Beckett. London: Faber and Faber, 1984.

Compagnie. Paris: Les Editions de Minuit, 1985.

Company. London: John Calder, 1980.

Disjecta. London: John Calder, 1985.

Dream of Fair to Middling Women. RUL MS. 1227/7/16/8, 9, ca. 1932.

Dream of Fair to Middling Women. Dublin: The Black Cat Press, 1992.

How It Is. London: John Calder, 1964.

Ill Seen Ill Said. RUL MS. 2202–7, 1979–80.

Ill Seen Ill Said. London: John Calder, 1982.

Long Observation of the Ray. RUL MS. 2909, 20 October 1975–19 November 1976.

Malone Dies. Harmondsworth: Penguin Books, 1962.

Mercier and Camier. London: John Calder, 1974.

Mercier et Camier/Mercier et Camier. RUL MSS 1396/4/17–24, 6 May 1970–ca. 1974.

Molloy. London: Jupiter Books, 1966.

More Pricks Than Kicks. London: John Calder, 1970.

Murphy. London: John Calder, 1977.

Nohow On. London: John Calder, 1990.

"Sedendo et Quiesciendo". *transition* 21 (March 1932): 13–20.

"Sottisier/Mirlitonnades/Company". MS notebook, RUL MS. 2901, 1976–82.

Sounds. *Essays in Criticism* 28, no. 2 (1978): 156.

Still 3. *Essays in Criticism* 28 no. 2 (1978): 157.

"Stirrings Still: Fragments for Barney Rosset". RUL MSS 2935–38, 1984–87.

The Unnamable. London: John Calder, 1958.

Waiting for Godot. London: Faber and Faber, 1965.

Watt. London: John Calder, 1976.

Worstward Ho. London: John Calder, 1983.

With S. Dumesnil. "F-", *transition* 48 (January 1949): 19–21.

With G. Duthuit. *Proust and Three Dialogues with Georges Duthuit.* London: John Calder, 1965.

With Marcel Brion, Frank Budgen, Stuart Gilbert, Eugene Jolas, Victor Llana, Robert McAlmon, Thomas McGreevy, Elliot Paul, John Rodker, Robert Sage, and William Carlos Williams. *Our Exagmination Round His Factification for Incamination of Work in Progress.* London: Faber and Faber, 1961.

Works on Samuel Beckett

BOOKS

Acheson, J., and K. Arthur, eds. *Beckett's Later Fiction and Drama.* London and Basingstoke: Macmillan, 1987.

Admussen, R. L. *The Samuel Beckett Manuscripts: A Study.* Boston: G. K. Hall, 1978.

Alvarez, A. *Beckett.* London: Fontana, 1973.

Barnard, G. C. *Samuel Beckett: A New Approach.* London: Dent, 1970.

Bair, D. *Samuel Beckett: A Biography.* London: Jonathan Cape, 1979.

Baldwin, H. L. *Samuel Beckett's Real Silence.* University Park: Pennsylvania State University Press, 1981.

Brater, E., ed. *Beckett at 80/Beckett in Context.* New York: Oxford University Press, 1986.

Brienza, S. D. *Samuel Beckett's New Worlds.* Norman: University of Oklahoma Press, 1987.

Bryden, M., and J. Pilling, eds. *The Ideal Core of the Onion: Reading Beckett Archives.* Reading, England: Beckett International Foundation, 1992.

Butler, L. St. J. *Samuel Beckett and the Meaning of Being.* London: Macmillan, 1984.

Büttner, G. *Samuel Beckett's Novel "Watt."* Translated by J. Dolan. Philadelphia: University of Pennsylvania Press, 1984.

Coe, R. N. *Samuel Beckett.* New York: Grove Press, 1970.

Cohn, R. *Back to Beckett.* Princeton: Princeton University Press, 1973.

Connor, S. *Samuel Beckett: Repetition, Theory and Text.* Oxford: Basil Blackwell, 1988.

Cooke, V., ed. *Beckett on File.* London: Methuen, 1985.

Doll, M. A. *Beckett and Myth: An Archetypal Approach.* Syracuse, N.Y.: Syracuse University Press, 1988.

Federman, R., and J. Fletcher. *Samuel Beckett: His Works and His Critics. An Essay in Bibliography,* Berkeley, London, Los Angeles: University of California Press, 1970.

Fitch, B. T. *Beckett and Babel: An Investigation into the Status of the Bilingual Work.* Toronto, Buffalo, London: University of Toronto Press, 1988.

Fletcher, J. *The Novels of Samuel Beckett.* London: Chatto and Windus, 1964.

———. *Samuel Beckett's Art.* London: Chatto and Windus, 1967.

Foster, P. *Beckett and Zen.* London: Wisdom Publications, 1989.

Friedman, A. W., C. Rossman, and D. Sherzer, eds. *Beckett Translating/Translating Beckett.* University Park and London: Pennsylvania State University Press, 1987.

Friedman, M. J., ed. *Samuel Beckett Now.* Chicago and London: University of Chicago Press, 1970.

Gontarski, S. E., ed. *On Beckett: Essays and Criticism.* New York: Grove Press, 1986.

———. ed. *Modern Fiction Studies* (Beckett issue) 29 no. 1, (1983).

Hamilton, A., and K. Hamilton. *Condemned to Life: The World of Samuel Beckett.* Grand Rapids, Mich.: William B. Eerdmans, 1976.

Hansford, H. J. *Skullscapes: Imaginative Strategies in the Late Prose of Samuel Beckett.* Ph.D. thesis, Reading University, 1983.

Harvey, L. E. *Samuel Beckett: Poet and Critic.* Princeton: Princeton University Press, 1970.

Hesla, D. *The Shape of Chaos.* Minneapolis: University of Minnesota Press, 1971.

Hill, L. *Beckett's Fiction: In Different Words.* Cambridge: Cambridge University Press, 1990.

Jacobson, J., and W. R. Müller. *The Testament of Samuel Beckett.* London: Faber and Faber, 1966.

Kennedy, A. *Samuel Beckett.* Cambridge: Cambridge University Press, 1989.

Kenner, H. *Samuel Beckett.* Berkeley and Los Angeles: University of California Press, 1968.

Knowlson, J. *Light and Darkness in the Theatre of Samuel Beckett.* London: Turret Books, 1972.

Knowlson, J., and J. Pilling. *Frescoes of the Skull.* London: John Calder, 1979.

Lake, C. *No Symbols Where None Intended.* Austin: University of Texas Press, 1984.

Levy, E. P. *Beckett and the Voice of Species.* Totowa, N.J.: Gill and Macmillan, 1980.

Locatelli, C. *Unwording the World: Samuel Beckett's Prose Works after the Nobel Prize.* Philadelphia: University of Pennsylvania Press, 1990.

McCarthy, P. A., ed. *Critical Essays on Samuel Beckett.* Boston: G. K. Hall, 1986.

Mercier, V. *Beckett/Beckett.* New York: Oxford University Press, 1977.

Murphy, P. J. *Language and Being in the Prose Works of Samuel Beckett.* Ph.D. thesis, Reading University, 1979.

———. *Reconstructing Beckett.* Toronto, Buffalo, London: University of Toronto Press, 1990.

O'Brien, E. D. *The Beckett Country.* Dublin: Black Cat Press, 1986.

Pilling, J. *Samuel Beckett.* London and Henley: Routledge and Kegan Paul, 1976.

———. ed. *The Cambridge Beckett Companion.* Cambridge: Cambridge University Press, 1993.

Pilling, J., and J. Knowlson. *Frescoes of the Skull.* London: John Calder, 1979.

Reid, A. *All I Can Manage, More Than I Could.* Dublin: Dolmen Press, 1968.

Robinson, M. *The Long Sonata of the Dead.* London: Rupert Hart-Davis, 1969

Scott, N. A. *Samuel Beckett.* London: Bowes and Bowes, 1965.

Smith, J. H., ed. *The World of Samuel Beckett.* Baltimore and London: Johns Hopkins University Press, 1991.

Tseng, L. *The "Syntax of Weakness" in Samuel Beckett's Later Short Prose.* Master's Thesis, Reading University, 1987.

Watson, D. *Paradox and Desire in Samuel Beckett's Fiction.* London: Macmillan, 1990.

Worth, K., ed. *Beckett the Shape Changer.* London: Routledge and Kegan Paul, 1975.

Zurbrugg, N. *Beckett and Proust.* Gerard's Cross/Totowa, N.J.: Colin Smythe/Barnes and Noble Books, 1988.

ARTICLES AND ESSAYS

Auster, P. "A Note on Beckett's French." In *The Art of Hunger and Other Essays,* p. 50–55. London: Menard Press, 1982.

Bataille, G. "Review Article, *Molloy.*" In *Samuel Beckett, The Critical Heritage,* ed. L. Graver, and R. Federman, 55–64. London: Routledge and Kegan Paul, 1979.

Davies, P. "Twilight and Universal Vision: Samuel Beckett's *Ill Seen Ill Said.*" *Temenos* 11 (1990): 88–103.

Harvey, J. R. "La Vieille Voix Faible." *Cambridge Quarterly* 1, no. 4 (1966): 384–95.

Murphy, P. "The Nature and Art of Love in *Enough.*" *Journal of Beckett Studies* 4 (Spring 1979): 14–34.

———. "Review Article: *All Strange Away.*" *Journal of Beckett Studies* 5 (Autumn 1979): 99–113.

O'Brien, G. "On Not Writing about Samuel Beckett." *Cambridge Quarterly* 9, no. 3 (1980): 285–88.

Pilling, J. "A Criticism of Indigence: *Ill Seen Ill Said.*" In *Critical Essays on Samuel Beckett,* ed. P. A. McCarthy, 136–51. Boston: G. K. Hall, 1986.

———. "Nohow J. On: *Worstward Ho.*" In *Beckett at Eighty: A Celebration,* ed. J. Knowlson, The Beckett Archive, Reading, 1986, 25–26.

———. "The Significance of Beckett's *Still.*" *Essays in Criticism* 28, no. 2 (1978): 143–54.

Read, D. "In Search of the Unseeable and Unmakeable: *Company and Ill Seen Ill Said.*" *Modern Fiction Studies* 29, no. 1, (1983): 111–26.

Scruton, R. "Beckett and the Cartesian Soul." In *The Aesthetic Understanding,* 222–41. Manchester: Carcanet Press, 1983.

Solomon, P. "Purgatory Unpurged: Time, Space and Language in *Lessness.*" *Journal of Beckett Studies* 6 (Autumn 1980): 63–72.

General Works

Aristotle. Translated by J. A. K. Thompson. *Ethics.* Harmondsworth: Penguin, 1955.

———. *Nicomachean Ethics.* Edited by J. Burnet. London: Methuen, 1900.

Austin, J. L. *How To Do Things With Words.* Edited by J. O. Urmson and M. Sbisa. Oxford: Oxford University Press, 1975.

Barfield, O. *Poetic Diction.* London: Faber and Gwyer, 1928.

———. *Romanticism Comes of Age.* London: Rudolf Steiner Press, 1966.

———. *What Coleridge Thought.* London: Oxford University Press, 1971.

Blake, William. *Complete Writings.* Edited by G. Keynes. Oxford: Oxford University Press, 1966.

Böhme, J. Translated by J. R. Earle. *Six Theosophic Points and Other Writings.* Ann Arbor: University of Michigan Press, 1958.

Bok, S. *Lying: Moral Choice in Public and Private Life.* Brighton: Harvester Press, 1978.

Burckhardt, T. *Alchemy.* Shaftesbury: Element Books, 1986.

Butler, C. *After the Wake: An Essay on the Contemporary Avant-Garde.* Oxford: Oxford University Press, 1980.

Capra, F. *The Tao of Physics.* London: Collins, 1976.

Coleridge, S. T. *Aids to Reflection and An Essay on Faith.* London: George Bell, 1893.

———. *Biographia Literaria.* London: Dent, 1906.

———. *Miscellanies, Aesthetic and Literary.* London: George Bell, 1911.

———. *Table Talk.* Edited by H. Morley. London: George Routledge, 1884.

Coleridge, S. T., and K. Coburn. *Notebooks.* Vol. 1. New York: Pantheon, 1957.

Corbin, H. *Creative Imagination in the Sufism of Ibn Arabi.* Translated by R. Manheim. Princeton: Princeton University Press, 1969.

———. "Mundus Imaginalis, or the Imaginary and the Imaginal," in *Spring,* trans. R. Horine, 1–19. 1972. Reprint. Ipswich: Golgonooza Press, 1975.

Culler, J. *Structuralist Poetics: Structuralism, Linguistics and the Study of Literature.* Ithaca, N.Y.: Cornell University Press, 1975.

Damon, S. F. *A Blake Dictionary.* London: Thames and Hudson, 1965.

Dobrez, L. A. C. *The Existential and Its Exits.* London: Athlone Press, 1986.

Eagleton, T. *Literary Theory: An Introduction.* Oxford: Basil Blackwell, 1983.

Eliot, T. S. *The Sacred Wood: Essays on Poetry and Criticism.* London: Methuen, 1948.

Ellmann, R. *James Joyce: A Biography.* Oxford: Oxford University Press, 1959.

Ghazzali. *The Mysteries of the Human Soul.* Edited and translated by A. Q. Hazarvi. Lahore: Sh. Muhammad Ashraf, 1981.

Goethe, J. W. von. *Goethes Werke.* Edited by E. Trunz. 14 vols. München: Verlag CH Beck, 1978.

Guénon, R. *The Reign of Quantity and the Signs of the Times.* Translated by Lord Northbourne. London: Luzac & Co., 1953.

Guirdham, A. *Man: Divine or Social.* London: Vincent Stuart, 1960.

Hartman, G. H. *The Unremarkable Wordsworth.* Edited by D. G. Marshall. London: Methuen, 1987.

———. *Wordsworth's Poetry, 1787–1814.* New Haven and London: Yale University Press, 1964.

Hazlitt, W. *Sketches and Essays.* Oxford: World's Classics, 1907.

———. *"The Spirit of the Age" and "Lectures on the English Poets."* Dent: Everyman, 1910.

Heidegger, M. *Basic Writings.* Edited by D. Farrell Krell. London and Henley: Routledge and Kegan Paul, 1977.

———. *Existence and Being.* Translated by A. Crick, R. F. C. Hull, and D. Scott. Chicago: Regnery-Gateway, 1949.

Heller, E. *The Ironic German.* Cambridge: Cambridge University Press, 1980.

Johnson, S. *Rasselas and Other Tales.* Edited by G. J. Kolb. New Haven and London: Yale University Press, 1990.

———. *Ulysses.* Edited by H. W. Gabler, C. Melchior, and W. Steppe. 3 vols. New York and London: Garland, 1984.

Joyce, J. *The Essential James Joyce.* Edited by H. Levin. Harmondsworth: Penguin, 1967.

Jung, C. G. *The Spirit in Man, Art and Literature.* Translated by R. F. C. Hull. London and Henley: Ark, 1984.

Keats, J. *Poetical Works.* Edited by H. W. Garrod. Oxford: Oxford University Press, 1939.

Keats, J. *The Complete Poems.* Edited by John Barnard. Harmondsworth: Penguin Books, 1973.

Lawrence, D. H. *Fantasia of the Unconscious.* London: Martin Secker, 1933.

Lings, M. *Symbol and Archetype: A Study of the Meaning of Existence,* Cambridge: Quinta Essentia, 1987.

Macmillan, D. *Transition, 1927–1938: The History of a Literary Era.* London: John Calder, 1980.

Miller, H. *The Time of the Assassins: A Study of Rimbaud.* New York: New Directions, 1962.

Nisbet, H. B. *Goethe and the Scientific Tradition.* London: Institute of Germanic Studies, University of London, 1972.

Norris, C. "The Margins of Meaning." *Cambridge Quarterly* 9, no. 3 (1980): 283.

Novalis, (Friedrich von Hardenberg). *Hymnen An Die Nacht/Geistige Lieder/ Jugendwerke.* Herrsching: Deutsche Klassiker, 1978.

Prawer, S. S., ed. and trans. *The Penguin Book of Lieder.* Harmondsworth: Penguin, 1968.

Raine, K. *Defending Ancient Springs.* Ipswich: Golgonooza Press, 1985.

———. *What Is Man?* Ipswich: Golgonooza Press, 1980.

———. *William Blake.* London: Thames and Hudson, 1970.

Rauf, B. *Addresses.* Sherborne: Beshara Press, 1986.

Ricks, C. B. *The Force of Poetry.* Oxford: Oxford University Press, 1984.

Russell, B. *The Problems of Philosophy.* 1912. Oxford University Press. Reprint, Oxford: Oxford University Press, 1976.

Santomasso, A. *Origins and Aims of German Expressionist Architecture.* Ph.D. thesis, Columbia University, 1972.

Shelley, P. B. *The Complete Poetical Works of P. B. Shelley,* Edited by Rogers. Vols. 1 and 2. Oxford: Oxford University Press, 1975.

———. *Essays and Letters.* Edited by E. Rhys. London: Camelot Classics, 1886.

———. *Poetical Works.* Edited by Hutchinson. Oxford: Oxford University Press, 1908.

Steiner, G. *In Bluebeard's Castle: Or, Some Notes towards the Redefinition of Culture.* London: Faber, 1971.

Sugerman, S., ed. *Evolution of Consciousness: Studies in Polarity.* Middletown, Conn.: Wesleyan University Press, 1976.

Weil, S. *Waiting for God.* Translated by E. Craufurd. New York: Harper and Row, 1973.

Wittgenstein, L. *Culture and Value (Vermischte Bemerkungen).* Translated by P. Winch, Oxford: Basil Blackwell, 1980.

Wordsworth, W. *The Pedlar/Tintern Abbey/The Two-Part Prelude.* Edited by J. Wordsworth. Cambridge: Cambridge University Press, 1985.

———. *Poems of Wordsworth.* Edited by M. Arnold. London: Macmillan, 1911.

———. *The Prelude: A Parallel Text.* Edited by J. Maxwell. Harmondsworth: Penguin Books, 1974.

Wordsworth, W., et al. *Penguin Critical Anthologies: Wordsworth.* Edited by G. McMaster. Harmondsworth: Penguin Books, 1972.

Yeats, W. B. *Selected Criticism.* Edited by A. N. Jeffares. London: Pan Books, 1976.

Index